The Super Analysts
Conversations with the World's Leading Stock Market Investors and Analysts

The Super Analysts
Conversations with the World's Leading Stock Market Investors and Analysts

Andrew Leeming

John Wiley & Sons (Asia) Pte Ltd

Singapore   New York   Chichester
Brisbane   Toronto   Weinheim

Other Wiley Editorial Offices

John Wiley & Sons, Inc., 605 Third Avenue, New York, NY 10158-0012, USA
John Wiley & Sons Ltd, Baffins Lane, Chichester, West Sussex PO19 1UD, England
John Wiley & Sons (Canada) Ltd, 22 Worcester Road, Rexdale, Ontario M9W 1L1, Canada
John Wiley & Sons Australia Ltd, 33 Park Road (PO Box 1226), Milton, Queensland 4064, Australia
Wiley-VCH, Pappelallee 3, 69469 Weinheim, Germany

Library of Congress Cataloging-in-Publication Data

Leeming, Andrew.
    The super analysts: conversations with the world's leading stock market investors and analysts/ Andrew Leeming.
        p. cm.
    Includes bibliographical references.
    ISBN 0-471-84310-5 (cased) — ISBN 0-471-47904-7 (paper)
        1. Investment analysis. 2. Stocks. 3. Investment advisors. I. Title.

    HG4529.L446 2000
    332.63'22–dc21

                                                                        00-040811

Typeset in 11/15 points, Garamond by Linographic Services Pte Ltd
Printed in Singapore by Craft Print International Ltd
10 9 8 7 6 5 4 3 2 1

For Don and Daphne

Contents

Acknowledgements

I would like to thank all of the people who gave their time so freely and willingly to participate in this project. In an industry where time is money and knowledge is viewed as the competitive advantage, the sharing of your experience and insights for the benefit of others is greatly appreciated.

Furthermore, this book would not have been possible without the considerable efforts and support of a number of people — Catherine Marr who spent many hours in typing the original manuscript under considerable time pressure; Robyn Flemming, who edited the manuscript and made many helpful suggestions; and Nick Wallwork and Gael Lee at John Wiley & Sons, who helped see the project through to completion.

I would also like to thank my friends and colleagues in the ING Barings Asian regional banking team, Ng Hon Mun, Tay Chin Seng and Warren Blight, who provided enthusiastic support for this project and who also gave me valuable feedback on the early draft chapters (e.g., "this makes no sense at all"). To Melinda Lim, whose outstanding logistical and organizational skills always ensured that I never missed an appointment or a courier delivery, many thanks as well.

Finally to my family, Erica, Eleanor, and Meredith, who more than anyone else, gave so generously of their time so that this book could be written, a very special thank you.

Introduction

It has been said that stock markets are ninety-nine percent confusion and one percent commission, and to many people, making money in the stock market is a black art. Moreover, having both a relatively unique ecology and language, the stock market at times resembles the Tower of Babel. But does it really require any special talent to succeed in the stock market? What is the best way to value an Internet or New Economy stock? What is it that separates the great investors and analysts from the crowd? How did some of the best investment minds get started?

Through the course of the interviews in this book, we try to answer these questions as well as address many other key issues regarding investing or working in the stock market. Furthermore, as this book is intended for a wide audience, the people selected for the interviews come from a variety of backgrounds and cover a wide spectrum of industry and geographic groups — from Australian mining companies to U.S. retailers; from developed to emerging markets; as well as Old Economy and New Economy stocks. The interviewees have also been selected from both sides of the stock market; the *buy-side*, who are the fund managers and institutional analysts who invest money on behalf of their clients, as well as the *sell-side*, who either work for stockbrokers or investment banks and whose main activity is to analyze companies and industry sectors and publish research that contains stock recommendations and earnings forecasts.

To an outsider, the pursuit of analysts and fund managers may appear to be an intellectual one. However the reality is that analysts and fund managers don't exist to prove how smart they are. They exist to make money for their clients and their employers, and qualities such as common sense, discipline, humility, and objectivity are viewed as being more valuable than an high I.Q. For example, David Fisher, who is chairman of the board of Capital Group International Inc., believes that "while I think you need a certain level of intelligence in order to be successful . . . I'm absolutely persuaded that there is no correlation between increased intelligence and increased success. From that point on, give me common sense, street smarts, all those types of qualities. That, I think, is incredibly more important." In fact, when asked about what it takes to be successful, the investment professionals frequently singled out common sense as one of the most important qualities. But as Emerson noted "Common sense is as rare as genius." maybe Emerson was too harsh and the view that common sense is not so common is closer to the mark.

Another important quality that was consistently cited by the buy- and sell-side alike was humility. For example, Michael Maubossin, who is chief U.S. investment strategist and co-chair of Credit Suisse First Boston's Investment Policy Committee, believes that "I don't see how anybody can't be humble in this business. I believe that markets are very smart. My assumption has always been that the market understands, and I don't. Not the other way round — which is the usual way of thinking." And Murdoch Murchison, who is the global banking and global mining analyst for the Templeton Funds Group, believes that " . . . humility is essential, you also have to have the self-confidence to make tough decisions and to see them through and bear the consequences, good or bad."

Nevertheless, in trying to divine the qualities that make for a great analyst or investor it was necessary to pose a number of core questions to all of the interviewees (e.g., "what was your worst ever call and what did you learn from it" or "what's the ratio between talent and sheer hard work"). That way, it was possible to identify some of the key principles and areas of focus required to succeed on either the buy- or the sell-side.

Management

A common theme throughout the course of the interviews was the importance of management. In many cases outstanding companies are run by outstanding people and that ultimately translates into an outstanding stock. On the other hand, some of the worst stock calls by analysts and investors were due to overestimating what company management could deliver. Consequently, understanding management — their backgrounds, motives, and capabilities — is perhaps one of the most important (but often overlooked) aspects of security analysis.

Valuation

Valuation can be a slippery concept, and with valuation tools and techniques continuing to ebb and flow, the process of valuing a stock was largely viewed as much of an art as a science. Moreover, understanding the behavioral aspects of markets — that is, the behavior of crowds and crowd psychology — were viewed as essential in understanding what drives stock prices and stock markets. In particular, understanding what the market values at a particular point in time in an investment cycle and whether the market is becoming too optimistic or pessimistic over a company's prospects was also regarded as a fundamental part of successful investing. For those readers with an interest this area, Charles Mackay's classic text *Extraordinary Popular Delusions and the Madness of Crowds*[1] which was written in 1841 is highly recommended. Moreover, Mackay's text is still regarded as mandatory reading for analysts and portfolio managers in a number of the world's largest money management firms.

John Maynard Keynes, the influential British economist and highly successful stock market investor, also understood the risk of looking for precision in stock markets. Keynes believed that, "There is nothing so dangerous as the pursuit of a rational investment policy in an irrational world." And in the context of the Internet and NASDAQ fever that gripped the U.S. market last year, Keynes' views were especially prescient.

This does not mean, however, that investors should eschew the use of objective and disciplined techniques to gauge the value of a stock or company, but Keynes also believed that, "I would rather be vaguely right than precisely wrong" and he was most likely emphasizing the risk of regarding mathematical models as *infallible* guides of value or market equilibrium. In the context of today's investment climate, financial models and algorithms are perhaps best used as guides and tools in understanding the difference the difference between *price* and *value*. In fact, the stock market truism that the price you pay determines your rate of return also has an important axiom — *price is what you pay, but value is what you get.*

Another key theme that emerged from the interviews was the importance of understanding that a stock's (or market's) valuation can be significantly distorted by supply/demand imbalances in scrip as well as broader market liquidity issues. That is especially true when it comes to investing in emerging markets. It was also the case for U.S. Internet stocks in 1998 and 1999, where a chronic undersupply of scrip combined with overwhelming institutional demand helped drive prices to stratospheric levels. Understanding the power and direction of these dynamics is an important component of successful investing. And as Stuart Baker, who is head of mining research at Macquarie Bank in Australia, attests, " . . . the market is just a whole bunch of buyers and sellers — it's like a sale at a department store, and you are competing to buy that last suit on the shelf that is going to get bid up."

Common mistakes

Too often investors or analysts expect instant gratification from a stock call or investment. The market professionals agreed that in order for a stock call or investment to work out, patience is required, but many investors sell far too early. What is more, one of the main criticisms of the buy-side of sell-side analysts was that they change their stock calls far too frequently, and quite often, on the thinnest of arguments.

The reality though, is that very few professional investors or analysts consistently buy at the bottom or sell at the top. In fact, the market professionals often cited timing as one of the most difficult aspects of their jobs. But if it is so hard for the professionals, then what chance does the average investor have?

For example, assume that there are four investors. The first was regarded as the world's best investor and always bought the market (i.e., the Dow Jones Index) at its yearly low. The second investor was the world's worst investor and always bought at the Dow's yearly high. The third investor had no idea about timing, and just bought at the end of each month. And the fourth investor always bought in January of each year. How would they have done between January 1990 and December 1999?

The investor who bought at the bottom of the market for each of the ten years would have enjoyed a compound annual rate of return of 19.1% (pre-commissions and taxes). The investor who always bought at the market's yearly high returned a compound annual rate of return of 15.6%. The investor who bought in January of each year returned 18.6% p.a. and the investor who invested at regular intervals every month enjoyed a return of 17.2% p.a.

Astonishingly, there is only a 3.5% difference in return between the *best* and the *worst* investor. Furthermore, there is only a 0.5% and 1.9% difference between the best market timer and the investor who bought either at the beginning of each year or at regular intervals through each of the ten years. The results over a twenty-year period are just as impressive: 14.2% compound annual return from buying at the top of the market each year, 16.2% p.a. from buying at the market's low each year, 15.7% p.a. from buying in January of each year, and 15.1% from buying at the end of each month.

These statistics provide strong support for the view that with the exception of the mining and oil service sectors, it's not your timing *of* the market, but your time *in* the market that counts. But despite these statistics, nearly three quarters of U.S. fund managers cannot outperform the market index. Perhaps the best advice about trying to time the market comes from Pierre Prentice from Jardine Capital Partners, who believes that,"the mindset has to be one of getting rich slowly." And one of the best examples of the value of taking a long-term view is illustrated by the fact that if at the end of 1991, if you had invested in Citicorp (now Citigroup) instead of Microsoft, you would have made a gain of 1,627% against Microsoft's 1,468%. However, you had to take a long-term view as well as have a strong stomach. But someone once said that successful investing is as much about having a strong stomach than a fine mind.

Another key issue that emerged for the buy-side was that it was not the binary stock call or timing of a call that ultimately determined success, but rather, correctly, *weighting* a stock in a portfolio that is more critical. For example, Alistair Veitch from BlackRock International believes that with respect to stock calls," . . . if you get it right 51% of the time you'll be better than the market, but the real measure of your success or performance will be down to the issue of how you weighted that portfolio." There are two strands to this. First, money management is equally, if not more, important than the binary stock call. Second, as you are always going to make mistakes, it's important not to compound your error by overweighting a bad stock call.

Another common error cited was holding stubborn or dogmatic views over companies or their managements. In other words, having a closed mind. For example, Tim Jensen from Oaktree Capital LLC believes that, "When there is a reputation good *or* bad, respect the fact that it exists, but then test it and see if it is still correct. The wonderful opportunities are when the perception of a company changes. That's a wonderful chance for outperformance."

Likewise, Michael Mauboussin believes that one of the greatest errors made by sell-side analysts is falling into what he calls the confirmation trap. That is, once you have made a decision, in an effort to remain *consistent* with that decision, you fall into the trap where you highlight every piece of information that confirms your hypothesis and you discount or ignore every piece of data or information that threatens to disprove or challenges your hypothesis. Keynes' bromide that, "When the facts change, I change my mind. What do you do?" is perhaps a good antidote to the confirmation trap.

Another common mistake cited was getting too emotional over companies or their managements and losing objectivity and perspective. Falling in love with a stock and believing that it was always a buy, or alternatively, holding an entrenched negative view and believing that things could *never* improve was viewed as a major risk and a common trap. But no matter how good or poor the prospects for a company are, the moderating variable is always price. That is, what are you being asked to pay for growth, or how much risk has already been priced in by the market? And as Stuart Baker succinctly puts it, ". . . To me a company is nothing other than a chip to make money out of. Capitalism in its purest sense."

Nonetheless, despite the merits of objective analysis, markets are heavily influenced by sentiment and emotion, and there have been a variety of metaphors and analogies used to describe stock markets. Keynes likened it to a beauty contest where he believed that it wasn't important to pick who *you* thought was the most attractive contestant, it was about picking who you thought the *judges* thought who was the most attractive contestant. He later improved on that analogy and said that, "We have reached the third degree when we devote our intelligences to anticipating what average opinion expects the average opinion to be."

And Roger F. Murray, who helped write the fifth edition of the value investor's bible, *Security Analysis*[2], likened the stock market to a broken clock and argued that, "Price, will tend to fluctuate around value. The price of a security is like a stopped clock — it will be right twice a day, and will be wrong all the rest of the time. The main principle in what we are saying is that securities are chronically mispriced in relation to their instrinsic value."

But whether you believe that the stock market is like a beauty contest or a broken clock, perhaps the best metaphor was one that emerged during one of the interviews for this book. That was, that successful security analysis and investing is like a diet. The principles are simple in theory, but very hard in practice. Moreover, it's also important to find a diet that works for you.

---

[1]   Charles Mackay, *Extraordinary Popular Delusions and the Madness of Crowds* was first published in 1841 and studies the psychology of crowds and various manias throughout history. It includes accounts of various swindles, scams, and deceptions such as the Mississippi scheme that swept France in 1720, the South Sea bubble that bankrupted thousands of English investors, and the Dutch tulip mania of 1637.

[2]   Benjamin Graham and David L. Dodd, *Security Analysis*, fifth edition (New York: McGraw-Hill, 1987).

1

Stuart Baker:
All that Glitters
is not Gold

"Treat them all as liars and crooks until proven otherwise."

Stuart Baker is one of Australia's top-rated and most experienced oil analysts. He spent the first eight-and-a-half years of his career working mainly for Schlumberger on oil platforms throughout Southeast Asia and then left the oil industry in 1985 to study for an MBA. Like many analysts, Baker just fell into stockbroking and after a fairly tentative start at the boutique stockbroker EL&C Baillieu, he eventually went on to head the highly rated mining team at BT Alex. Brown for just under six years, where he was also rated as the industry's number one oil analyst. Following the acquisition of Bankers Trust by Deutsche Bank in 1999, Baker joined Macquarie Bank, Australia's leading investment bank, as head of the mining research team. In the volatile and risky world of calling mining stocks, Baker's success is due in no small part to a healthy degree of skeptiscm and to the fact that he rarely takes things at face value. And while industry experience and cynicism have been necessary ingredients in Baker's success, they are not sufficient. Hard work and persistence have also played a significant role, with seventy-hour weeks a regular requirement.

How did you get started in this business?

By accident, really. Which is probably the way most people get into
this business. I knew something about the broking industry from
when I was working in the oil industry. I had a stockbroker I used to
deal with who I thought was a god and a guru — until I
subsequently learnt that retail brokers aren't much different from
used-car salesmen. They know little other than what's on the piece of
paper they're reading from. Thankfully, that's changed now. But they
had an oil analyst and he used to ring me after I had finished
speaking to their retail advisor. In other words, he thought: "Here's a
guy in the field who might have some mail." I would happily tell the
analyst what I thought was happening on the rig, and he used to get
some snippets that he would use in his research for his institutional
clients. That was in the early 1980s. That's how research was put
together then — in the days before spreadsheets, the analyst would
talk to real people in the field.

   After I left the oil industry in 1985, I did an MBA. I did it because
the oil industry was collapsing rapidly. I hadn't known this when I
was working in the jungles; I only really discovered it when I
returned to civilization. Maybe the industry collapsed because I left,
or maybe I left because it had collapsed — I'm not quite sure which
came first, but it forced a change of direction; there was no going
back to the oil patch. I had no idea about what to do, so I did the
MBA because some friends of mine had done it and recommended it.
During the next two years, doors opened up that I wouldn't have
thought about. Life is like that; things happen over time, and there are
events you can't foresee or plan for.

You qualified as an electrical engineer first?

Yes.

When did you finish that?

In 1977.

And then you worked on oil rigs and oil platforms — that sort of thing?

Yes, between 1977 and 1985. Thanks to OPEC, which had tripled the price of oil, the industry was booming.

And then you decided to get into stockbroking because you figured ...

Well, not really. What happened was, I was living in Asia and just about to turn thirty. I had made a lot of money, but I'd been living out of a suitcase. One year here, one year there, starting in Sorong in the extreme west of Irian Jaya. It's the first bit of mangrove you hit after flying directly east from Jakarta for three-and-a-half hours. Basically, I had worked in the jungles: Balikpapan in Borneo, Java, Sumatra, India, Papua New Guinea. And I'd had a gutful of moving around the world, and I'd often promised myself that the day I stopped enjoying the job would be the day I would quit. Well, you know how it is — there are always days when your job isn't enjoyable, but you hope tomorrow will be better. By October 1985, though, I'd had enough. I had been working for an extended period in the highlands of PNG. It was cold and wet — it rained eighteen hours every day. I got really sick of getting wet just walking to and from the shower block. I rang the boss in Sydney, who made serious efforts to keep me by offering me other assignments in the Middle East. Less rain there, I suppose!

The first thing I did after leaving PNG was return to Australia with the aim of walking into a cozy job in air-conditioned comfort with one of the local oil companies. But the oil price was going down — we're talking October 1985 here. It had fallen from US$30/bbl the year before to the low teens. The companies I wrote to — BHP, Woodside, Esso, etc. — were all putting staff *off*, so there was really nothing going in the industry. So I enrolled in an MBA course because I had few other options at that time. Going back to college would give me something to do to fill in time. It was either an MBA or a Master of Science, and I thought, "Well I'll do the MBA thing because a few of my mates from Schlumberger[1] had done the course and recommended it." I had no real idea where it would lead. It may sound like a stupid thing to do, to just up and leave a successful career with no real plan for the future, but years of working for Schlumberger in the oil industry imbue one with confidence, arrogance, and money. The world was just waiting for me!

In terms of your success as an analyst, what was of more value to you — industry experience or your MBA?

The industry experience. There's no doubt about that. But the MBA was a passport. It got me in because, although the oil industry was collapsing, the financial markets were booming. You would read the *Australian Financial Review* on a Friday morning with all your MBA colleagues and you would see job after job after job in investment banking, funds management, stockbroking. None of us really understood what those businesses were, except there were big dollar signs at the bottom and we thought, "Yes, hey — *now* you're talking!"

How did you first start in broking?

I started with the small family-owned Melbourne firm, EL&C Baillieu on January 2, 1988. When I say I fell into broking by accident, it was a series of coincidences that resulted in my meeting the firm's chairman, the late John Baillieu, deputy chairman of Elders IXL at the time and a pillar of Melbourne business. My wife (fiancée at the time) used to mind their dog.

She used to what?

She used to mind their dog.

I thought you were referring to their stock portfolio!

No, a barking dog. When the Baillieus went away on business, they couldn't take the dog. So, my wife used to care for it. Through my wife, I met John Baillieu, who asked me, "What do you want to do?" I said, "I'm doing an MBA. The financial markets are booming, and I'm going to come out the other side and get a job in the financial services industry, preferably stockbroking." John thought about this and invited me to talk to some of the people in the firm, in particular Malcolm Brodie who was one of the firm's more senior partners. I spoke to Malcolm and we got on well, and at the end of the week they offered me a job. Wow! Although I was a raw recruit, I made the right noises, shook the right hands, wore the right clothes, and drove a red Ferrari — that may have helped. I started on January 2, 1988, just after the crash of October 1987. I had had other job offers, which after the crash looked shaky. But the Baillieu offer was firm. This, I thought, was a big commitment. They showed a lot of faith in me, and they stood by their word.

In terms of getting started, what was your first big stock call?

I was going to tell you something about John Baillieu that I thought would be interesting, because he gave me some advice that has helped me a lot. As a green guy, I had never spoken to a company before. I had the view that everyone that I would come across in this industry would be successful businessmen or successful managers. And why *wouldn't* they be, if they were running companies? John Baillieu, who was very experienced in these things, sat me down one day and said something like, "Son, when you go out and talk to these companies, when you come back with a story, I'll give you some advice you should never forget. Treat them all as liars and crooks until proven otherwise." I was horrified, but that's exactly the advice that *should* be given.

My dilemma at the time was that I was about to go and meet the managing director of a mining company who had obviously made a fortune, so how could it possibly be a bad company? But John was right, because the first three company visits I ever did, I was hoodwinked — absolutely. The first company I visited was a respectable diamond miner. I had been looking at this company for a while, watching the stock price come down. The rumor was that the price was coming down because the market was concerned that there was going to be a rights issue. It had just bought a gold mining asset and it was thought it might need external funding to complete the deal. They weren't sure how to fund the thing; there were gold loans, debt, and all that sort of stuff, and the market was probably right in being concerned about a rights issue. So I did some digging into it and came up with some profit forecasts that said the company was going to make A$25 million and I couldn't see that they really needed to do an equity issue — they could do a gold loan or debt issue. I thought the market had really got it wrong. But I needed to talk to the company.

I went down there, accompanied by one of the very cynical senior guys who had been around a long time, and we met the managing director, a Ph.D. Now, this is a warning sign. When you meet a Ph.D. who calls himself "Doctor," that's the first red flag. And the Doctor sat behind this big desk with not a scrap of paper on it — the second warning sign. The third warning sign: we went through the research, and the feedback was that our profit forecasts looked okay. We were told that we had got the story right, and that all that stuff about a rights issue was a load of baloney because there are gold loans etc. that could be used, etc., etc., etc. We had a scoop! I went back to the office and wrote up the meeting, rang around everybody, all the institutions, telling them that the rights issue just wasn't on. The profit release was coming in three weeks, so we put people into the stock big time. Three weeks later, out comes the profit result. My profit forecast of A$25 million was bang on. I felt great for about twenty seconds, until the rest of the story emerged over the squawk box. There was also a one-for-three renounceable partly paid new share issue. Not a rights issue, not quite a rights issue, but a partly paid issue! *Bang*, wrong. We just got life!

What was the lesson you learned?

Well, we were lied to and therefore you've got to be cynical in this business. The managing director had either lied to us, or allowed us to believe in a falsehood because we hadn't asked the right questions. What's the difference? When I rang the Managing Director and talked it through with him, he said he had discussed funding options openly with us, but ultimately such things are board decisions, etc. I'd asked the wrong questions, and the market was right. Probably the market had been sounded out by underwriters that this company needed to raise some equity, which is what they did, and here was the sucker. A lamb to the slaughter!

So, what follows from that? Do you learn more from your bad calls than the good calls?

Yes. I learned that one has to be a lot more prepared and to listen to the market. I mean, I was a green analyst and my contact with institutions at that point was very, very limited. I think the market probably knew that the company was looking for equity. I hadn't heeded the warnings. I hadn't known the company long enough to read the body language, and I'd never dealt with the managing director before. It was just totally inappropriate to go in headfirst. Also, when you are talking to companies about equity raisings, it's always a sensitive topic. It's like, "Are you going to acquire company XYZ next week?" You're not going to go in there on day one and get what is probably ultrasensitive information after a one-hour meeting. It's just unrealistic to go in with the expectation that you can get that. Even today, I see people on the buy-side doing exactly that, going into a meeting with the managing director after a few days of preparation, at best, and no real depth of knowledge. As for my lesson, it took time to sink in and there were other lessons yet to be learnt.

For example?

Well, about a year-and-a-half later I was looking at AGL. AGL was the New South Wales gas company that had been around since 1840, but it had gone through a couple of bad years as it struggled to find a growth path. In 1989 it had big debt, sub two times interest cover, single-digit returns, and the prior three years' earnings per share and dividends per share were flattish. It had been engaged in all sorts of corporate machinations during the booming 1980s and had equity stakes in small gold mining and oil companies. They dabbled in property investment and development. It looked a real mess. The stock price was performing badly despite the market's appetite for utility-type companies during the upcoming recession. In 1990 a new managing director was appointed and the board got an infusion of fresh blood. The market was basically told that the company would focus on gas and get rid of all the peripheral assets, get the debt down, and grow earnings. I thought, "Well, this is interesting — a turnaround story." It was all, "We'll do this, this, and this." It was all "gunna, gunna, gunna, gunna." To me it sounded like trying to turn the *Titanic* around in a meandering stream. You can't possibly do all those things. It would take an army of McKinsey-type people plus a lot of money to do it. It's going to take years and years, and it's all too hard.

My view was, if you have any stock, sell it, and we'll have a look at it again in a couple of years. Well, that was when the stock price was about A$1.80; over the next ten years it went from A$1.80 to a high of A$12.80 in early 1998, or a compound return of 24% p.a. Add to that the dividend growth. Dividends have risen from 13 cents per share in 1990 to around 50 cents per share now, or a compound annual dividend growth of 16%. Earnings per share has grown similarly, even during the recession years. The debt mountain fell from A$1.3 billion to A$300 million within four years and this enabled AGL to start acquiring businesses. So, basically, the new management delivered, and earnings and the stock price went up, up, up. So, *bang*, this was my second major bad call, and again it was a result of my inexperience and total lack of understanding of the people who ran the company and of what they could do. I thought I knew something about the history of the company, I had read the annual reports, and I had been to the show-and-tells. But this is another example of lack of experience and no real understanding of the history of the company. Yet the job of an analyst is to make calls, and you don't have three years or five years to do your homework. You have days or weeks, and then the desk and clients want to see product. The company had been around for 150 years; I'd looked at it for three months and reckoned I was an expert! Was I qualified to make a call? Not even close!

But that's a fairly common mistake in this business, isn't it?

Absolutely. In a perfect world there would be time to fully understand every company in every sector, but time is scarce, so you have to compromise. You do what you can, given the limited time.

What's interesting here is that Mark Mobius makes a similar point. He says he puts a lot of emphasis on the character of the people running the company and on actually knowing and understanding the management. He thinks that the sell-side has a pretty poor track record in this regard.

Yes, getting to meet and know all the key people. He's right.

How did you manage the AGL call, because it must have looked like being life-threatening at some stage?

Well, I took that lesson and the pain, and I could see that my view was starting to go wrong within about a year, because the stock price kept going up and you could see management doing the things they said they were going to do. After a year I changed that recommendation, even though the stock was then over A$3, and we kept that buy call for several years thereafter. But what I learnt from that was, I needed to be much more thorough, because the way I *had* been approaching the industry was by trying to do lots and lots of things and looking at bits and pieces, and then having a view. You know, the instant call. So, I said to myself, "What I'm going to do now is I'm going to pick on a couple of stocks where I reckon I can get to the bottom of them and make a good recommendation." In other words, make one call, but get it right.

Get a sharper focus?

Yes, just get focused. So what I took away from the AGL thing, what it taught me, was just to get focused and learn much more. The next one up on my list was SAGASCO. SAGASCO had been formed in 1987 as the result of a merger between an upstream oil and gas company based in South Australia and a downstream utility. The institutions were looking at it, and the company was raising equity. It started to look like it could become a serious utility stock after AGL. What I did there was, before I put pen to paper, and before I put any numbers in boxes, I spent a year talking to the senior management and getting close enough to them so that they would let me go down to the next level and talk to their line managers and division managers. I got to know probably a dozen or more people within the company. It takes a lot of effort for nil immediate brokerage, but it's the only way.

Were you still at Baillieu's then?

Yes. Shortly thereafter I went across to Prudential Bache, owned at that time by Prudential Securities. I just continued this process there. I spent a year just learning about that company. I made it my business to speak to the managing director, the finance director, and some of the senior managers about once a week. I got to the point where the secretaries in most of the divisions knew me, and whenever I rang up, I would be put straight through. The company was also very helpful. They could have said, "Get lost." After about a year, I felt confident enough to write something about the company, not just teenage scribblings, but about their strategy, the way the people thought, and what they really wanted to do. Then I started to model some numbers and grew some confidence in them. I then took those numbers to the market and said, "Look, here's the story." By now we were getting into the recessionary years of 1990/91 and gas utilities are, of course, great recession-proof businesses. So maybe there was some fortunate timing there as well, and I thought that this is a company that has just been transformed, like AGL had, by merging two upstream and downstream companies. It had good cash flow, low debt, and we're going to get this good profit growth out of it — you know, 10% or 15%-plus profit and dividend growth at a time when all of the Australian banks were losing money and every second company on the main board of the stock exchange was also losing money. No other companies were recording profit growth, but this one was going to record profit growth *and* dividend growth. That was a tough story to broker, given the times, but I was absolutely confident of it by now. And management were right — you could see it coming through in the numbers over a period of about two years. And in the recessionary period of 1991, from late 1990 through to about 1992, the company tripled its market capitalization without raising capital. The stock went up over 250%, dividends grew about 10 cents a share to about 18 cents, or something like that, at a time when everyone was in recession and companies were losing money. It made money, and the share market rewarded the stock price.

So, you were right for all the right reasons?

Yes, because anyone can be right for all the wrong reasons — it's harder to be right for all the right reasons, and that being the case, that stock call put me on the map — for all the *right* reasons. It got me in the door and gave me some experience in how to do it right. If you are going to make stock recommendations on companies that are run by people who have been in the business twenty or thirty years, then you've got to invest at least a year of your human capital in trying to understand what they are doing, and getting as close to them as possible. Sometimes you're not even going to get in there, but you've got to spend *at least* that amount of time; if you don't, you're on the back foot to start with. You see, it takes at least a year to test whether they are liars and crooks after all!

Do you think your early mistakes were partly due to attending business school?

Maybe, but it's hard to know how little you know until you know more. As a raw business school graduate you would go away and put everything into a Porter[2] framework and then think, "I'm now an industry expert." I used to laugh when I visited our counterparts at BT Alex. Brown in the United States. I would meet these twenty-six-year-old analysts who would say, "Well, I do the food and consumer sector in America and its 220 stocks with a capitalization of $150 billion. I just finished modeling McDonald's last week, this week I'm doing Zippy's, and the week after I'm doing Starbucks Coffee, and then I'll be *totally* on top of it." I've heard that sort of thing so often, and I thought to myself that from what I'd learned back in Australia, "It'll take you a decade, pal — if you're lucky — to get on top of *anything*." The MBA thing teaches you to be a guru, or at least to *think* that you're a guru, and you come pre-armed with this inbuilt arrogance and a recipe book that you believe will solve all of the world's problems. So, you put things in boxes, you do a Porter framework or use some other analytical tool, and invariably you end up making mistakes. Why? You still need to talk to people and to understand the personality of companies.

It sounds like you ended up throwing away everything they taught you in business school.

Not totally. I just woke up to the fact that learning goes on long after you've put the Masters certificate up on the study wall. The diamond miner and the AGL call taught me that you need to go backwards before going forwards. You have to chuck away your preconceptions and assume you know very little. It was like saying, "I assume I know *nothing* about this company," which really was the case. You might think you know a bit about the oil and gas industry, but you've got to strip it right back and say to yourself, "I know *nothing*. It's a blank piece of paper and I'll start from scratch to learn about this company." It's hard to face this and to admit it.

What is the hardest part of your job?

Getting up at 4.30 a.m. to catch a plane to somewhere, anywhere, or maybe nowhere. Seriously though, I need to think about that one a little bit because it's a question of degree.

How important is courage in this business?

I'm not sure that you need to be courageous. Certainly not arrogant, though — the market is a big leveler.

Would it help if you were humble?

Maybe. You might get some sympathy along the track and possibly some help. This industry is notorious for not helping; everyone is expected to be experts. You dare exhibit weakness, though, and you'll get run over in the rush for your chair. You'll get run over by salesmen, for sure. But if you're working for one of the major American investment banks and you're a timid sort of person, then I suppose the two probably don't fit well together. I think the problem you've got is that, yes, you need to be courageous in front of your own dealing desk and with your clients. However, when you are going into a company, if you take a go-and-kick-heads type of attitude, you're not going to get very far.

An ounce of humility and empathy can go a long way?

Yes, especially empathy, which can be very important. If we look at
organizations or companies, they are run by people. The MBA course
doesn't teach you that. It teaches you that basically an organization is
shaped by a set of industry conditions, and you put them all in a box
and you look at the inputs — capital and intellect — and you look at
the output, being the buyers, whether they are Japanese steel
producers or consumers at a supermarket. And then you just break it
down into analytical things and diagnostics. But at the end of the day,
they are organizations *run by people*. The manager you talk to has
probably clawed his way up through the organization after thirty
years, and what he wants to do with the company is probably
completely different to what the shareholders expect, and also
probably completely at odds with what the management books tell
him to do, because it's a whole bunch of people, social relationships,
ego factors, and all those sorts of things.

**Yes. And companies don't make bad decisions, only people
do.**

Correct. We'll come back to it when we talk about picking targets or
companies that are going to be successful and looking at how
corporate objectives are met by individuals who have different
objectives — and BHP[3] is perhaps a classic case. It will be interesting
to see if one man can unwind fifteen years of corporate arrogance
and error.

**You almost have to be a political analyst and behavioral
psychologist to understand how some companies work and
how they make and implement decisions.**

Yes, especially in large organizations. Some of them aren't
homogenous organizations, but rather a loose confederation of
warring tribes or divisions.

In terms of becoming a rated analyst, because it's a long, hard slog, how important is the name of the house? For example, if you had worked for Merrill Lynch instead of Bankers Trust, would you have achieved success sooner?

Probably — a bit quicker, maybe — but it's hard to know. I've thought about that a lot, because you see some well-rated analysts at less well-rated firms, and on the other hand, you see more rated analysts at the big firms anyway. So, do the big firms help the analysts rate, or do the big firms go and actively get analysts that do rate if their own don't? In any case, it's harder at a small firm. It's a lot harder to get into companies, harder to get noticed, harder to get access to information. I think it's a lot harder, but as to whether you would rate in a big firm, I don't know. Big firms can impose all sorts of rules and constraints as well, so it's difficult to know.

You talked about doing your homework and due diligence, and you spent a year just researching SAGASCO. How many stocks do you think an analyst can cover properly?

Ten or fewer. It's hard to be explicit because it depends upon how homogenous the sector is. Obviously, the more you try to cover, the thinner will be the quality. And then there is the question of the degree of difficulty, and there are some very good examples of this. For example, if I take a stock like Santos,[4] which is very much a homogenous company with a single style of asset. While it's large, it has an economy of scale in its business, and it's very simple to model and understand and do numbers on. It's a relatively straightforward job. You could give it to a junior analyst. Yet there is another company — for example — Novus,[5] which isn't even a tenth of the market capitalization of Santos. Novus operates in at least eight different financial and political jurisdictions with different production sharing agreements, and they are unique. Each one is complex to understand — Iran, Pakistan, Qatar, and Indonesia, all these places. It's far harder to model that company and project numbers than for a company like

Santos. And your modeling can be way, way out, because it's easy to get the numbers wrong. So, it's a question of difficulty. But I would say as a general rule of thumb that once you get to ten or a dozen companies, that's about it.

Where is the highest degree of forecasting risk?

In small companies.

What are the variables that make it so difficult — production or price, for example?

Well, it's a combination of factors, but I think also in terms of if you are just trying to project a straight profitability figure, small companies have inherently high cost bases, so what you are really trying to do is forecast an error. The profit margin is almost an error factor. If they get their administrative costs wrong — if their administration bill blows up by a million dollars — it can wipe out the profit. You might have been forecasting a $3 million profit on a $100 million revenue, and it comes in at a $3 million loss. So you're 1000% out! Yet in your model at the total cost line, you're only 6% out! Whereas a big company like Woodside,[6] where you are projecting a $300 million profit, isn't going to deliver a $300 million loss — well, one would hope that they're not going to do that in this age of efficient markets. So, with small companies you are really faced with a high error and forecasting risk, whereas big companies, through their PR machine, their investor relations department, their websites, and the fact that they are out there lunching all the time, they keep the market in a much narrower range, so the degree of error or risk is perhaps a lot less.

Do you enjoy following the small ones or the bigger ones?

The smaller ones are much more fun. You can see the impact of individual effort and personality. You can spot a press release written by the managing director — it contains vibes. Big companies lack personality. They are full of lawyers who draft investor releases that are boring to read and contain as little information as possible. These same companies complain if you don't understand the company! Quite so!

Which can you make more money out of?

The smaller companies — if you get them right, the leverage is huge. With big companies it's difficult to get the leverage. Mind you, the leverage can work in reverse. However, the risk is large. Look at AGL, though. It's big and, hey, a small investment in 1990 could have been a real mortgage buster!

What do you think are the popular misconceptions that people have about your job and the stock market in general?

The man in the street probably thinks the average advisor or analyst they listen to over the phone is an expert in either commodities or economics with a Ph.D. behind him, when in fact they are more likely to be a retired schoolteacher that the firm has put in front of a machine and who is reading through the daily research. I think there is a perception out there that the people in this industry are super-normal financial types, when in fact you see some very, very ordinary people. It never ceases to amaze me how many ordinary people you come across, not just behind a screen, but also on the other side, on the buy-side. As a result, the man in the street thinks we are experts, and perfection is expected. We are viewed as experts, as being "in the know," so if we totally stuff-up a call, there's little understanding as to how that could happen.

I mentioned before, you can be right but for all the wrong reasons. The other thing is that there is an assumption that you must know everything. You might be a number-one-rated oil analyst, or the number one bank analyst, but with the information flow being what it is, and the Internet, there is so much material that goes out to the public on a daily basis, you can simply miss it because there is just a flood of it there. Unless you have a whole team of people combing through reports and bringing things to your attention, you can easily miss something.

Do you ever say to clients, "I don't know?"

Yes.

Too often, you see people trying to wing it.

Definitely, and that's the worst thing you can ever do. It's what junior or inexperienced analysts tend to do. They have to, because they are under pressure; they are employed to write product and to come up with ideas.

What advice would you give to someone just starting out?

Be patient and diligent, and don't be too ambitious. Pick the one stock that you think you can do. Pick the one that's reasonably easy in terms of not having all sort of complexities. You are eventually going to add value in the most difficult stock, but that's not where you're going to start out. Pick the easiest one. It might sound trite, but pick the easiest one, and make sure you do it better than anyone else. There are three reasons for doing that: one, it's easy; two, it will build your self-confidence; and three, you've got a chance that your competitor at Merrill Lynch who did that company five years ago is perhaps not so interested in it now, and he is out there chewing the top end of town. Quite often the second-line companies tend not to be done as well, so maybe that's a place to start. So do that small company, get it right, and don't be too brave. Don't go out there picking the big companies and going out with a heroic call. Get a small company, build your self-confidence, and get the story right, and use that as your way into the game. When you are confident that you've got that one right, then pick the next one off the list. Then when you've got a few of those ones right, and this might take probably three years, then you can go for the big end of town. I think if you start with the big end of town, if you pick off National Australia Bank,[7] BHP, or Telstra[8] as your first stock and you are three months in, if you get it right, the fund managers that you talk to won't know whether it was due to your corporate finance department, luck, or your uncle was the managing director. They won't know, and they won't give you the benefit of the doubt anyway, because you are out there competing against the big firms. If you get it wrong, however, which is more than likely the case, then you just set back your career three to five years — if you're *lucky* — and that's assuming that you don't get iced.

So, the point you are making is the need to develop credibility. If you can develop credibility, know your limits, and be diligent, you'll be very successful. How long do you think it takes to be a good analyst?

I think a long, long time. I think you have to go through an apprenticeship and make mistakes. I don't think there is anyone out there, even at the top end of town — that is, the number one and two rated analysts — who hasn't made mistakes. You are going to make mistakes, but hopefully you'll have enough of a reputation and track record to work through that. But bottom line, I think it takes a minimum of three years, but more than likely five.

And a lot of success in this job is grind. It might look glamorous, but it's a grind — 90% grind and 10% gravy. Would you agree?

Probably almost 100% grind. When we take on juniors and analysts and graduates, they come in thinking they are going to be a big Wall Street type surrounded by screens, with phones ringing and people yelling, and you've got some guy on the end of the phone who is just going to give you a billion-dollar deal. That's so far from the truth.

This can be a very boring job with you sitting in front of your Excel spreadsheet late at night, talking to people out there who don't want to tell you anything, reading the news reports that come through, and scrambling in this big gray area called *the competition* to try and find out where you fit on that big screen. It can be very tedious work.

But all the same, it can be the worst job in the world but also the best job in the world. The highs are very high and the lows are very low.

Yes, the highs and lows parallel your stock calls.

Is the pleasure of a good stock call as intense as the pain of a bad one?

People remind you of the bad ones more often. You get phone calls from investors you've never heard of that read your report and bought some stock three years ago, and they chew you out because they paid $6 for it and it's now worth 40 cents, but your name was on the piece of paper. It goes on and on and on. Whereas the good stock calls, people tend to forget about and they never ring you and say, "Hey, well done, I became a millionaire from your efforts." However, when people *do* acknowledge a good call, it feels great.

The other thing, too, about a bad stock call is when something has really gone wrong, it's tremendous. I mean the market is a big leveler, and you can get it wrong for all the right reasons, but at the end of the day there is this nagging feeling because you know you lost and you're like a Wimbledon tennis player. You might be holding the cup today, but next year you could be bundled out in the first round. You think to yourself constantly, "Did I screw up because my time has gone and I'm not as sharp as I was or I wasn't putting the hours in, or did I genuinely do everything possible and if anyone else had done the same thing they would have screwed up too?" You don't know. So you start to become filled with self-doubt and that's bad, because this whole business is like a Grand Slam tennis tournament or a golfing major. You've got your skill level, and you've got your self-esteem and confidence level on top of that. You have your contacts and industry sources — however, all your competitors have got this too, and it's that little bit extra that makes the difference. The last thing you want is indecision, because clients are making decisions daily.

How do you handle a bad streak?

That's easy. Take some leave and go away and take a holiday. And then when I come back, I look for an opportunity to say, "Gee, I got that call wrong — it's not a sell after all, it's really a buy." And the clients tend to say, "We were waiting for you to say that, Baker. You were only about six months too late on the call, but finally you admitted it." But you need to have confidence in your numbers. Sometimes stock prices can move powerfully for or against you. If you believe in your numbers, tough it out and wait. The call will come good.

Is there blood lust when there is a bad call?

In what sense?

When you got rated number one, I remember you were apprehensive and said to me ...

Only one way to go from here, and that's down.

Yes, that's right.

Well, yes and no. But I know that when I came into the industry, the big driver behind everything I did was that I just had to get rated and it took five, eight years. Being unrated means a tenuous position on a lousy salary, so everything you did was about ratings. You looked at the surveys, you read your competitors' research, you spent your nights laying awake, worrying about what your competitors were doing, and if you took a week off that was the week they'd be writing research and be in front of your clients and you'd be forgotten. You didn't dare relax. Then when you get rated, the thing I find now, whether you are one, two, or three, or whatever, I find that I worry about it less and worry about it more. There are always fresh people coming into the industry who are going to want to cut my lunch. So, what I'm trying to think about now is not about staying number one, but about how to *relax* and stay number one. Again, it's like being a Wimbledon champion. You ask yourself, "Should I retire with the cup, or should I play just one more year? Maybe next year I'll get the cup again, but maybe I'll get bundled out. Maybe I just want to play some tennis for fun! And good tennis, not bad."

So the issues are different now?

Yes. It becomes one of how long you are going to sit at the top. What effort are you going to put in to stay there?

The buy-side live in a state of tension too, because they also have their good and bad years, and fund redemptions can be just a click of the mouse away.

Yes, it's a similar issue. Everyone in this industry lives with stress and tension. You never relax. It's just a different source of frustration. Different irritations. When you are an unrated analyst, you look up at all the highly rated analysts above you. When you go to the show-and-tell, it's all these guys standing around and you're in awe of them because they are rated and you're not. The managing director knows all their names, but not yours! You're in awe because they get to speak to the managing director. When *you're* the highly rated analyst, you go to the show-and-tell and they are all standing around looking at you talking to the managing director and trying to eavesdrop, and you think, "These guys are just waiting to eat my cake."

What is it about the industry that you like? What is it about the job that keeps you there?

There are lifestyle dividends to it and if you look around at what most of us are doing, as a general rule, if you look at people who are in this business, particularly in mining research, they have come from a mine or an oil field. They've come from somewhere really horrible. What this business allows you to do is to live someplace nice, it probably allows you to travel, it allows you to have some free weekends. I think it's a good industry to be in if you want to make some money. It's not the tough existence, in many respects, it would be out in the real world. Just imagine if you were working for, say, BHP at the moment, notwithstanding the fact that the company is going through hell and everyone's in fear of losing their job, but you are probably running an iron ore mine, and you are worried that when you come to work on Monday morning, the union has gone out on strike. You are worried that a tornado or a natural disaster is just about to occur and will wash the railway line away. You are worried that the iron ore carrier that has just pulled up in port, registered in Liberia, will capsize and you will have a massive loss of life, cargo, and the greenies suing you. And if you are the mine manager, you've got to go to the coronial inquiry — you know, that's real-world stress. Then when you've got all those things right and you've got your pile of iron ore in the boat, then you've got to front up to the Japanese to get paid for it. Then they turn around and say, "Sorry, our mill has just gone out of business and our economy is flat. We're not paying you."

And you are on an award wage.

Yes. And after thirty years, if the mine hasn't been closed down and your health holds, you might just have enough retirement money to treat yourself to a round-the-world cruise. On the cruise you may see an iron ore carrier on the horizon, steaming for the hungry mills of Asia, and feel a sense of loss because it's not your pile of ore anymore.

If we choose, we can knock off on a Friday night, and at the end of the day the worst thing that can happen to you is that you can lose someone's money. And unless you get iced, generally speaking you are safe. Some people may try to sue you, and some may try to put a knife in your back. Either way, you're dead. But that's the worst that can happen. More likely, someone might abuse you on the phone. But it doesn't compare to the stress that a twenty-five-year-old doctor saving lives in the casualty ward has to cope with, or a middle manager running a coal mine that has just caved in burying his whole shift and some of his friends.

It's not your life, it's not your wife, it's a job.

It is a career, but I never did understand the subtle difference between a career and job. I think one pays more. Only recruiting people know the real difference between a job and a career.

Do you ever look at charts?

I didn't use to, because they teach you in business school not to. But as a truism, a chart captures a lot of history, and history is the base of future knowledge. On a daily basis you know what your stocks are doing. You need to know if a stock is going sideways, or breaking new highs and lows. You need to know how a stock behaved in the past, in order to understand how it may behave in the future. A chart can be a powerful tool coupled up with other ideas, and that is that the stock has just reached a ten-year high and you can see a few cracks out there and you have to be commercial. If it's the little bit that you need to put into a story saying, "Look, this company is about to tip over" and you look at the chart and everyone is sitting on profit … However, there is no substitute for a good predictive model, knowledge of the company, industry, etc.

Is there a natural conflict of interest between the broker and the investor?

Yes, there is. Investors may be best served by holding a stock on certain occasions. But brokers need turnover; they are only interested in buys or sells. Skip all the maintenance.

How do you resolve or cope with that and maintain your integrity?

I think that if you work for a firm like BT, which was used to losing money in the agency business which were offset by profits from other equity products, it's not a problem, and you can be honest with your recommendations. However, if you work for a firm that is aggressively desk-driven or commission-driven, or if you are a retail salesperson on 40% commission, or if you work in a firm that is driven by the corporate finance department and it needs some buy recommendations, then you've got a problem. I think it's an ongoing industry problem. One of the greatest barriers to wealth creation is analysts doing what I call a practical, commercial job, rather than analytical research. Analysts are under increasing pressure to pump out buy and sell notes that lead to immediate stock transactions. There's no time for research, no market for analysis. In fact, "business journalist" would be a better label than "research analyst." And then there is the "hold" report on a stock that should really be a "sell." There is an increasing trend now to write less, because there are increasing internal and external constraints on what is written. I see the industry going back full-circle, with face-to-face contact with clients, over lunch or a coffee, which frees the analyst to express what he really thinks rather than what he may be forced to write.

One client pointed out to me that there were something like 2500 financial stocks listed in the United States, and he asked me how many I thought had sell recommendations on them.

Probably ten or a dozen.

Nineteen.

Nineteen, that many? Things must really be bad in banking!

The client concluded that Wall Street is a great place for information but it's a lousy place for investment advice. And as commissions continue to be cut, it has forced brokers to look at other avenues of revenue, and naturally this has increased the scope for conflict and a lack of objectivity. So there is some circularity there. And you have to ask yourself, "Who do I primarily work for, the buyers of equity or the issuers of equity?"

Correct. Your corporate finance department has to make the money, or your own firm from principal or trading positions, so there is cross-subsidization due to the thin commissions and high fixed cost base of this industry. The other thing is, there are clients out there who say they respect analysts who thump the table and call a sell a sell, and who put the size ten boots in. There is one broker I know of who likes to do that, and there are a couple of funds that like to do it too, but it's not rewarding. It's not commercial in the long run. If you adopt that approach, you'll be excluded by the company and the information dries up. That is the truth. The second thing is that the institution that requires you to make those aggressive calls will just as happily turn to the next broker in the queue once you are out of business and they won't necessarily reward you for it anyway.

Yes, sell recommendations are always harder to implement and can have more severe consequences.

True. And I think that logic would dictate that you should always have a buy on a stock. If you don't, then don't even bother to write it. If you put a buy on a company, your target audience to capture brokerage and generate revenue is the entire universe of investors, full stop. Assuming investors don't have this stock, then your target audience is wide open. Also, you might find that a lot of people have some stock already. Fine, you can always sell them some more.

Basically, if you've got a buy and your story is good, you can sell the stock to anyone.

As most people are optimists by nature?

Correct. People want to make money and they are looking to buy. Those people who already have the stock will feel very happy about their investment, as you have just given it a tick. And those people who don't have it will look at it as an opportunity to get rich. No-one starts out to make money by seeing prices fall. People spend nine-tenths of their time looking at the buy-side of the story. No-one is out there looking for sell recommendations; it goes against human nature. The second thing with a sell recommendation is, unless you can short sell the stock or if people don't own the stock, there is no capacity to make money from your call. And short selling only appeals to a few people. Third, if you have to meet a client who has got the stock, and you tell him it's a sell, then the first thing that you are telling him is that he has made a mistake, and he isn't going to like that. Moreover, it's going to take a lot of convincing to get him to sell it, and he probably won't sell it through *you*, anyway. He'll most likely sell it through the broker he bought it through. And if you get the call wrong, you'll be iced.

So, sell recommendations take a lot of thinking through?

Yes, those calls are really hard to implement successfully. And of course, then there is the company as well and the repercussions, not to mention your corporate finance department. Unless it's a situation where it's a clear overvaluation, where the stock has just doubled in a week for no particular reason and the company doesn't know why, you can say, "Look, take some profits, because the fundamental value is out of line with the stock price."

But it also depends on the maturity of the company. Some companies are actually happy to see the price come off, as

too strong a share price can put too much pressure on management to perform above their capabilities.

Yes, that's true. But you cover banks, and bankers tend to be a bit more level-headed than miners! But in general, company folk don't like to see sells; they take it personally.

Do you think that mining analysis is easier than industrial analysis? What are the essential differences?

It's different. With industrial analysis, you use different valuation tools and measures. You use EBIT[9] margins, GDP growth, margin contraction, market share gains or losses, premium or discount to market multiple, etc. With mines, it's reserves and NPV.[10] The value is finite, deterministic, and absolute.

But in industrials, you don't get the same degree of operational leverage as you do in a mining company.

Yes, that's right. In a mining company, for example, people may be looking for very bad fundamentals, such as a company with high debt and high costs, but which offers profit leverage should commodities run. This is very much a commodity-driven equity strategy. Consider MIM,[11] which has a high level of debt and a poor record of profitability, or lack thereof. It has doubled in the past few months because of an uplift in the copper price. It's widely recognized as a "copper play." All you have to do is get the copper call right, and if you do, the returns can be huge. You can double your money in months. While the company has problems, investors who make rapid gains would think of it very favorably indeed.

So, while understanding the micro issues of the company is necessary, you also have to get the macro commodity price call right, and your timing is also crucial.

Yes, absolutely. The mining cycle is about a six-year wavelength. Five to six years amplitude from peak to trough, and the cycle is about 200% to 300%. So you have to try to pick it at the bottom, which is when everyone has sold it and then wait three years for the industrial cycle to turn, or for something else to happen to the commodity cycle, and then go out on the sell side. So you get two moneymaking opportunities every three years. One is to put everyone in, and the second is to get everyone out, and then along the way the job gets harder when you reach some sort of inflection point. But in calling the mining sector, that's what you are trying to do. Really, it's macro-driven.

How do you formulate your views on where commodity prices are headed?

We read all the material by the professional forecasters, plus we have our commodity specialists; we marry it up with the economics, look at which way the industrial production cycle is going, have a look at the last couple of cycles, and have a look at stock levels. It's a relatively inexact science, because there are so many parameters that you can throw in. But I think you can strip it down to basically bond rates, global industrial production, commodity stock levels, and the supply/demand balance. What we have found just from looking at the price cycles is that in a typical mining cycle, the gold sector will turn first. It turns about six to nine months before, and it might not be a very big turn, it can be quite subtle, but it turns about a year before the mining stocks, like metals, and then three months later you'll find things like bond rates ticking up and industrial production picking up. Industrial production is the ultimate driver, however — a bit like global GDP, and it's industrial production that drives metal consumption. Typically what you find, though, is that the pattern is boom-bust, boom-bust, with some sort of continuation on the amplitude as the ping-pong game with the global banks goes on, as they try to squeeze out the cycle and eliminate inflation etc., etc. But what you find is that the worst thing from a mining point of view is periods of recession or periods of stability. Now this is where the gold cycle comes in. The thing with gold is that it's a leading indicator. Gold stocks do poorly in any environment where people are comfortable with the immediate-term outlook. Uncertainty drives gold. Typically we find maximum uncertainty at the end of a cycle, such as when you come from a period of stable economic growth and before you go into recession, or vice versa. Once you know whether you are heading into a growth or a recession scenario, you can set a portfolio that will capitalize on either outcome. For example, if economic indicators point to a growth period, you go for growth stocks. Conversely, if you are headed into a recession, you buy real estate companies, utilities, etc. The transitions are periods of uncertainty. The last such period, August 1998, was a classic example when we had the big banks blowing up in Europe, markets were coming off, Asia was going through the floor, and there were concerns about an interest rate hike in the United States. Gold stocks performed briefly in August and September 1998 and flagged the imminent start of the current mining cycle.

Gold's role has changed, then, from being a hedge against inflation to more of a leading indicator of a change in economic sentiment?

Yes. What you find now, in the context of the global industrial production cycle, is that gold stocks go first as an indicator of change. About three months later, we start to see some other mining companies pick up from very low levels, and mining stocks typically lead basically a troughing in industrial production globally by about nine months. And then what you find a month or two after that is that bond rates start to pick up, and that's what we've seen in this cycle. The first quarter of 1998 was probably the bottom of the bond rate cycle and of industrial production globally, not just in the U.S. but everywhere else. So, industrial production is starting to pick up, the U.S. is up there, and now we are seeing Europe pick up a little bit and certainly Asia is coming through. So, the mining sector is pretty straightforward. You've got to look for gold as the leading indicator, and you have to look at the bond rate cycle, you have to look at the global industrial production cycle and, of course, stock prices. The last thing you look for is fundamentals such as PERs[12] and price to cash flow. They will look absolutely bloody awful, but this is when stock prices will be the absolute cheapest.

So if mining stock prices are reflecting what are recessionary-type lows, then that is the right time to go in?

Absolutely. And the final thing that nails the coffin is that when you go and talk that story to fund managers, the average fund manager will tell you there is absolutely no reason why he should be buying mining companies now. You know, the usual response that we get is, "You show me when the turn is going to come" — that's what you hear. We wrote a piece of research that gave every reason to buy mining stocks in March or April 1999 at the latest, but all we heard was, "I have absolutely no reason to own them." People had been selling these things for three years, and the stock prices were one-third of what they were.

It's similar to one of my favorite examples, which was back in December 1991. If you had had a chance to buy either Microsoft or Citicorp, what would you have bought?

Probably Microsoft.

That's what most people say, and you'd have made forteen times your money. However, if you had bought Citicorp, you would have made sixteen times. What sort of valuation methods do you use?

What we do with all the mining stocks, whether they are single mine-type companies or conglomerates like Rio Tinto[13] or BHP, is we use the NPV, method. NPV, of course, is related to EVA[14] analysis in another form. But for a finite resource company, it's a fair way to go because you can put an absolute value on the ore body in the ground. There are your basic inputs obviously, like what are the costs of extracting the ore and the long-term commodity price. The long-term commodity price is the hardest one to predict, and this is where your sensitivity is. I pick a long-term price that is constant over ten or twenty years, or whatever the oil field or mine life is for a particular asset. I'll use oil as an example. I put in \$19/bbl for oil for my NPVs. Why \$19? That's what it has averaged for the past twelve years, or near enough to it. The past twelve-year price history of oil ranges between US\$10/bbl and over US\$25/bbl. The daily oil prices are normally distributed, or close to it, with a mean of \$19.28. The sort of things that have shaped this historical oil price are global growth, recession, OPEC action, technology shift, and wars. You asked about charts before. Well, here's the historical chart that captures much that shapes oil prices. Going forward, I expect similar factors to influence the price. I don't believe in new price paradigms. Unless I think there is a good reason why the value of this commodity should shift structurally — that is, it should block shift up or down — then it's as good a reason as any to pick \$19 for the next ten years as it was for the last ten. And in NPV work, the twenty-year price is more important than next week's.

Unless you've got a Gulf War coming along.

That's right, unless you've got a war or a global embargo, as happened in 1973. These are rare, but real, events. It's even longer since the world went to war over the price of copper or coal! Nevertheless, predicting wars is best left to the CIA.

Wars end, anyway.

Correct. So we'll use the long-run historical average price as a first pass, and what we'll do in our modeling is we'll continue to use it, and I use it irrespective of whether the spot price is US$15 or US$25/bbl. I'll use that price for the long-term number, and what that gives me is an NPV for the resource in the ground. Now, the only other variable in the equation will be bond rates. How do we pick that up in the NPV? Well, it feeds into our discount rate, so even if we leave the $19 oil price constant, if the ten-year bond rate goes from 10% to 5%, our discount rate will go from 12% to 7%. And what that does when you feed it into the NPV of Woodside, for example, it goes from $5 to $8. What has the stock price done over the past five years? It's gone from $5 to $12, so you pick up the market mechanism through the discount rate. We can fiddle around with the long-term oil price and we can do sensitivity analysis for those people who aren't happy with my commodity call. But what I'm unlikely to do if the spot oil price is, say, $20 today is suddenly redo all my numbers and stick $20 in, because what I'm going to find over time is that I'll get scatter gun values, or NPVs if you prefer, that are reacting to today's commodity price. It doesn't reflect the long-term value of the company.

So you remove the white noise from your valuation process.

White noise, yes, that's right. Otherwise, you end up confused and might never have a true feeling of what the underlying value is. Why else do we pick a constant oil price? Well, let's get back to how companies work and add value. The managements of these companies are sitting down making the same sort of decisions. They're not going to open a new oil field or mount a takeover if they think the oil price is going to be $15 or whatever. What the serious ones will do is tip in a long-term price, and that's what they are going to have to assume to get that oil field to work over the eight or fifteen years they intend to drain it. In other words, real oil companies can't react to today's spot oil price.

If it's that straightforward, why don't we see price and value converging more often?

Well, they do converge from time to time. Stock prices tend to react much more closely to short-term information, white noise, the latest drilling reports, etc., and consequently they'll be much more volatile than the NPVs. But the NPV is useful because it gives us the anchor value. If the stock price is moving a long way above or below its valuation range, and if we have a history of it, we can typically say with confidence that the stock doesn't trade at this premium or this discount and therefore it's a strong buy or sell. The final thing that we have to worry about, and this is the hard bit and this is where all your skills and experience come into play, because the NPV is the measure of the future after-tax value of cash flows, is can the company, or more precisely its management, can they grow the NPV? Can they add value to that cash stream coming back, or were they just lucky, and are they going to take all that cash flow and blow it on the next exploration phase and lose it all? This is key. Because as an equity investor or shareholder, you never get the cash flow. The custodians of the cash flow are the management and the board and all the workers. And you have to gauge whether they can reinvest it sensibly and manage it wisely for the shareholders. The reason I raise this is because, as a general rule, what you find in the mining sector is the mining sector erodes wealth. It's a value destroyer. No doubt about it. Given a dollar of cash flow, your average mining company will return about 70 cents. They'll destroy 30 cents in the dollar trying to find the next big oil field, trying to find the next big mine, until they finally figure out that finding the first one was an accident or they were just lucky.

So, on average, a dollar of value created and retained in the company isn't as good as if it had been put in the hands of shareholders?

In most cases, that's right. We're looking for the exceptions, the wealth generators. So then we've got to come back and have a look at the management. Are these people capable of reinvesting the money wisely? Some of them are. Will they return the money to you if they discover they're not finding the next big mine or oil field? Answer, no.

So, this isn't a strong investment case for mining companies, is it?

That's right. And there are lots of cases. If you look at the compound rates of return from the Australian Stock Exchange's accumulation indices for the major subcategories in the mining industry, you'll see that the energy sector has returned about 13% compound average annual growth, and that's even with the crash in oil prices in 1998 in the sector being off about 30%. So, in other words, the energy sector has created wealth over ten years, and it has over five and over seven years as well. And that's a commodity-based industry with the oil price over ten years down in real terms. But look at the gold industry, which is also a commodity-based industry, and the gold price, which has also been down in real terms. The gold industry over the past ten years has returned about negative 5% p.a.! Quite different! And if you look at some of the other extractive industry companies, returns aren't much above zero. What it tells you is that, with the exception of the oil industry, the mining sector, generally speaking, erodes wealth. That's over ten years, which captures booms, busts, technology shifts, etc. And the irony is that while much of the mining sector in Australia is generally efficient in terms of world practice, low-cost ore bodies, etc., and despite the fact that you have a commodity-based currency, it still wastes and erodes shareholders' capital!

A brilliantly run mining company isn't necessarily a brilliant investment?

Correct.

So, in short (a) you don't have pricing power (you're a price taker), (b) you're also faced with high ongoing capital expenditure requirements (which is a drain on free cash

flow), and (c) exploration costs can take a big chunk out of what's left, and that means there isn't much left over for shareholders. These aren't especially compelling investment fundamentals.

That's right. They're very poor, and you're better off out of these industries over the long run. But there is still a strong case for trading mining stocks during a commodity cycle. But they're not "buy and hold" stocks.

So, timing becomes more important when it comes to investing in mining companies. And you have to bear in mind that price and value are separate concepts?

Yes. For example, you can still make huge money by investing at the bottom of the cycle. In the first quarter of 1999, for example, oil was at US$10 a barrel. You had to adopt a view and ask, "Is this a structurally lower price? Are we going to have $10 forever?" Answer, most probably not. You could do some research and within thirty seconds work out that it would rebound, while at the same time the economists were telling everyone that oil was doomed. So, people were staying away from the sector and it was a great time to enter. The issue was timing. The oil price is now 250% higher. Likewise, base metals are rising, and mining stocks this year have risen 30–100%. That's a big gain.

And what about the gold sector?

If you look at gold at the moment, likewise it's been absolutely flattened, down to US$250 an ounce. Will it recover? Probably — it's a question of timing. But would you still invest in the gold-mining sector? Maybe, maybe not, as this is a different animal. If you look at the industry generally, and it doesn't matter what the trend in the gold price is, because over ten years it's made negative returns, and back in 1993/94 we had a good gold rally, and we had a lesser one in

1998. But in 1993/94 the gold sector doubled in the space of three months, again because we were in that sort of transition period between a recession and a growth phase and the gold price responded. So again, there is money to be made in the stocks. Lousy prices wring out excess and expose value. It's worth a close look. But the gold *industry* destroys wealth. Now, why is that? We've got good gold mines, we've got some very efficient pits, so where does the money go? Well, what you find is that in these companies it goes into exploration, or corporate excess, or whatever. What we find is that the first thing a gold company will do when it has found a super ore body is start looking for the next one. There are numerous examples of small start-up outfits finding a gold mine and then waiting to find a second one. There is a fixed amount of rent in the ground from the gold mine, and the first thing that happens is a third of it is wasted on looking for the next one. So, what drives this?

Ego?

Yes, exactly. It's driven by people who have just found a gold mine and who want to be the next Newmont[15] or the next Rio Tinto.

Was Big Pit[16] an ego-driven venture, or did it make sense economically?

It was one of the exceptions. Economically, it made sense. And if that money had been captured and returned as dividends, then those businesses would have done very well for their shareholders. Now, there have been some very good high-yielding gold stocks in the past that have never grown and have simply returned the money from the pit, and that's just fine. But when you want to grow, the big risk is, where are you going to find another big pit? Unfortunately, the exploration industry has lost a lot of money, and I can only put it down to looking for the next big pit. And the gold sector is one that has never had a shortage of capital. There has always been excess capital to come into the business which has found its way into drilling exploration holes. You go back until the early 1990s, and it wasn't taxed. You were paying no tax. You can go back to the period pre-1990, when you had a whole series of gold booms and raising equity capital if you were a gold miner was very, very easy. You had no secondary or primary taxes if you were a gold miner. Conversely, oil companies paid in excess of 70% in taxes until 1990. And if you needed some money, you did an equity issue and there was never a shortage of capital. It was a one-way trip, and yet the ten-year returns from the sector are negative, despite the tax breaks and the availability of capital!

Is there any compelling reason, then, to hold mining stocks, especially gold miners, as a long-term investment?

Yes and no. Some miners have done badly, and some of the diversified miners have delivered double-digit returns. Rio Tinto does, and has done so for a long time. But you have to be very selective. For example, there are reasons why Rio Tinto has delivered exceptional returns to its shareholders. How do they achieve it? Because it has a capital discipline at the top of the company. But little companies will drill the next prospect and open another mine even if it's marginal, because they have nothing else.

So the message isn't quite that bad, and investors should go for the larger, diversified, well-managed companies that show responsible capital management and have a reasonable dividend yield?

Correct, in general. Over ten years, Rio Tinto has beaten lots of industrial companies!

At the other end of the spectrum, if you are going to be in a small company, are you better off just going for outright explorers?

No, that's not the case. What you have to do if you are going for the small end is sit down and ask what really drives the people running these companies, because this is where the ego factor comes in. If it's a bunch of guys who have just started up a company and they've got an ore body that looks like it's going to be great, but they don't have all the necessary skills and need to get in consultants to build the plant and someone else to joint venture it, then there's a good chance that it's going to be knocked off at some point if it really is a good ore body — it's going to get taken over. Anaconda[17] is a classic case. The people running it aren't technical. It floated at 25 cents, and within a couple of years it was $5. You get in on a couple of those and you can make over a tenfold return. But the time to be out of it is before they turn the plant on, and Anaconda is a sell right now. They have just started to produce, or are trying to produce. People will be looking at that, and the big mutual funds will be looking at it, and thinking, "Ah, it's a producer now. It's got some future cash flow. It might pay some dividends. It has a market capitalization of $1 billion, and it's in the MSCI.[18] We can buy some for the fund." Wrong! Get out! That cash flow, if those guys take it and don't give it back to the shareholders, will most probably be burnt up.

So the key is to split them into two camps — diversified miners and start-ups — and timing is very important. And watch management very, very carefully.

Yes. But I think go for the start-ups. Go for the floats. Go for those miners that have got an ore body that might shape up. Chances are that one in five will probably be a loser, but if you've got enough winners it won't matter, because you'll make more on the upside when one does come through. It takes fortitude, though.

And with the diversified mining companies, go for the big guys at the bottom of the cycle?

Yes, that's right. Rio Tinto, Western Mining[19], Pasminco[20], Comalco[21], and the like.

And always remember John Baillieu's advice?

Yes. "Treat them all as liars and crooks until proven otherwise." With the mining sector, you can relate a lot of the issues and risks for investors back to management theory. You've got companies which, when they get a mine up and running and they are just about to turn on a cash flow from a billion-dollar-type investment, that's at a maturity stage for a lot of these companies. But that's also where the challenges start, rather than finish. They're also going to have to invest seriously in growing staff, their operational and production skill sets, and importantly, exploration capabilities going forward or deciding that they will just exit. Now that's where you have to sit down and talk to the management to find out what they really want to do and whether they've got the interest to grow the organization to the next level. Some of them don't have the attributes or skills required. And if they are just going to take the cash flow and continue to explore without the organization structure behind them to keep finding and developing these big mines, then you are going to find a good part of that rent is going to wasted. If you're lucky, they'll stop wasting money before the whole thing goes belly-up. You can find lots of examples of single-mine companies that started out with a stockbroker, a lawyer, an accountant, and maybe a consultant. That's how many small companies start life, but it's rarely how any of them finish life.

Which means that prices move first and fundamentals second.

Correct. You'll find analysts doing research on the company saying that the nickel mine or the gold mine or oil field is now just about to produce and, assuming it gets through commissioning and the technical risk disappears, the company will get some cash flow and be re-rated by the market. Wrong. They never get re-rated. They go down in price, because once you've got that re-rating, it's in the stock price already unless the company is on a PER of six and a cash flow multiple of three, which isn't usually the case. They are always fairly priced assuming that the plant operates okay and the cash costs will come in and the commodity price will stay there. And you find, almost without exception, that the stock prices for all these single-mine start-ups peak about three to six months *before* the mine starts producing.

Why three to six months?

Because that's when the beauty parades take place. You know, the analysts and journalists have begun visiting the new mine, the big brokers have written their research, and the big mutual funds have just taken a slab of stock. That's the wrong time for anyone to buy. You have to buy on a bet, and sell into the certainty. You sell into that strength and then sit back for three years and have a look and say, "Okay, now let's assume this mine really does make money and they take that cash flow and grow the organization." That's worth a look, because really what all these little companies are trying to do is what Rio Tinto is doing, and Rio Tinto has been in business for a thousand years. By comparison, Anaconda was floated only four years ago. You're not going to build a Rio Tinto or an Exxon[22] within a space of four years. So that's when you need to figure out the ego factor. What's in it for these executives? And at what point do they want to get out? Do they just want to fatten this thing up a bit and get it taken over? If so, that's great. You can make a lot of money if you can find a managing director who just wants to fatten a company and have it taken out. You see a lot of these types in the mining industry.

You previously mentioned price/earnings ratios, but in view of the NPV methodology you outlined, do PERs have any utility when it comes to looking at the value of mining stocks?

No. Earnings are either going up with new development, or down due to depletion. Spot comparisons of multiples don't tell the story. Earnings, cash flow multiples, are only proxies for value and a poor substitute if value can be more accurately calculated in other ways.

But the average investor probably still uses them as a benchmark measure of value?

There is no doubt about that, and it creates stock price anomalies. But that's the way the stocks are marketed in a research piece that may say, "This mine is about to start up, it's going to produce cash next year, it's on a PER of eight and a cash flow multiple of four times, it will pay a dividend, and they are going to explore and there are lots of opportunities, blah blah blah."

Which is the worst thing you could ever believe.

Yes.

How would you summarize the sector?

Basically, you have two camps. You have start-up jobs, backing some people who might have an ore body, and at the other end of town, it's really the big end, with guys like Rio Tinto who have got capital discipline. All the ones in the middle are just fodder for the M&A game. Some investors look on it as a casino. You know, "Let's go and find a little oil company that's about to drill a well and we can make some money," so it's the fast end of town. At the other extreme, if people are asking stories about what's the dividend, they've also got the wrong mindset. You're not going to get a dividend; you're in there for the capital gains. And in the middle you have the seasoned investor who understands the risks, the returns, and the cycles. You can make money anywhere in this sector, but you'll only score a run if you play with the right bat. By that I mean, learn the rules that govern stock prices, and know where absolute, not relative, value exists.

Does the mining industry realize that there are diseconomies in their business?

No, they don't, because the ego factor stops it. You have a level of M&A activity, but it's usually driven by distress and isn't what I would call merger for growth. Look at the oil industry. When we had a US$10–$12 oil price, in early 1999, albeit for three months, we had Exxon and Mobil merge — two global majors. We had BP and Amoco merge. And then Total and Petrofina — one is French and the other's Belgian! And there was Repsol and YPF. Four global mega-mergers because we had oil at US$10–$12 for three or four months! It drove these companies to merge when at any other time they wouldn't have considered doing so. Meanwhile, gold goes down the drain, takes the industry with it, and companies just have to sit and tough it out.

Desperate measures?

Global oil companies were quick to react to the lower oil prices. They merged to get their costs down. And the focus of those organizations now is to reduce costs. They've all cut their capital spending, after three months of US$10 oil, all slashed their capital budgets, so they figure that the only way they'll get capital out of their businesses is to cut the costs, and that's pretty fair. Now that oil prices have rallied, those merged oil majors will reap a big reward. It hasn't happened in Australia, though.

Why not?

It simple terms, because oil companies here do deliver financial returns and pay dividends. Some smaller companies are very poor financial performers, but people still buy because the industry is healthy. Where is the pressure to merge?

And what about BHP?

Well, BHP is a classic. There will be case studies written about this. I had to do one recently for a major Australian oil producer who is thinking of going the global route, and they wanted to see what mistakes they could learn from BHP. Well, there are lots. How much time do you have? If you go back, BHP was an Australian icon, and there was an arrogance level there that was evident when you were dealing with some of the middle management — guys that I knew from the oil industry or from business school days. You could see the corporate façade when you spoke to them. They knew everything, you couldn't tell them a thing. You could point to their competitors doing something better, and these guys could think of three reasons why it wasn't really better after all, and their competitors were just going to blow up at some point. Well, guess who blew up? And the real problem with BHP was the success of their Bass Strait oil fields. Ever since they found Bass Strait, the whole focus in the petroleum division and corporate culture for the next fifteen years was to replace it. So, they were no different from a little gold miner who thinks, "We've just found this golden goose. Gee, that was easy. Let's go and find another one!" Ditto with Escondida,[23] an excellent copper asset, which naturally led to Magma.[24] What a joke. The whole world knew this was a dog, but BHP weren't listening.

It sounds like they were complacent.

Yes. That was BHP. From about 1975 to about 1989, out of every dollar of cash flow earned from the entire company, 50 cents was reinvested in the petroleum division. The coal and iron ore divisions, and all those very efficient and profitable businesses, could have had an equal claim on the cash. And the cash flow being generated was scarce capital. When BHP made their coal acquisitions, when they grew those iron ore mines in the 1960s, BHP was the god of the mining industry and the capital discipline was much tighter than what it was in the 1980s and 1990s. But they became *too flush* with money. And what they did was, through the 1970s, 1980s, and 1990s, they started to explore globally, and you would read in their financial reports and statements and hear at their show-and-tells, "We are a globally significant company. We are top ten now in terms of production. We have to be internationally competitive." Not a mention anywhere of being big in terms of shareholder returns.

And the corporate logo and media slogan became "BHP, The Big Australian."

Yes, that's right — all these sorts of things. All feathers and no meat. There was nothing you would ever read like, "We aim to deliver 15% compound return in shareholder value and a 20% return on capital. We aim to grow the dividend by such and such amount." There was never any mention anywhere in the annual or other reports of the financial discipline or the financial rewards that would go to the stockholders. It was all about, "We're now global." Who were they running the company for?

So Robert Holmes à Court[25] was right?

Yes. He should have broken it up in 1985. It may have saved them, but Holmes à Court's methods were probably premature by fifteen years. But getting back to the petroleum division, in the late 1980s they went off and bought a bunch of companies around the world and lost a fortune. Then they did the same thing on the mining side with Magma. And they ended up wasting over A$10 billion of shareholders' money. Even though the present management are trying to turn the company around, and the current stock price is up, I would argue that you can't waste $10 billion of shareholders' money and retain your previously strong competitive position. You can't waste $10 billion, or a quarter of your shareholders' capital, over a period of time and then expect to turn the company around quickly and reclaim the mantle. Because in the meantime, you have starved all of your efficient operating businesses — the coal, the iron ore, and the copper mines — to take this capital out. And while you were doing that, your competitors in Brazil and Rio Tinto have fattened those businesses, so when you crawl out from under the wreck and go to compete again, you'll find that your competitors have repositioned themselves on the cost curve, and that they are faster, better, bigger, and cheaper producers. It will be interesting to see if BHP's new approach succeeds in the longer run.

So, scale — excess capital — can be a problem, as it can breed arrogance and complacency. Is there an optimum size or operating structure, say like an asset trust, for an extractive industry company?

Probably not. Rio Tinto operates like a closed-end asset trust, and that's not a bad model, and a lot of companies would do better to understand that structure. It would stop the erosion of capital, because that's where the wealth destruction happens. It's not because people can't make money out of extracting some dirt and making ore; it's fundamentally a very profitable business once you have sunk in your capital. And if you get lucky first time around, and it's a generally low-cost ore body, you can make a fortune out of it. But as I've mentioned, companies tend to blow up when they take the cash flow out and then think, "Gee, that was easy. We found the world's biggest mine. Let's spend all this cash flow trying to reproduce that." And they spend the next fifteen years trying to reproduce it and burn a lot of shareholders' money in the process. But if you work like an asset trust, and send the money upstairs to your asset trust board, who say, "Wrong, we were just lucky. There aren't any more Eldorados or King Solomon's mines left. We're going to reinvest that cash flow into our iron ore mine, or spend it elsewhere," then that structure and capital discipline would add a lot more value to shareholders.

In the banking sector, we have a lot of companies that work under a holding company structure and are very strict about

leaving surplus capital behind because some bankers realise that you can't sit on surplus capital forever. There comes a point where you have to start spinning it back to the shareholders.

They sound like smart guys. That model should also work in the mining sector, because you can buy companies and mines as efficiently as you can explore if you are patient. But, unfortunately, you find it doesn't happen. Companies are driven by people with big egos who don't focus on earning 15% return on capital for their shareholders.

Do you think that people can make money in the mining stocks by following gurus?

Yes, but you can also make money by tossing a coin. But I think there are some simple rules.

What are they?

Don't buy a company when they are about to start production and everyone is all over them and there is lots of hype. Again, it gets back to an efficient market hypothesis. That's when everyone's buying them. And, as you know, the market is just a whole bunch of buyers and sellers — it's like a sale at a department store, and you are competing to buy that last suit on the shelf that is going to get bid up. I think the average investor should look seriously at the small floats that come through, and I think there is money to be made out of the M&A cycle, certainly. You have to bet, and buy in the face of uncertainty. Certainty costs money. I also think there is money to be made out of some big companies when they are down on their luck and people aren't writing the stories anymore. Some of these companies aren't going to disappear overnight, their stock prices have halved, and people are selling. You should take advantage of those situations. Big stocks can double or triple over a cycle. Buy at the bottom. We have been critical of BHP. But it halved over the past few years. That's a big downward move, and there was value. At A$10–$12, it was a *great* buy.

Any other advice?

You are always going to have a story coming around about a company that is going to drill up a batch of wells, and while that can be a recipe for losing money, there could be a sentiment wave there, so you have to look at whether you are getting in at the front end or the back end of the wave. You can make money, but I think the thing about it is that you have to trade. If you make 20% in a week, don't buy more, sell. The other thing I see people doing is they go into a quick trade, and the broker will tell them that they have to buy this stock because "there is a drilling program coming through and if the drilling program doesn't work, it still has an NTA (net tangible asset backing) of $1 and you can buy it today for 80 cents. If the drilling program works and they find something, it will be worth $2." Now, at the end of the day, the NTA is still $1. If the stock price goes from 80 cents to $1.20, sell it. If it goes from 80 cents to $1, sell it. If it goes from 80 cents to $1.60, sell it — but don't hang on to it at $1.60 and see it come back to $1 thinking that it's going to stay there because that's what the NTA says. It will go back to 80 cents, less whatever they spent. If you have bought stock thinking it's going to go up during the drilling program, then sell it when it goes up. Don't ever hold it thinking there's a backup strategy, because other people don't buy backup strategies!

So, with drilling programs you'll never lose money taking a profit?

Correct. But even if the stock price goes down, it's a mistake to hang on to it thinking there will be a natural level beyond which it won't go. It may do. It might settle up, but it might sit there for three years.

What's the typical size of the junior to mid-cap oil explorers?

Anything under a billion dollars. That takes in most of them, and if you've made your quick 20%, then sell it. The worst thing you can do is buy more on the way up, and you see that happen often. Or when it goes up and then comes down, people buy more. You have to trade these situations, and when you've made your supernormal return, get out. Then you take the supernormal return and buy some blue chip industrials or banks, and sit it out until the next story.

As an analyst, what is the ratio between sheer hard work and talent?

You need a combination of both. I think it comes down more on the side of hard work, probably a 90:10% proposition, because you see a lot of people who I would call normally qualified, with a degree or two, but who aren't rockct scientists. Put it this way, if you want to become an astronaut or you want to design rocket ships for NASA, you're going to have to be one talented sonofabitch, and you're going to have to have flown navy jets and landed on an aircraft carrier pitching in a raging sea. You're going to have to have an IQ of 197, a Ph.D. in nuclear physics, and to have studied all your life. Or if you want to be an Olympic athlete and race against Linford Christie, you're going to have to be very fast. Bottom line in these pursuits is that talent is the starting point. Now in broking, you don't need a Ph.D., you don't need to land jets on an aircraft carrier or to run a ten-second 100 meters. You can take a whole lot of normal people and overlay on that the hard work element — that is, a willingness just to persevere through all the grind and late nights — and they'll be successful. But not a lot of people want to do that, or they get bored with it. So, hard work is the key. And in this business, you're on your own; no-one is going to give you much advice. The market will give you feedback, and you'll know if you're getting the story wrong or you're going in the wrong direction. There is no "How to Do It" book. You are in a fairly ambiguous environment and you just have to learn how to adapt to it and grind it out.

How difficult is it not to have too rigid a view on a stock? You know, the view that "management of XYZ Mining N.L. just reinvent the wheel every three years and then proceed to run themselves over."

Or as a mining analyst, never have a buy recommendation on any company that starts with the letter C or P! By the way, one of those companies was taken over and made everyone a lot of money! Two of them did. But it's true, you can get stuck in a rut and think that a company is never going to change, and that's dangerous.

How hard is it to separate your emotions from objective analysis?

It can be tough. I think you have to be objective about the work. And when we go and talk about companies, we split out the human factor. We are talking about companies as simply chips at the casino. A company is a commodity, it's a thing to be traded by your client, and we all make money out of that process — client and broker. You've got to look at the financial terms, and that requires objectivity. People ask me whether I like or hate company ABC. It's not a question of passion — only of stock price versus valuation.

That's a good analogy. Do you know the origin of the term "blue chip"? It's the most expensive chip at the casino in Monte Carlo.

Is that right? No, I didn't know that. Sounds fair enough, though. From the point of view of the people investing in stocks, if I was going to the buy-side, to me a company is nothing more than a chip to make money out of. Capitalism in its purest sense. Yes, companies are run by people and all that sort of stuff, and you can read their corporate brochures that say they are very sensitive to the environment and they have a great human relations track record, etc. Rubbish! It's got to come down to how much money you can make out of their stock. There are five pillars that need to be satisfied in this whole financial services industry. It's a bit like Maslow's[26] hierarchy of needs. And there is a hierarchy of needs in broking and funds management; it's money, money, money, money, and money. And nothing matters unless you make money for your clients. If you make money for your clients, the clients will reward your business. If they reward your business, you'll get rewarded. So coming back to the point about objective analysis, everything has got to come back to a set of objective financial numbers. Is the stock at a discount to whatever it's fundamentally worth? If it is, can it be taken over and broken up and the value realized for the shareholders?

Analysts don't exist to prove how smart they are; they exist to make money for their clients and employers.

Correct. You exist to make money for your clients, they make money for the firm, and the firm will make money for you. The three are related. Get me a dumb guy that makes money — that's fine.

How valuable is historical analysis?

I think that if you approach life asking, "What can I get out of that piece of historical information," you are probably going to get more out of that, and what's more, you can take that into your research and your dealings with people, more so than you can by looking forward. For example, no-one wants to hear about what Nostradamus had to say. He was written up in the paper today, saying the world is going to end today. You sell more newspapers by writing up what we *already* know, which was that last night Pat Rafter got beaten by André Agassi at Wimbeldon. You will sell more newspapers by talking about Rafter as opposed to Nostradamus telling us the world is going to end today or tomorrow.

Is too much success a risk?

I think so. I think that the ego factor is the greatest destroyer of personal ambition and wealth, and everything else that comes along, because no-one is bigger than the market. The market is a big leveler, and it's made up of a lot of stupid people. The smartest people in this industry can get it wrong because they don't realize how stupid everyone else is. Stupid people can make a fortune, so does it matter if they weren't smart? You're only going to make money if you bring yourself to the level that allows you to see what drives the market.

Do you have to pull yourself back sometimes though?

You have to. Ego is a big destroyer, and I think bearing that in mind also helps you to deal with others. If you assume that your client is a normal person on day one, then you have a better chance of servicing him. I mean, it's still a human business, too. We're dealing with people, not machines, and because we're dealing with people's wallets, we're as close to the nerve as the dentist is with the drill.

So, a big ego is a liability?

Absolutely. I think the ego thing is the biggest barrier to any analyst's performance, really. I've seen some talented analysts where the ego factor has just gone over the top. It makes the job harder than it should be. Some of these people have been successful, but they would have been a lot more successful if they had been better able to relate to their colleagues and clients.

What are the fundamental business principles that you live by?

It might sound like Pollyanna stuff, but there are two. The first is that honesty and integrity are critical, and you must always look after your client's interests. From time to time, corporates come along and pressure you to write such-and-such. If you don't feel comfortable, don't do it. Sometimes it's a mutual fund that is putting the pressure on you because they have a big position, or its corporate finance department, or you're not happy with the company in its representations. If you are uncomfortable about it, then don't write. I have found that if you do and you make a mistake, then it's a killer and comes back to haunt you because it's *your* signature on the piece of research. It's *your* work. It doesn't matter what inputs went into it, as no-one will ever know what they were. You've got to feel 110% responsible for any piece of paper that goes out with your recommendations and numbers. You could have a whole army of juniors doing the numbers for you, but if there's a mistake in the numbers, it's *your* mistake, not a junior's mistake. It's *your* recommendation, not your corporate finance department's, so you've got to do your work honestly and if you're not happy with it, then don't do it.

What is the second rule that you live by?

It's a client business, a people business. You have to treat everyone with respect as a human being with a job to do. I see some adversarial relationships where people view the client as an enemy, or they go out there with a point to prove, such as that the client is a turkey, I don't like him, I'm going to belt him over the head and embarrass him and extract an order out of him — you know, that kind of thing. Wrong! You've got to talk to the clients, find out what drives them. If they are under pressure because they've just lost one-third of their funds and they're about to get fired the next day, you had better understand that. Otherwise, you're wasting the client's time and yours. So, spend some time understanding the client. Talk to them. In the first meeting I go to with a new client, for example, the first thing I do in the first hour, is I don't even tell them, "This is my story. This is my stock pitch." I don't do any of that. Instead, I explain the principles by which I do my research. I tell them what I'm looking for, which is an NPV. These are the inputs I tip into it. I emphasize that this is what I do, and if they think that's of some help, then that's what I can do for them.

Everybody brings something different to the market, and so they have to know what is your value added.

Correct. I'll tell them up front what I can do and what I can't do. If a client wants to know where the drill is with every oil well every day, then sorry, I can't do it. I'm not even in that part of the game. Others can do that better. However, if they want to find out how all the businesses run, what is the value of all the businesses, and if they want a twenty-year profit forecast, then yes, I can provide that, and I'll send them my model on a disk if they want it. Whatever they want, if I can give it to them, I'll give it to them. I'm not about to say, "I can't give you the numbers, that's confidential." That's rubbish. I'll give the clients everything I have in return for the fee or commission, understanding that we'll get paid for our efforts. If there are things I can't do, I'll be straight up-front with them and say, "I don't do that, or I won't do it, or I can't, or I don't have time." So, after about an hour the fund manager knows what sort of service he or she can expect, and in return I've assessed the likelihood that we'll get paid for our efforts. If it's a little fund that has no money and they want you to model things fifteen different ways by next week, then you might say, "Well, that looks unrealistic for me; we're not on your panel, and it's unrealistic for me to do that. But what I *can* do is send you some numbers from time to time, or whatever." But always give the client the benefit of having got something out of it without having been overly pressured into it. I leave pressure tactics to the vacuum cleaner telemarketers.

How do you judge success?

By the speed of the car in the garage. I've got two cars out there, one of which would be lucky to do 60 miles an hour! I judge success in a professional sense by whether or not you are still married after ten years, and whether or not your kids are drug addicts. It might sound silly, but I see a lot of people go into this industry at the front end to grow themselves a personal success, to have a happy family life, etc., and they end up with none of that. They might have the wealth without the family, or they might have the family without the wealth. But I think at the end of the day you've got to look at the family. You have to look at yourself in the mirror every morning and ask, "Why am I getting up at 6 a.m. and going to work?" You've got to like what you do, you've got to like talking to your clients and like the people you work with. If you have to force yourself to go to work, you're in the wrong business. Schlumberger always used to say, "If you like the job, you would do it for half the money. If you hate the job, you wouldn't do it for twice the money," and I think there is a truism in that. You see in broking a lot of people who are doing the job for twice the money, and they work for firms that blow up their analysts or dealers quite regularly. So these people move on, or they get iced. And they don't get back into the industry. The ones who survive at the firms that pay twice as much as anyone else, if they're not balancing their professional life with their personal life, then they risk ending up divorced. Their wife will end up with all their money and they'll end up with nothing. Thanks for coming! So, I think that's the wrong game plan. You have to have a balanced view of life. You've got to provide some financial security for your family, and you're not doing your wife or family any favors by growing a fancy lifestyle, only to find yourself fired two years into the job, with three kids in private schools and a huge mortgage and car lease. You'll get no thanks from anyone for that. I think you really have to provide balance to all those people around you, your family, and your workmates. There's no point in going to work if you are a complete jerk and abuse everybody all the time. That doesn't work either. You have a responsibility to conduct yourself properly, ethically, and professionally. And don't come home and abuse your family and kick the dog every night, either. So those are the important issues for me, and if you can do that and catch the trappings along the way, then you will have succeeded.

Finally, what advice would you give a novice analyst?

Your first three recommendations should be "holds."

✳ ✳ ✳

Stuart Baker's experiences will be of interest to anyone, whether analyst or investor, who has suffered setbacks or losses early in their career. There are probably three things that stand out about Baker's approach to analyzing stocks and investing.

First, have a healthy dose of skepticism. While Baker's comment about treating management as "liars and crooks until proven otherwise" may sound a little harsh, unless you know and understand a company and its management very well, you must be prepared to invest at least twelve months of your time in studying the company and, more importantly, management and their philosophy about running the business. As Baker admitted in relation to his early mistake with AGL, "The company had been around for 150 years; I'd looked at it for three months and reckoned I was an expert! Was I qualified to make a call? Not even close!"

Second, there is nothing wrong with making mistakes, but it can be fatal if you don't learn from them. When it comes to investing or making stock recommendations, everyone makes mistakes. Be prepared to regard bad stock recommendations or investments as powerful learning experiences, rather than as something to hide from or get embarrassed about. After all, when it comes to investing you can be right for all the wrong reasons. Humility is therefore an important part of stock-market investing, as it's easy to get carried away with your successes. Be more concerned about how to manage and learn from your failures. Baker firmly believes that no matter how experienced or qualified you are, you never stop learning, and sometimes you have to take two steps back for every step forward.

Third, investing in mining stocks can seriously damage your wealth. While the Australian energy sector has returned about 13% p.a. for the last ten years, gold stocks have returned around minus 5% p.a., and some of the other sectors have returned not much above zero. So, even a brilliantly run mining company isn't necessarily a brilliant investment. Therefore, adopting a "buy and hold" investment strategy is relatively risky, and investors need to be very aware of at what point of the industrial production and commodity price cycle they are buying. With larger stocks, Baker favors buying at the bottom of the cycle, and even then, he says, you have to be very selective. With respect to small or medium-sized mining companies, he believes that investors would be better off going for start-ups and floats, but you must be prepared to take some losses. However, a portfolio approach should deliver good profits over the longer term. Moreover, the best time to sell is when a mine or oil field is about to produce, because that's when the company will start to look attractive to the larger fund managers on traditional pricing benchmarks.

Finally, despite Baker's twenty-plus years either working in or tracking the mining industry, as well as his obvious intelligence, he rather modestly claims that success has more to do with hard work than any special talent or gift. Moreover, he says, at times the job can be boring and dull, and sustaining motivation and enthusiasm is one of the main challenges for the analyst.

---

[1] Schlumberger Limited provides resource management services and technology products, services, and systems for the oil industry. The company offers seismic data acquisition, well construction, and productivity services, wireline logging, and other oil field services. It also provides services to utilities, energy service providers, and other industries. At the time of writing, the company had a stock-market capitalization of US$43.9 billion.

[2] Michael Porter is professor of business administration at Harvard Business School and author of *Competitive Strategy: Techniques for Analyzing Industries and Competitors* (Harvard Business School Publishing, 1998).

[3] Broken Hill Proprietary Company Limited is an Australian-based international resources company whose principal business lines are steel production, minerals

exploration and production (coal, iron ore, gold, copper concentrate), and petroleum exploration, production, and refining. At the time of writing, the company had a stock-market capitalization of A$32.4 billion.

[4] Santos Limited explores for and produces natural gas, crude oil, condensate, naphtha, and liquid petroleum gas. The company conducts major onshore and offshore petroleum exploration activities at oil and gas fields in Australia (Cooper/Eromanga Basins), the United States (Gulf of Mexico), Indonesia, and Papua New Guinea. At the time of writing, the company had a stock-market capitalization of A$2.5 billion.

[5] Novus Petroleum Limited explores for and produces crude oil, natural gas, and other petroleum products. The company has exploration activities located in Australia, Indonesia, Oman, and Thailand. At the time of writing, the company had a stock-market capitalization of A$218 million.

[6] Woodside Petroleum Limited explores for and produces oil and gas from offshore and onshore facilities located in Western Australia and the Northern Territory. The company also operates oil and gas fields and pipelines throughout Australia, Papua New Guinea, and Mauritania. At the time of writing, the company had a stock-market capitalization of A$7.3 billion.

[7] National Australia Bank Limited is an international banking group operating in Australia, New Zealand, Europe, Asia, and the United States. At the time of writing, the company had a stock-market capitalization of A$36.3 billion.

[8] Telstra Corporation Limited is a full-service domestic and international telecommunications provider for Australia. At the time of writing, the company had a stock-market capitalization of A$45.5 billion.

[9] Earnings before interest expense and taxes.

[10] Net present value.

[11] MIM Holdings Limited is an international minerals and metals exploration company whose activities include the mining of copper, gold, zinc-lead-silver, and coal. At the time of writing, the company had a stock-market capitalization of A$1.6 billion.

[12] Price to earnings ratio (also referred to as price/earnings ratio).

[13] Rio Tinto plc is an international mining company with interests in aluminum, borax, coal, copper, gold, iron ore, lead, silver, tin, uranium, zinc, titanium dioxide feedstock, and diamonds. The group's mining operations are located in New Zealand, Australia, South Africa, South America, the United States, Europe, and Canada. At the time of writing, the company had a stock-market capitalization of £11.8 billion.

[14] Economic value added, or EVA as it is often referred to, differs from most other measures of corporate performance by charging profit for the cost of all the capital a company employs, debt as well as equity. Capital is also adjusted to reflect economic reality by taking into account off-balance-sheet debt and adding back unwarranted write-offs against equity. The result is better information and insight about a company for its managers, which enables them to make better decisions. EVA is not particularly new, as the concept, a registered trademark of Stern Stewart & Co., was first written about by Alfred Marshall, the English economist, in 1890.

[15] Newmont Mining Corporation explores and produces gold, as well as acquires and develops gold properties. The company operates in the United States, and in Peru, Indonesia, Mexico, and Uzbekistan. At the time of writing, the company had a stock-market capitalization of US$4.4 billion.

[16] A large open-pit gold mine proposed in the mid-1980s in Western Australia.

[17] Anaconda Nickel Limited is a mineral exploration company. At the time of writing, the company had a stock-market capitalization of A$822 million.

[18] Morgan Stanley Capital International World Index tracks the performance of twenty-two of the world's major stock markets.

[19] WMC Limited's activities include the mining, processing, and marketing of copper, uranium, alumina, nickel, gold, fertilizers, and industrial minerals. The company's operations are focused in Australia, North and South America, Europe, and Asia. At the time of writing, the company had a stock-market capitalization of A$8.5 billion.

[20] Pasminco Limited's activities include exploration, mining, smelting, and marketing of zinc and lead concentrates, and zinc, lead and silver metals, together with alloys and by-products. At the time of writing, the company had a stock-market capitalization of A$1.0 billion.

[21] Comalco Limited produces and explores for aluminum and bauxite through mines in Australia, New Zealand, and Guinea and West Africa. At the time of writing, the company had a stock-market capitalization of A$5.4 billion.

[22] Exxon Mobil Corporation operates petroleum and petrochemicals businesses on a worldwide basis. At the time of writing, the company had a stock-market capitalization of US$272.3 billion.

[23] BHP produces copper concentrate from its 57.5%-owned Escondida mine in Chile.

[24] In 1996, BHP bought Arizona-based Magma Copper for A$3.2 billion, but plunging world copper prices forced an A$2.16 billion million write-down and closure.

[25] South African born Robert Holmes a Court (1938-1990) was one of Australia's most astute investors and deal makers during the 1980s, and at one stage was Australia's richest man before his business empire was ravaged by the October 1987 sharemarket crash. In 1983, Holmes a Court stunned the Australian business community with an ambitious bid, to take over Australia's largest company, and mining giant, BHP. The bid ultimately failed, although the manner of the bid, through a relatively unknown road haulage and engineering company, enhanced his reputation as a master of unorthodoxy in corporate deal making and takeovers.

[26] Dr. Abraham Maslow, a psychologist, coauthored with Robert Frager and James Fadiman, *Motivation and Personality* (Reading, MA: Addison-Wesley Publishing Company 3rd ed. 1987).

2

Mark Mobius:
The True Believer

"When it comes to investing, you have to do your own analysis, you have to draw your own conclusions, and you have to be ready to live by your decisions."

Born in Germany, raised and educated in the United States, and the author of two books on investing in emerging markets, Dr. Mark Mobius is managing director of the Templeton Emerging Markets Fund as well as a number of other funds in the Franklin Templeton Group. His original Templeton Emerging Markets Fund, which was the first emerging markets fund to be listed on the New York Stock Exchange twelve years ago, was valued at just over US$100 million. Today, even after the shocks of the Asian and emerging markets crisis, Mobius has US$11 billion in funds under management. As part of his philosophy of undertaking on-the-ground fundamental research, Mobius spends at least eight months of the year traveling in a Gulfstream IV jet with his team of analysts, visiting companies and meeting with managers all over the world. Mobius and his team of twenty-seven analysts, who work in eleven offices worldwide, speak eighteen different languages, and travel to forty countries each year, make nearly a thousand company visits a year. One of Mobius's mentors was Sir John Templeton, who pioneered international investing in the early 1950s, well before it became fashionable, and who subsequently became known as "the dean of global investing." The legacy of Sir John Templeton is sixteen rules for investment success, which are set out at the end of this chapter. Despite the fact that Sir John Templeton no longer has an association with Templeton Funds Group, his sixteen principles still form the foundation of Mobius's investment philosophy. This is illustrated by the fact that Mobius's letterhead contains three words, "Value, Patience, Bottom-up," to which three more words could be added which summarize the principles Mobius emphasized throughout our discussion — that successful investing is also about common sense, hard work, and humility.

How did you get started in the investment management business?

I began my fund management career in 1984 with Vickers De Costa. I was sent to open their office in Taipei, and a few years after that I became president of International Investment Trust — a joint venture with a number of Taiwan banks and some other brokers and fund managers, including Citibank, Lazard, Gartmore, and Jardine Fleming — set up to manage an offshore Taiwan fund. This was the first vehicle through which foreigners could invest in Taiwan, and it was fairly successful. We then started a domestic fund in Taiwan which proved to be very successful as well. So, that was my first direct experience in managing funds.

What was your first big stock call?

I would say Formosa Plastics,[1] which was owned by Taiwan Plastics.

What attracted you to the stock?

The company that ran Formosa Plastics was very dynamic and entrepreneurial, very disciplined, and had very strong management. I noticed that the company was tightly run, almost like an army, with very strict controls. I was very impressed by that, and I was also impressed by the company's size. Moreover, at that stage it was a world leader in its business, as management had acquired technology from all over the world, particularly America. So, the company impressed me from a variety of perspectives and I felt that it would be a good investment going forward, especially as the plastics industry was doing very well at the time.

Do you learn more from good or bad stock calls?

I think my first, and most valuable, lesson came from a bad stock call. One of the very first investments I ever made in Hong Kong was a company called Mosbert Holdings, which eventually went bankrupt. It was a very good lesson, because I remembered trying to call the company to get information and being refused anything. But, based on a hot tip from a friend of mine, I invested in the company anyway. And I think that's where I really learned the value of doing your own research and not relying too much on other people's analysis. When it comes to investing, you have to do your own analysis, you have to draw your own conclusions, and you have to be ready to live by your decisions.

What then do you value from sell-side analysts? Some fund managers have told me, "We don't value your stock calls, we don't even want your valuation — we just want your company and industry intelligence and data."

Well, I think that's a fair comment, and it's generally true for all of us here at Templeton. We love to get information about companies, even if it's just rumors. Anything that brokers hear about a company is grist for our mill. But we like to get as much unbiased information as possible. And we don't really value recommendations, whether to buy or sell and so forth, because very often these are time-sensitive. For example, somebody may say, "Look, this is a great buy," but if you read the report a month later, prices may have moved up to such an extent that the stock is a sell. So, we prefer to have the basic information so that we can fit it into our database.

Everyone brings something different to the market. Do you prefer analysts who think laterally and strategically, or analysts who are very good gatherers of data and have good modeling processes?

We prefer data gathers and people who will get information not only from the company, but also from the company's competitors and other people in the industry — this is particularly helpful to us. We like to have a full picture of the company, and we particularly like industry information, industry trends, or anything that has or might have an impact on the company. And, of course, any information about the people behind the companies is of great help to us. This is often lacking in sell-side research — there is, generally speaking, not enough information about who is running these companies; what their mindset is; what their background is; what the family connections are, etc.

Given the events of the last two years, have some of your premises changed — for example, that emerging markets will deliver twice as much growth twice as fast, relative to the developed markets? Are you still as enthusiastic as ever?

Yes, absolutely. It still holds because of the underlying demographic and technological trends that we see. Of course, as we have seen, there will be some setbacks, there will be some periods of slower growth, but overall these emerging markets countries are going to grow faster.

And does Indonesia still figure in your thinking?

Yes, definitely so. Indonesia is very important for us. It's one of the largest countries in the world, so we can't ignore it. But we look at Indonesia as having tremendous potential and, of course, greater risk.

So if we look at where we are heading in the emerging markets over the next five years, are geopolitical analytical skills more important than they were two or three years ago, or are we just going through, as you describe in your first book, "one of those bumpy periods that all markets suffer from"?

There's no question that the political dimension and political analysis is very important. The problem with both political and economic issues, particularly the economic numbers, is that they are, generally speaking, too late. That's a real problem, and as a result you get the warning too late and you get into trouble. That's why we always emphasize the "from-the-ground-up" approach, because we can understand the issues more readily by asking the companies what their problems are, rather than by reading about bad political or economic news in the newspapers.

In your book, you mentioned using common sense when it comes to investing. But someone once said that common sense isn't that common. How do you define common sense in terms of investing?

Well, I think using basic, simple logic. I think it's also very much tied to humility — you have to be humble whenever you are approaching a question, and you've got to be willing to say, "I don't know." Too often, people sit in meetings and are afraid to raise questions for fear of looking stupid. And common sense would dictate that you never look a gift horse in the mouth. You should always be prepared to say, "Look, I don't know," or "I don't understand. Please explain that to me."

So, there are no dumb questions, just dumb answers?

Exactly.

How do you go about finding the right questions?

Well, I think by listening. Again, humility is very important. You've got to listen to what the other guys are saying and then respond in a commonsense way.

And is singing karaoke with the chairman's son also part of the process?

If that's what it takes, then yes. Very often it doesn't require that, but if you are meeting people and saying, "I'm a potential investor, and I'd like to know as much as I can, I'd like to see as much as I can. Please tell me about what you're doing," then if that process also involves socializing, then yes, we have to do it.

When it comes to the emerging markets, and investing in general, what skills do you think can be taught and what skills can't?

I think all the number skills can be taught — there's no question about that. Any person can read a textbook and apply these things. What can't be taught, though, is attitude, this attitude of humility. That's something you need to develop, and I'm not so sure how you acquire that.

Probably by making enough mistakes and learning from them. Quite often I say to clients, "All I'm bringing to the table is seventeen years of mistakes."

Exactly. This is what you learn over the years, I guess. It's a psychological thing. You also have to be curious in this business. Intellectual curiosity is a very important ingredient.

Do you think that great analysts and fund managers have a special talent?

I don't think so. You can come from any field of endeavor and be an analyst or fund manager. The one thing that separates the good ones from the bad ones is their diligence, their curiosity, and their willingness to work hard and pursue every last detail.

How long does it take to get the right attitude and experience? It takes quite some time to master the craft of sell-side research, and the more gray or thinning hair you have, the better.

That's a very interesting point. It's very true in our business, and I think it's also true in your business. There's no doubt that the older you get, the better you get, because you have more experience, you know what questions to ask, you can look behind what people are saying. You've been through it all before. You've had those experiences where someone says one thing but does the complete opposite. These experiences are very important.

So the age of fund managers and analysts is probably going to continue to lengthen?

Very much, and I think the good ones are the older ones.

What do you think are the popular misconceptions about markets and about investing in emerging markets that tend to get people into trouble?

I think, paying too much attention to the short term and looking at things on a day-by-day basis without taking a longer view and putting things into perspective. I guess that's true of all markets, but it's especially true of emerging markets. You have to put things into the longer-term perspective, otherwise you'll end up seeing only the trees and not the forest.

There is probably also a popular misconception about the reward-for-effort equation in this business. This business is

probably 90% grind and 10% gravy, and that success is very, very hard work.

I agree — that's absolutely true.

How many hours a week would you work, for example?

Lots. For example, I was here until 1 a.m. last night and then I was back in the office by 7.30 a.m. Twenty-hour days are not uncommon. You end up working so many hours because you're so involved.

So you have to have energy, passion, and enthusiasm?

Yes — those are absolutely essential.

What is the ratio between talent and sheer hard work, though?

I would say effort is 80% of the equation. That is really the bottom line. And as we discussed earlier, experience counts for a lot as well.

Is it easier to be popular or contrarian? Which is more profitable in your view?

I'm tempted to say contrarian, but I think one of the fundamental rules is that you really can't go against the market in the sense of being consistently in the opposite direction, because very often the market is correct — and in the long run, the market is *always* correct. You shouldn't go against the market consistently, because there will be many times that you'll be wrong. At the same time, you must be willing to take a different view from everybody else, because you want to outperform everyone else and so you've got to do things differently. You have to take a balanced view. You can say, "Okay, I'm a contrarian," but you can't make it a religion. And as we all know, change is with us all the time.

Can too much success be a risk in this business?

Undoubtedly. You can get carried away with your own success. Again, this is where humility comes into the picture. You can have good years, but for every good year you have to expect a bad year, and when that happens you mustn't lose heart.

Are there any years that stand out for you as good or bad?

I'm not avoiding your question, but it really depends on how you define good or bad. For example, if performance is very good in any year, I'm usually quite unhappy because I know it will be difficult to sustain. On the other hand, if the performance is bad, then of course I'm struggling to make it better. Therefore, you are constantly in this state of tension. A large part of this job is psychological — self-control and discipline. You've also got to become sympathetic on the one hand, and at the same time you have to become painfully objective, otherwise you're not doing your job properly.

Do prices move first and fundamentals second?

Yes, I would say that's a fair comment, which is why I mentioned earlier that the market is ultimately never wrong, because as fund managers we are based on what happened to the market. But hopefully what you can do is anticipate the market by looking at the fundamentals.

Which is similar to Keynes'[2] view that we have reached the third degree when we begin to spend more time thinking about what we think average opinion expects the average opinion to be.

That's a very good way of putting it.

Do you use charts?

Yes. Charts are a road map, and anything that is graphic is very useful because you can get a very good picture of what has been happening relatively quickly and efficiently. But they are only one part of the equation, and I wouldn't want to give the impression that I'm a closet technician, because at the end of the day you have to look at a lot more than that.

So charts are just another piece of data?

Yes, but they can be a fantastic tool.

What are the pros and cons of spreadsheets? Has the craft of stock picking and equity analysis suffered or benefited from the impact of technology?

The avalanche of information that is available has been helpful, really. The Internet, for example, and all of the various information sources have been a tremendous boon for investors. But at the end of the day, you also have to have the discipline to separate the wheat from the chaff. But notwithstanding this, it's a terrific help to have this kind of information. We don't look at everything, but we find what we can look at very useful.

What was your experience in October 1987?

It was pretty much of a shock, as we had just started the Templeton Emerging Markets Fund and were about 70% invested. Then the market collapsed. So it was the first real test of character for me, because the philosophy, of course, when that sort of thing happens, is to buy when others are despondently selling, and that's exactly what I did. It turned out to be a great lesson for me because it worked beautifully and started us out on the right foot. Nevertheless, it was painful at the time and very difficult. It was the right thing to do and it gave us the courage to do it again when the opportunity presented itself. Really, it was one of the key reasons why we survived.

So, courage and self-discipline were important ingredients?

No doubt about it.

But even so, emotions must come into play at some stage. Is the pleasure of a good stock call as intense as the pain of a bad one, for example?

Oh yes, absolutely. But remember, we are generally looking at performance in the context of an overall portfolio, so we are trying to make as many good calls as possible and to minimize the bad calls. So it's not like we are waiting with bated breath for a particular stock that we picked to go up. We're always looking at the total portfolio performance and taking our knocks along with our successes.

And as your portfolio grows, it becomes harder to achieve outperformance, doesn't it?

Yes, unfortunately, that's also true.

Do you get to a point where your success starts to create future problems insofar as the more successful you are the more money you attract, and the larger you get the harder it becomes to achieve outperformance?

Again, unfortunately, yes. And that's the reason why I keep stressing this issue of humility. Unless you are going to be humble, and say, "Look, this isn't going to last," and remind yourself that these things are transient, unless you keep your nose to the grindstone, you can really get caught and suffer a lot.

It's interesting that you keep stressing this issue of humility, as it's a quality that you don't come across very often in this industry. A popular belief is that in order to be perceived as successful or good at your job, all you have to do is be quoted in the newspapers or keep getting your face on television and be loud.

That's absolutely correct. I agree entirely. A lot of the analyst surveys are more about being a good marketer or media star than being a good analyst. You have to strike a balance. I mean, I'm regarded as a media star and that's a necessary part of marketing, but at the end of the day our job is to make money for our clients.

Has the turmoil in the emerging markets over the last two years altered or changed your investment philosophy and approach?

Well, a lot of things have changed. In fact, the emerging markets themselves have changed. We've gone from six markets in 1987 to forty today. The amount of money that we manage has gone from US$100 million to US$11 billion. So, there have been tremendous changes not only in the markets, but also for us here at Templeton. But what *hasn't* changed is the need to perform, to make the right investment decisions, to do the research, and all the other things that are so critical, like sticking to your fundamental investment philosophy and methods. And from that perspective we haven't changed, insofar as we are still fundamentally driven, value-orientated investors. So, even though the amount of money we manage has gone up by a factor of 110, the fundamental parts of our approach and philosophy haven't changed. With respect to our faith in the emerging markets, our enthusiasm and optimism are even stronger as a result of what has happened over the last two years. In fact, it has probably strengthened our belief that we are in the right place.

So your emerging markets investment thematic of rising income levels against a background of a large and growing population base still holds?

Most definitely. I see no reason for that to change, and our enthusiasm for the emerging markets has probably gotten stronger as a result of some of the issues that have been addressed as a result of the crisis.

What have been the main lessons that you have learned from Thailand and Indonesia over the last two years, for example?

The human or political aspects of investing are areas that we probably have to pay a lot more attention to — especially in the context of the individual company investment. It's not sufficient to look at the generality of what is happening in a particular country; you have to do more detailed analysis of what's happening on the ground, especially the political aspects — that is very, very significant. The other issue here is the increased need for shareholder activism, and we are becoming much more active and much more concentrated on what we want to do.

How do you know or develop the resolve about what it is you want to do?

One of the reasons why we do intense on-the-ground research is partly to know what decisions to make. Another aspect that is often overlooked is that it helps us psychologically in sticking to our decisions, because one of the biggest mistakes that people make in the investment business is changing their minds too often. By being on the ground, and by having met the company and having asked them about the business, etc., we become more confident in our decisions.

You sleep better at night.

Yes, that's right. It helps you to stick to your decisions. You won't be jumping from one thing to another. I think that's very important.

That sounds similar to something I read about Warren Buffett.[3] He was reputed to have said that the average investor would be better off if they didn't make more than twenty investment decisions in their lifetime, and that when you buy something, you should want to buy it for keeps.

Exactly, and the only way you can do that and hold to your decisions psychologically is by being very confident. The way you can be confident is by visiting the company, talking to the people, and so forth.

Can we talk about portfolio diversification, because one thing that you advocate is diversification. However, there are differing views on diversification. Keynes believed in putting all your eggs in one basket, and watching that basket very carefully. As mentioned earlier, Warren Buffett reputedly said that twenty investment decisions in a lifetime would be enough for the average investor. And at the other end of the spectrum you have Mike Milken[4] with his junk bond theory. What do you think are the pros and cons of those investment philosophies?

Well, diversification really saved us, because it saved us from many of our mistakes. In this business, you are going to make mistakes, no matter how lucky or how smart you may be. So, I think the philosophies that you mentioned were made in different contexts. For example, for the entrepreneur, the self-made man who is concentrated on one business, the idea of putting your eggs in one basket and watching that basket very carefully is very, very good, and many people have made a lot of money doing that. But that's not appropriate when you're managing public funds, because the volatility and risk are too great. And that is, of course, one of the contributions of modern portfolio theory, and the reason why pension funds around the world adopt these theories, because it saves them from the extreme volatility of having all their eggs in one basket. But notwithstanding this, there is relevance in both approaches, because you have to have diversification, but then you try to concentrate as much as possible by knowing each element in your portfolio and watching it very, very closely. So, it is possible to have the best of both worlds — that is, to have the very best companies that you can find, but in a diversified portfolio. So, when something happens through no fault of your own — by the way, there are many things that can happen over which you have no control — you have some degree of protection.

Do you tend to favor countries over sectors, or sectors over countries?

We favor companies. Companies come first, sectors second, but in the context of the company. Basically, we are evaluating companies in the context of their environment and their industry.

When you find these undervalued companies, what is the catalyst for price discovery and the realization of their potential value?

I would say a *fall* in the price. Too often the sell-side comes to us with a stock that has already gone up a lot in price, and we have to try to train the analysts to come to us with stocks that have gone *down* in price a lot. There is a bias from the sell-side because they want liquidity and volume, and volume comes in a rising price.

Which is understandable, given that the sell-side earns its living based on volume and turnover. But are you implying that this may not always be in the interest of long-term investors?

To a degree. But liquidity *is* important for us, or anyone in the mutual funds industry, because without liquidity we're in trouble when those redemptions start rolling in. We appreciate that brokers are generating liquidity, but there is a tendency, because of their commission structure, to emphasize those stocks that are liquid, and liquid stocks tend to be the ones that are rising or have already risen to great heights.

If you were to publish a new edition of your first book, *Mobius on Emerging Markets*, what would you add, subtract, or change?

I would probably put in more about the people and the political aspects that I mentioned earlier. Unfortunately, it's a very difficult area to write about if you want to write good examples, as you would probably spend most of your time defending libel actions! But I would probably emphasize that part of the business more.

It's one of the fundamentals of banking or lending money — character. Can you trust what management are telling you?

Absolutely. That's a key issue.

While we're talking about risk, a fundamental tenet of investing is the unit of return per unit of risk. In emerging markets, how do you measure risk, what sort of criteria do you use to measure your performance, and do you use proxies or measures beyond the traditional actuarial or statistical metrics?

We know what the risks are in portfolio management terms — that's volatility — but in terms of assessing the risk in layman's terms, no-one has mastered that. This is well-illustrated by the fact that the credit ratings agencies failed to warn investors and lenders about the Asian crisis — they were all left flat-footed. But to be fair, they were given an impossible task. That's one of the reasons why our business is a qualitative business, rather than a quantitative one.

A good example of that was when we saw the baht devalued in 1997. One fund manager said to us that this could find its way all the way to Wall Street. There was no spreadsheet or quantitative analysis behind that conclusion.

Sounds like a very smart guy!

I suppose that also raises the issue of market timing — you can sift all the data, draw the right conclusions, but implementation and timing can still cause you headaches. If timing the market consistently is nearly impossible, is it best just to buy and hold and let time take care of the rest?

As a general rule, yes. We've demonstrated that in our funds as well, and being fully invested most of the time is what we find works over the long term. Perhaps the *lowest* we have ever been is 80%. And we are probably never going to go there again because, as you say, being fully invested is very, very important.

Perhaps the other important variable apart from time in the market is tax. In your book, you argue that capital gains are the natural enemy of the equity investor. However, there are a number of markets that have performed very well but have a capital gains tax regime. Does this mean that you are automatically excluded from investing in what by most criteria would be attractive markets?

Well, it does depend on what the capital gains taxes are, but generally speaking, we cater to international investors who have portfolios that are taxed in their home countries. If they are taxed in the host country as well, then that tends to affect their total returns. So, the valuations may be attractive, but taxation considerations must also be considered.

On the issue of valuation, what are your preferred benchmarks or valuation tools?

In recent years, there has been a lot of talk about EBITDA,[5] enterprise value,[6] etc., but at the end of the day, you want to know about earnings, because that's what investing is all about. A company has to earn money for its shareholders *after taxes*, so you have to keep your eye on that objective. Now, what we do is say, okay, let's not look at earnings this year. Let's look at it in five years, because at the end of the day, that's when it's going to be critical. So, the price we pay for earnings *five years* out is what interests us.

Finally, what money management advice would you give to the average investor when it comes to investing in emerging markets?

In view of the volatility of emerging markets, I would recommend that dollar cost averaging is a sensible strategy for the average investor. Also, don't put your money in unless you are willing to buy at the absolute bottom of markets when things are really bad and very, very negative. Most people would be far better off putting their money in gradually over a period of time, rather than trying to be greedy and make a quick killing.

❇ ❇ ❇

Mark Mobius is passionate about the virtues of investing in emerging markets. The fundamental premise of his 1996 book, *Mobius on Emerging Markets*, is that "emerging markets will continue to grow at about double the rate of the developed world." He also argues that emerging stock-market capitalizations should grow faster still, as stock-market capitalization to GDP ratios should advance toward that of the more developed markets. Mobius emphasizes the importance of portfolio diversification, and this extends right through to his belief that investors should not adopt a single-country investment approach in the volatile world of emerging markets, because "the markets which lead the pack in one year, few appear even in the top five in subsequent years." But whether you are an investor in emerging markets or not, the investment principles that Mobius outlines can be equally applied to developed markets:

- Quality of management is a key investment variable.
- You have to be curious when it comes to investing, and always be prepared to say "I don't know."

- You have to be prepared to work hard in finding and managing your investments. Mobius believes that effort accounts for 80% of success.
- Have a fundamental investment philosophy and method, and stick to it.
- Take a long-term view — at least five years.
- Don't be afraid to buy quality stocks when everybody else is selling them.
- It's not your timing *of* the market, but your time *in* the market. In volatile markets, dollar cost averaging is perhaps the most sensible strategy for the average investor.

Sir John Templeton's Sixteen Rules for Investment Success

1. If you begin with a prayer, you can think more clearly and make fewer mistakes.

2. Outperforming the market is a difficult task.
    The challenge is not simply making better investment decisions than the average investor. The real challenge is making investment decisions that are better than those of the professionals who manage the big institutions.

3. Invest — don't trade or speculate.
    The stock market is not a casino, but if you move in and out of stocks every time they move a point or two, the market will be your casino. And you may lose eventually — or frequently.

4. Buy value, not market trends or the economic outlook.
    Ultimately, it is the individual stocks that determine the market, not vice versa. Individual stocks can rise in a bear market and fall in a bull market. So buy individual stocks, not the market trend or the economic outlook.

5. When buying stocks, search for bargains among quality stocks.
    Determining quality in a stock is like reviewing a restaurant. You don't expect it to be 100% perfect, but before it gets three or four stars you want it to be superior.

6. Buy low. So simple in concept. So difficult in execution.
    When prices are high, a lot of investors are buying a lot of stocks. Prices are low when demand is low. Investors have pulled back, people are discouraged and pessimistic. But, if you buy the same securities everyone else is buying, you'll have the same results as everyone else. By definition, you can't outperform the market.

7. There's no free lunch. Never invest on sentiment. Never invest solely on a tip.

    You would be surprised how many investors do exactly this. Unfortunately there is something compelling about a tip. Its very nature suggests inside information, a way to turn a fast profit.

8. Do your homework, or hire wise experts to help you.

    People will tell you: investigate before you invest. Listen to them. Study companies to learn what makes them successful.

9. Diversify — by company, by industry.

    In stocks and bonds, there is safety in numbers. No matter how careful you are, you can neither predict nor control the future. So you must diversify.

10. Invest for maximum total real return.

    This means the return after taxes and inflation. This is the only rational objective for most long-term investors.

11. Learn from your mistakes.

    The only way to avoid mistakes is not to invest — which is the biggest mistake of all. So forgive yourself for your errors and certainly don't try to recoup your losses by taking bigger risks. Instead, turn each mistake into a learning experience.

12. Aggressively monitor your investments. Remember, no investment is forever.

    Expect and react to change. And there are no stocks that you can buy and forget. Being relaxed doesn't mean being complacent.

13. An investor who has all the answers doesn't even understand all the questions.

    A cocksure approach to investing will lead, probably sooner than later, to disappointment if not outright disaster. The wise investor recognizes that success is a process of continually seeking answers to new questions.

14. Remain flexible and open-minded about types of investment.

   There are times to buy blue-chip stocks, cyclical stocks, and convertible bonds, and there are times to sit on cash. The fact is there is no one kind of investment that is always best.

15. Don't panic.

   Sometimes you won't have sold when everyone else is selling, and you will be caught in a market crash. Don't rush to sell the next day. Instead, study your portfolio. If you can't find more attractive stocks, hold on to what you have.

16. Do not be fearful or negative too often.

   There will, of course, be corrections, perhaps even crashes. But over time our studies indicate, stocks do go up ... and up ... and up. In this century or the next, it's still "Buy low, sell high."

[1] Formosa Plastics Corporation manufactures and markets PVC resins, high-density polyethylene, acrylic fiber, acrylics, carbon fiber, caustic soda, PVC modifier, and calcium carbonate. At the time of writing, the company had a stock-market capitialization of TWD 220.9 billion.

[2] John Maynard Keynes (1883–1946) was one of the twentieth century's most influential thinkers and economists. His principal legacy was his book, *The General Theory of Employment, Interest, and Money*, as well as the international banking institutions, The International Monetary Fund and the World Bank, which were established as a result of the post-World War II Bretton Woods conference in the United States, which was dominated by the presence and works of Keynes.

[3] Warren Buffett is chairman and CEO of Berkshire Hathaway and is widely regarded as one of the globe's most astute investors. He is the third-wealthiest person in the United States, with an estimated net worth of US$31 billion.

[4] Michael Milken, former junk bond chief at the defunct Drexel Burnham Lambert Inc., who pioneered the high-yield junk bond market in the early 1980s. "Even junk has its uses" was a favorite expression of Milken's, who was convicted of insider trading.

[5] Earnings before interest expense, depreciation, amortization, and taxes.

[6] Enterprise value is defined as a company's market capitalization plus the market value of its debt less cash plus long-term liabilities plus deferred tax plus minority interests.

3

Brian Johnson: A Champion Team will Always Beat a Team of Champions

"It's about surrounding yourself with good people. That's a very important part of it."

Brian Johnson is Australia's number-one banking analyst and head of research at Ord Minnett, widely regarded as one of Australia's most successful independent stockbroking companies. Johnson started his working life as a chartered accountant auditing the Australian Stock Exchange. He began his career as an equity analyst a few weeks before the October 1987 stock-market crash and, despite this harrowing start to his equities career, Johnson admits that, in spite of all the uncertainty back then, he would not have contemplated returning to chartered accounting. Johnson is perhaps one of the hardest-working analysts you would ever meet. During reporting season, he averages anywhere from zero to two hours' sleep a night as he and his team grind out fifty or more pages of analysis. While he is one of the hardest-working analysts in the market, Johnson is also one of the most modest, and largely attributes his success to a combination of sheer hard work and having good people around him. Moreover, Johnson believes that while discipline and effort are an important part of the job, as a sell-side analyst, the house you work for also has an important bearing on success. For example, when Johnson left Macquarie Bank in 1994 he was a middle-ranked analyst, but his move to Ord Minnett was a major turning point in his career and helped him climb the last few rungs of the ladder to become Australia's number-one banking analyst.

How did you get started in this business?

I was a chartered accountant with Peat Marwick, who used to audit the Australian Stock Exchange. I did a bit of the work when they were merging all the various state stock exchanges, and one of my friends was a financial controller at a small stockbroker and I subsequently became the assistant financial controller. But I later found myself drifting more and more toward the analysis side, so it went from there.

And you started out as a banking analyst?

No, I didn't. I started as an analyst that did A to P.

A to P? Okay, stocks from Amcor through to Pacific Dunlop.

I might not have started at that point in the alphabet, but I started out on industrials, building materials, News Corp, Palmercorp — which is a fashion company.

That's interesting, because it probably adds to your analysis.

Very much so.

Are there any issues or techniques from industrial stock analysis that are useful in analyzing banks?

Probably more the other way around. One of the biggest issues that I find probably isn't adequately covered in a lot of other industrial research is sustainable capital expenditure and the ability of a business to generate capital to fund ongoing capital expenditure.

That is really a critical issue for banks, for example. Although it might not be capital expenditure to actually fund a fixed asset, it's about funding balance sheet growth. So, I think there are a number of parallel issues between the two sets of stock classes. In addition, I'm finding increasingly a lot of the work that I'm doing translates and crosses back into industrial companies.

At Bankers Trust, we also believed that one of the biggest determinants of earnings per share (EPS) was capital expenditure. You know, estimating stay-in-business capex and expansion capex. Whereas in banking, what you are saying is that the equivalent concept is how much qualifying or regulatory capital you can generate and how much you need to leave in the business to generate future growth.

Exactly.

And then it's all about how that links into a bank's capital management philosophy and how that drives dividends, EPS growth, and, ultimately, valuation.

I completely agree. That's what it's all about.

What was your first big stock call?

TNT.[1]

Was it a buy or a sell?

It was a buy.

And what was the price then?

I couldn't tell you what the price was, but TNT was a stock that had always looked cheap on just a straight cash flow multiple. But if you actually looked at TNT and thought about your sustainable capital expenditure — because depreciation for a company like that actually becomes a cash flow — it actually didn't look cheap at all. In fact, it looked quite expensive. And basically the turning point for TNT was a succession of disasters. This was a long time ago.

When?

The pilot strike of around 1990/91. I called it just before the end of the pilot strike. That was pretty much my first really big stock call.

What did you learn from that?

I suppose what I learned was that there is nothing wrong with going out and making a big call and having a different view to the market. Unfortunately, my next big stock call didn't work quite as well as that. The next one was an absolute disaster.

Which was?

Westpac.[2] And there is a report out there, a big red report that I wrote when I was at Jardine Fleming, that still haunts me to this day. People still bring it out. In that report I predicted that Westpac would make a A$1 billion profit in either 1991 or 1992. They actually *lost* a billion dollars. I was only out by minus 100% [*laughs*].

So you just forgot to put the minus sign in?

That's right. But the stupid thing was that in the report I had written a lot about asset quality and how highly leveraged transactions coming out of the United States could have undone it all, but I just came to the wrong conclusion. I had the bare bones of the right story there, but I just came to the wrong conclusion. Interestingly, the report included a bit from our quantitative/technical analyst, and he said it was the worst stock price chart that he had ever seen. He turned out to be right. So, I published the negatives and the pluses, but unfortunately I went out on the plus side, which was pretty dumb in retrospect.

That must have got you noticed!

Yes, it did. It put me on the map big time as probably one of the worst analysts around for many, many years. And despite all the good work on TNT, Westpac still comes back and haunts me now.

People always seem to remember the bad calls a lot longer than the good ones. What lesson did you learn from the Westpac call?

If you are going to make a big call against the market, you want to make sure of your numbers inside out. That doesn't necessarily mean you'll get the call right, but at least you'll have a second line of defense if you're wrong.

Did it worry you at the time that guys like Kerry Packer[3] were buying Westpac? Did you think, "What does he see that I don't?"

Well, I've got to tell you — and I can remember it quite clearly, because I was working for Macquarie Bank at the time — Ord Minnett, who were then a wholly owned subsidiary of Westpac, were actually *buying* the shares for Kerry Packer, which was quite funny in retrospect. But the valuation case to buy Westpac then was pretty ordinary. Now, what I had failed to appreciate — and I've got to say that this is the thing about trying always to improve your analysis by learning from your past mistakes — but the fundamental mistake I had made, was that if you had looked at Westpac's balance sheet at that point in time, they had something in the order of 30% of their balance sheet in commercial property. Westpac had gone from being a property lender to being a property developer. Which meant that you had 30% of a very big balance sheet overhanging the commercial property market in Australia, which is quite a small market. And what I had failed to anticipate was the crushing impact that Westpac's own oversupply of property actually had on property prices.

What was the turning point?

If you look at what actually happened, the turning point for Westpac was, and you can nearly track it down to the day, and I didn't, I've got to be honest and say I got it wrong for a long time after, the turning point for Westpac was when they came out and recapitalized the bank based on the *market* value of the assets. Because the minute that you did that, you took Westpac out as being a desperate seller of the assets, which meant that property values rose and they actually ended up with surplus capital. And I believe that the big key to Asia at the moment is if you can be certain that you can find a bank that has written down the value of its assets to market value, and has recapitalized its balance sheet on that basis, that bank will probably be the best buy of the century. For example, I think South Korea has an interesting dynamic to it as well, which is that recapitalization isn't going to work unless you have every participant in the market doing it at the same time. And if you look at what South Korea offers, the debt is incredibly concentrated and very high profile — in twenty very large companies. So, it's very measurable, and that's why Korea is going to rebound a lot faster than a lot of other Asian economies. Whereas if you look at a place like Thailand, it's a lot more opaque and dispersed.

Where does a banking analyst add the most value for their clients?

A lot of people would probably disagree with this, but I think being a good bank analyst isn't about stock picking; it's the actual sector call. There is no reason why you can't have buys on all four major banks,[4] especially if you've got very rational kinds of behavior from all four banks at the one time. That suggests, in fact, that it might even be prudent to spread the risk across all four.

How important is timing in that equation?

That's a good question, because I've done a lot of work looking at this, and if you look at the Australian banks — and you have to remember that basically two out of four were basket cases in 1990 and 1991 — the bad lending behind that was basically done between 1984 and 1989. And the *really* bad lending was probably done in around 1986. What caused that bad lending was deregulation following a period of quite strong commercial lending growth, and at the same time as the economy dipped out and capital expenditure actually fell. But the banks still felt obliged to meet asset growth targets, so they lent against speculative assets. The point I would make about that, is that the bad lending was between 1984 and 1989, and yet it didn't really manifest itself seriously until 1991 and 1992. There was, however, a slight escalation of bad debts in Australia between 1985 and 1988, but it wasn't out of control. And I would flag to you that one of the things about longevity, and learning from your mistakes, is that it's always worthwhile to go back and look at past cycles. And if you look at Australia at the moment, a lot of people think 1992 was an aberration and that 1990 was probably the norm. But I would say that 1990 was incredibly high as well. And to really get the most similar environment to what we see today, you really have to go back to 1984, 1985.

Are the cycles getting longer or shorter?

If you get the data for twenty years in Australia and you go back and you think that deregulation happened in 1984 — which caused the problem — a lot of people will tell you that the cycle is ten years. It's not. It's actually getting longer. If you look at the data for Australia, basically from 1980 through 1999, there has been only one blip, which was 1992. So in Australia, people who say the cycle is ten years, I don't believe that's right. And what we spend a lot of time looking at as banking analysts is competition in the banking market. So let's talk about interest rates, competition, and behavior, because that's what you should really be looking at in the banking sector. And the great thing about being a banking analyst is that it doesn't necessarily mean when things turn that it's a bad problem when it first happens. You've normally got about a four- or five-year time frame before it actually manifests itself in big losses and significant underperformance.

Notwithstanding that, how important is gut feel and instinct in picking stocks?

I think it's probably the crucial thing, because if you look at the banking sector in Australia, the earnings are relatively predictable. But the flip side of that is that valuations are really driven off the bond market. Now, if you look at the bond market you'll get very disparate views on where bonds are going, and the moves tend to be incredibly volatile. I think gut feel does actually become a major component of what you do. And the other thing is the idea of looking at oligopoly-type behavior by the banks.

So it's a relatively different valuation paradigm because of the structure of the Australian banking sector and the market for banking services compared to, say, the United Kingdom or the United States?

Yes. And the great thing about it here in Australia is that if you look at the four major banks, they've got tremendous pricing power and tremendous scale. Any new players coming into the market have to put away more capital. They have to run on a higher Tier 1 ratio, because they're small. Furthermore, they tend not to have the geographical diversity, and they don't have the same operating scale or efficiencies on the cost or funding side. So, we have a bizarre situation where the new entrants are actually less profitable but they need to put away more capital, which means they can't compete on the basis of price. And that is essentially what has happened in Australia with the mortgage originators. They went from being incredibly price-competitive to being just another commodity-based service. Banks have repriced down and are now getting more scale on the cost side.

And unlike commodity or mining companies, who are price takers, the banks have pricing power.

Yes, and what's more, they have it both ways — on the supply and demand side. They can flick out their products at a certain price and they also have an incredible capacity to price their inputs. Moreover, when people start to talk about technology and its impact on the economy in Australia, banks are the only technology players that really exist!

People have been writing off the banks for a long, long time, but you seem to think that the banks in Australia still have tremendous appeal as an asset class.

Yes, and a lot of it comes down to assessing rational behavior. There are great parallels with this in the commodities market at the moment. I think it's to some extent a bit of a tragedy, in a way, that we have had a rebound in commodity prices and commodity stocks, because we were starting to see excess capacity taken out of the market. That excess capacity stems from poor management decisions in the past, so to some extent, you are now seeing a reversal of that. Some managers are getting their "get out of jail" card, and there are some companies that could have gone from being very ordinary companies to great companies but will now remain very ordinary companies. But looking at the banks, there is a general awareness that they are stewards of capital. It's quite amazing. The mood has gone from banks saying it's defeatist to hand back surplus capital, to saying it's more defeatist to try and generate an incrementally smaller return on surplus capital. So, you are getting a whole paradigm shift and it comes down to this idea of capital discipline.

At the end of the day, then, the best bank in the world could be one that has a high gearing ratio, but a good capital adequacy ratio due to efficient capital management, good provisioning, strong liquidity, and good asset quality. And the combination of those factors will probably drive ROE[5] to 25% or beyond. However, in Australia, as bank bashing is almost a national sport, that sort of financial performance would be politically unacceptable.

Yes. I think one of the other big issues for bankers is to ensure the sustainability of ROE. One of the biggest risks I believe banks face is the fact that they trade at discounted multiples relative to insurance companies. I have spent many years marketing the theme that you should see bank PER[6] multiples expand back up to the market multiple. And I'm still a firm believer in that. Logically, that should happen. But every time you flag it, once you start to see a bit of the PER expansion coming through, you see people selling into it. So it never quite happens.

Why do you think banks trade at a discount to the market?

Mainly because there is a generation of investors who believe that banks can't behave rationally. Now the flip side of that is, if you look at some of the great banks around the world — Lloyds TSB, for example — they have actually proved that if you aspire to do better than your peer group, you can succeed. And that highlights another thing that we look at closely, which is how management is remunerated and how that flows all the way down into adding shareholder value. It's a very big thing for Ord Minnett generally, so it's not just in banks. It's something we look at very closely for all companies.

Are you seeing a generational switch happening? Are you seeing signs that people are beginning to believe that this change in bank management behavior is sustainable?

To some extent. For example, most people are overweight banking stocks at the moment, and even though the PERs haven't been re-rated, they have had much better accumulation returns than other sectors and people are starting to think about that.

Another argument could be that as the banks are the arteries of any economy, they should trade at the market multiple because if the economy is in good health, banks are probably behaving rationally, and if companies are making money, then the banks are going to do just fine.

Yes, and their innate pricing power leverages that up even more.

But when things sour, banks are the first in and the first out.

That's true, too.

So in periods of economic prosperity, it's illogical that banks should trade at a discount?

Yes, it is. And what's also interesting is that fund managers will tell you that they should trade at a discount because they are highly geared. But I would argue that they take a totally different risk through leverage compared to industrial companies, as they have their borrowers' shareholders' funds subordinated to them. People often miss that point. But once again, it comes down to this idea of discipline, and it becomes very apparent when the banks aren't behaving rationally.

What is interesting about the capital and leverage issues is that, at the end of the day, capital never saved a bank. You can have 15% or even 20% capital adequacy ratios, but that's not going to save a bank. Asia proved that. The only thing that will save a bank is liquidity and depositor confidence.

Yes, it's quite bizarre. Moreover, I can see arguments why banks with superior profitability are going to be generating capital at such a rate that they should be able to run on lower Tier 1 ratios. For example, coming back to Lloyds TSB, it should be able to run on a lower Tier 1 ratio. The caveat on that, however, is that if you look at someone like Wells Fargo, the drive to maintain the high capital generation is an absolutely critical point and you don't want to pursue capital-dilutive acquisitions. The other factor to consider is return on risk. Over the time I have been analyzing banks, there has been a tremendous investment by banks in measuring and managing all aspects of risk, be it credit, market, country, or operating risk. The effort isn't directed toward minimizing risk, but rather toward optimizing the risk/reward profile. Before the big blowout in Australian loan losses in the early 1990s, I don't think banks could adequately identify all the potential risks they faced, let alone manage them to optimize returns. Better risk management practices, and, more importantly, a disciplined approach toward risk by all banks in a marketplace, must reduce the likelihood of failures. Conversely, excessive competition which sees risk ignored is what ultimately leads to bank failures.

What are the key fundamentals that you focus on in a bank stock?

I've got to tell you that mine aren't particularly imaginative. I just break it down into the drivers, which I believe are asset growth, lending spreads and margins — and they are two very different things — and what I see happening on fees, because a lot of fees aren't really about revenue, they are about costs. Other issues include noninterest expenses, bad debt, provisioning, and capital adequacy. If you break a bank down across those particular measures, invariably it will spit out the aggregate picture. I find a lot of banking disclosures about divisions incredibly useless because, for example, the allocation of capital between operations seems to be shuffled around, as well as the allocation of head office costs, so we tend to end up looking at everything in aggregate.

And the business divisions don't exist as legal entities, either.

No, they don't, so it makes return on capital difficult to assess as well.

What do you think of price-to-book ratios as a valuation yardstick?

I think price-to-book is totally irrelevant.

It's an outcome.

Absolutely. If you do any chart of a price-to-book ratio versus ROE, you'll get this incredible correlation. And what that is really telling you is that banks trade on earnings-based multiples and their yield on sustainable capital.

Consequently, a bank can be cheap at three times book and expensive at one times book.

Yes, and what it really comes down to is that a low multiple of price-to-book may well be telling you that a particular bank is under-earning, and the issue is then to assess management's capacity to turn that situation around. That's not to say that price-to-book is a driver of value, but it may well be a screen, and a limited one at that. You can't follow it slavishly.

So it's a question of looking at the right diagnostics and understanding their information content. What skills do you think can be taught in this business, and what skills do you think can't?

A lot of people will tell you that it's a black art and that a lot of it is magical, but I don't think it is at all. I think the only thing you really need to do is be close to your companies and not be afraid to offend them. But more importantly, be close to your clients and listen to what they want. What you will find is that your clients teach you. I find speaking to smart clients — and I spend a lot of time marketing, for this very reason — is the bit that really creates value for me. Every good piece of work I have ever done, I can quite honestly say was triggered by some client request, or some client comment that got me thinking in a slightly different way. So, what can you teach? I think you can teach all of it. I don't come from a banking background at all. I haven't had anyone teach me. I've learned just by listening to what my clients want, and learning from my mistakes.

So listening skills are important?

Yes, very, and listening to what companies say as well. We've got a slightly unusual market niche in Australia, in that we follow absolutely the minutest detail because the data here are incredible. But a lot of people would dismiss small things, but small things add up to big things. Look after the cents, and the dollars will look after themselves.

Yes. Small holes can sink big ships, and Henry Ford once said that a lot of men got very rich by paying attention to the detail that many ignored.

There is another slight nuance to that as well. Really, a lot of value-add in this industry is having reasons to speak to your clients.

Just to get a dialogue going?

Yes. I 've got a team of people who have the same work ethic and philosophy, and that's why we do pretty well.

What is the effort-for-reward equation?

I think people come into this industry thinking that they are going to work fifty hours a week, get their head on TV, and get quoted in the newspapers, and that's all you have to do to be successful. I would suggest that it's 150% grind, because the job is all-encompassing.

Anyone who works in this industry has been given the most tremendous opportunity and you've just got to make the most of it. What's more, you get paid a risk premium because you can be retrenched at any time. I wouldn't feel good about it unless I worked pretty hard. But I want to stress that it's not just me; it's also a matter of surrounding yourself with great people, and of promoting every single member of your team and yourself as a separate brand. One of the really important things is that my team is responsible for every product. So everything is branded not just with one name; it's branded from the most junior guy up to the most senior guy. All the names appear on the front cover. I'm increasingly finding that the value-add in this business is going out and speaking to clients, which means you are on the road a lot. My clients can get a great deal from speaking to the most junior person on the team up to the most senior members.

How long does it take to become a good analyst?

Well, I can say it personally took me about seven years. But it could take someone else a week. It basically comes down to when you become aware that there is a cycle and how long the cycle is. I think that's when you become a good analyst.

How important is the house you work for in getting that rating?

I think it's absolutely critical. There are three keys to success. The first is *wanting* success. The second is surrounding yourself with very good people. And the third is surrounding yourself with an excellent sales team, both domestically and offshore. For example, the sales team that I have the privilege of working with offshore is second to none. Those are the guys who go out and develop accounts from scratch. I have guys there who can market the most complex ideas. And we really do work as a team. Really good salesmen are worth their weight in gold.

Because at the end of the day you can have the best product in the world, but if you don't have good distributors, your product is never going to get out into the market.

That's right.

So how do you see the balance — do you think success is 50% marketing, 50% research? How would you blend the equation?

Because we have a niche where we kind of cover everything, it probably works out to be 60% marketing and 40% research.

Do you learn more from bad stock calls than good stock calls?

Yes, no doubt about it.

What sort of things do you learn from that?

I think you learn that you can make more money from actually reversing a call.

For example?

I've made some shocking calls over the years — for example, on ANZ.[7] When it hit me that I had got this stock fundamentally wrong and I reversed the call, the clients appreciated that I was up-front about it.

How do you make those big switches?

Just be bold about it. Changing calls by stealth isn't good for brokers, but, more importantly, it isn't good for the client because it affects the feeling of trust. I think it's very important to admit it if you have got something wrong, and to really go through and look at why you got it wrong, and if you got it wrong, admit it.

Have there been any major changes in calls that you've made more recently?

Yes, CBA.[8] I have been marketing overseas a piece about CBA and it explains why we got it so wrong. Even though we have had a buy recommendation on the stock, it was only ranked as our fourth-best buy out of the four major banks. But CBA has been the number-one-performing stock, so we've gone through it and looked at why we got it wrong. I wrote it from the point of view that it was still going to be my number-four pick. We were talking earlier about learning from one's mistakes. A weakness in my own research is that when I'm flat out looking at the minutiae, it's easy to forget the big picture. If you look at really great strategy in banks, it's not about a broad sweeping change; it's about very small steps in the same direction.

Incrementalism?

Yes. For example, CBA today is the exact opposite of what it was when it was floated in 1995. I think that's something that the market hasn't yet appreciated.

In which ways do you think they have changed?

I think it comes down to one thing. And that is that they have a strategic objective that is really shareholder value driven. In CBA's case, it's dual: they have to deliver total shareholder returns in the first quartile, and also expand RAROC[9] on both a group and divisional basis. Now, all four banks will say that's their goal as well. But CBA actually live it. They actually do it. The other thing with that particular stock is, while we can give CBA a big tick for strategic excellence and strategic execution, if you think about what they were in 1991 versus what they are now, it's a very different beast. And that's due to the change in management attitude and philosophy. It's not necessarily a matter of getting rid of some of the older guys; some of the older guys are fantastic retail bankers who can work in a new shareholder value paradigm.

They know their craft.

Yes. CBA have some excellent senior management who were pre-deregulation bankers, but they have also brought in some excellent guys and they all meld together very well. But the thing about CBA is that you've got to think about where they were versus where they are now. The next thing is that the market needs to really understand what they are doing. If you look at it, management consistently state those strategic objectives. Another factor is that you don't see any evidence of contradictory management behavior. Another thing that we really like about the stock is that management explicitly recognizes risk in the whole strategy. Reducing risk, turning the company into a less earnings-volatile stock, is a fundamental objective of management, and they live it.

Can we talk some more about bad calls, as we all have a few dogs in our portfolios. How do you handle a bad streak?

I think the worst thing you can do is retreat from it.

You need to take it head on?

Yes. I get out on the road and I market quite aggressively through it.

Get up there and just basically get through it. A lot of people hide, which is …

… the very worst thing you can do. If you really believe that you are right when the calls are going against you, it's actually a beautiful time to execute what you are saying.

So one day you're the dog, and the next day you're the lamppost?

Yes. And finding that next good call can make up for a lot of mistakes.

Do you find that the thrill of a good stock call is as intense as the pain of a bad one?

That's a good question. When I get something wrong, it certainly does concern me. I can tell you that the reason I would never be a good fund manager is because I lie awake at night worrying about whether I've got something fundamentally wrong.

Because you might be costing people money?

Yes, and that's why I think fund managers as a group have such a tremendous responsibility and should be remunerated accordingly. So I suppose the answer to your earlier question is that I find the pain of a bad call far worse than the pleasure of giving myself a pat on the back for a good call.

One fund manager has pointed out that, to them, the binary call isn't that important, as it's the portfolio performance that matters. So, perhaps the sell-side puts too much emphasis on the binary call.

That's interesting, as I've been told that my marketing seems to work quite well, but I would really flag that if I was doing a forty-five-minute presentation, forty-three minutes of that is talking about background, rather than the actual call.

And that's what people value.

Yes. They've got the facts there. They've got the good stuff and the bad stuff, and they can draw their own conclusions. The call is what's tacked on the end, but it's the "this is what I know" stuff at the beginning that's important. That's the value-adding bit, and good stockbroking is about understanding the stocks. I'm not demeaning it at all, but good brokers can take a fairly dull company and turn it into a story. I have sat through so many presentations where the stock isn't a story. There is no logical conversion. There is no point to what the company is trying to do, except that the story is that this company is stuffed! So quite often I think people are too afraid to draw a conclusion one way or the other. I'm not.

What is the toughest part of your job? For me, the maintenance side is the hardest part.

Yes, I agree. The way I approach reporting season is to see it as a once-a-year super-maintenance check.

How do you do that?

We have to work pretty amazing hours, and the toughest part of the job is finding the time to come up with something to tell your client the next day.

Is it easier to be popular or contrarian?

Popular. Without a shadow of a doubt. The reason being that you aren't creating any conflict with the client's existing decisions. But you should never let a bit of conflict deter you from making a recommendation that people may disagree with. It's the information, and the logic behind the recommendation, rather than the call itself, that is important.

Do you think there is an inherent conflict between brokers and investors, because brokers exist primarily to earn a commission and that generally requires generating a lot of stock turnover?

That's a very interesting point. One of the smartest people I have ever had the privilege to work with is a guy called Geoff Warren, who was a fund manager at AMP.[10] When Geoff came back to Ord Minnett, he came up with a vision statement. I think a lot of vision statements are a waste of time, but he came up with a great one. And it's one that really kind of homed into me. And it said that what he wanted people to do was aspire to be their clients' broker of choice. And that is really what I try and do.

What does that involve?

For some people, to be their clients' broker of choice may well mean being able to give them a rough overview and really big stock calls. For someone else, it might be being able to give them incredibly detailed valuation work. There's no one answer to that.

And that's the point, isn't it — every investor has different needs?

Yes, and the logical extension of that is that any fund manager who thinks they can get everything they need from one stockbroker is going to be disappointed.

That broker doesn't exist.

That's right.

And if you were a fund manager, you would probably only want to talk to three brokers, and then talk to them for very different reasons.

That's right, and a very good point. For example, there are people who still think my franchise is very much numbers-based, but in the last six months I've written more on strategy than in the last eight years.

But you've got to do the numbers. It's a credibility thing, and a comfort factor thing as well.

Yes. One thing that I would flag in my particular sector, and I can prove it quantitatively, is that bank analysts probably get the numbers correct more often than the rest of the market. Certainly, the consensus earnings revisions are less, and that's often one of the big things we market — that is, earnings certainty.

But don't the banks communicate their results pretty well to the market?

Yes, but if you look at it, people analyze the numbers to the nth degree.

And things take a long time to change in a bank, anyway.

Exactly.

And once they have momentum, they are hard to knock off track.

Yes. The other thing about banks that I have identified, and it's very clever on their part, is that they tend to undersell and outdeliver. That's one of the big paradigm shifts that we've seen in Australia.

But coming back to the earlier point, do you think brokers and investors have a natural conflict?

No. I think it's perverse, because I think salesmen and fund managers, or dealers and fund managers, probably do. It would be great to sit here and say my job is to generate as much commission as I can, but it's not. My job is to add as much value to my clients as I possibly can. And then it's up to the management of the firm where I work to extract that value from the clients one way or another.

Do you think the great analysts have any special talent?

I just keep coming back to the idea of being able to communicate. It's having the discipline to market, time after time after time.

But then you have to have a talent for being disciplined.

Yes, discipline is the key to success in any profession, and particularly in broking.

What is the ratio between talent and sheer hard work?

Well, I can quite honestly tell you that I'm not particularly smart. For example, I type with two fingers because I can't think that fast [*laughs*]! And I don't do a lot of finance-type analysis. So, in my case, my franchise is probably more work- or effort-based. But certainly there are other analysts out there who are smarter and who probably don't work as hard. One of the most amazing things is to work incredibly hard on a piece of research, spend days on it, on some obscure point, and then take it around to someone and they grasp it straight away. But it's important in this business to be good at assessing yourself and at going back and looking at where you made mistakes.

Being humble?

Yes. But also to share the glory as well. That's a big component of it.

What advice would you give a novice analyst or anyone thinking about entering the industry?

The very best advice I could give to people is to look at things where the broking industry probably doesn't have much talent. At the moment, I think that people with strong accounting backgrounds are valuable. So the best advice that I could give to anyone is to go and do your time in a chartered accountancy firm and really understand how the numbers fit together. Because once you understand that, everything else flows from it.

Talk to the numbers and the numbers will talk to you.

Yes. You can learn strategy by speaking to someone. But you can't learn the numbers by speaking to someone. You've got to understand how it all fits together, and that would be my number one piece of advice.

Can too much success be a risk?

I don't know. I don't think I'm successful enough to be able to give a complete answer to that. Honestly, at the moment I'm very lucky in that we are rating well. But I would imagine that if you have some success and then you start being complacent about what your clients want, then yes, success can be a risk. But you know, it's really funny, people ask me why I work so hard. And the answer is because I've been retrenched twice in six months and I live in fear of that happening again. Now, realistically, that's probably a very stupid fear.

Talking about history, do you look at charts?

That's really interesting, because a lot of people will tell you it's all chicken giblets, or that it's all filled with goat's intestines, and you throw them up in the air and see what comes down. But I must admit, I don't understand a lot of the mechanisms to actually get to it, but I have found some technical analysts that can make the most amazing predictions. I'm thinking of three people who I've worked with over the years who I don't recall ever getting something major wrong.

But have you ever met a rich chartist?

No [*laughs*], because the funny thing is, it's not valued, and it probably should be. But as I say, I feel very fortunate. I spend a lot of time speaking to our technical analysts who are very, very good. Earlier, we were talking about longevity. A lot of technical analysts have been around for a hell of a lot longer than a lot of the broking analysts. And then on top of that, they have charts that go back even further. So I spend a lot of time talking to our guys about what things were like in the 1960s.

In the 1960s, analysts did twenty-year forecasts. Do you look at the actual data as far back as the 1960s?

No I don't, but I do look at trends going back to the 1960s. For example, if you were to look at the Australian banks, as mentioned earlier, I could put a very strong case that these stocks should be re-rated. If you go back to the 1960s and 1970s, banks traded at the market multiple. If you look at the reason for that, it was because they had low volatility in earnings as they had very large hidden reserves. In a regulated environment they priced credit rationally, because they were forced to, and they couldn't really lend on bad credit. But more importantly, because of the pricing mechanism imposed on them, they generated enough capital that they never needed to raise capital. Now, if you look at what destroyed it, it was deregulation. We saw the exact reversal of that. And if you look at the period we are heading into now, there is clear evidence of disciplined risk pricing, and banks are basically forward provisioning, which, any way you cut it, will smooth the earnings going out in the future. So, it's really a hidden reserve that reduces the profit volatility. And the final point is that we are going from a period where banks used to raise capital every second year, to one where most banks will be returning capital. So, I could put a very strong case that banks should start to trade at premium multiples. And the issue about all the buybacks we are seeing is incredibly important, because if you think about the scrip dynamics, companies tend to buy back scrip from institutional shareholders, and it's the very sticky scrip that is with the retail shareholders. So that is continually tightening the supply of the scrip to the index managers.

A piece of research from the Federal Reserve Bank of New York[11] showed that in 1997 the top twenty-five U.S. bank holding companies paid back to their shareholders more by way of dividends and stock buybacks than they earned.

That shows real discipline. It probably also highlights the point that returning a dollar of capital instead of incrementally lending it out for an inappropriate return relative to the risk is a better thing for shareholders.

How difficult is it not to have too rigid a view of the stock?

If you speak to my competitors, they would probably say that I always have a favorable view of one particular Australian stock, which is far from the truth.

Which was Westpac?

Yes. And while Westpac is our number one stock again, that hasn't always been the case. It's only a very recent development.

And why do you rate it so highly?

I think because of the idea of bringing in some American management, who were bringing some disciplined capital management on top of a good earnings story.

Are sell recommendations harder to implement than buy recommendations?

No.

Do you enjoy sells more than buys? You said it was easier to be popular. Isn't the buy story more popular than the sell story?

It has been a bit of a one-way street in terms of share price performance on Australian banks for quite a while; they've all been heading north. But having been around in the past cycle where it was a bit of a one-way street the other way, the sell calls are actually good fun. A lot of that comes down to the fact that results weren't bland. The conflict between the broking and investment community and the management of these banks was an amazing thing to actually be a participant in around then. Analyzing banks now is boring compared to what it was like there for a while.

Were there times when the banks were playing the man and not the ball?

Yes, incredibly so. It's really funny — there is one other bank out there, for example, that I did some very specific research on. I went through some problems I had with the company. And in their results briefing, it was like they were addressing just this one particular piece of research I'd written, to the point where I had to deal with the question, "Is that response real, or are they just responding to my piece of research?" I really don't mind getting out there and annoying people. I have to tell you that the managements of banks that are really good are the ones that don't care about criticism, and they virtually use me as a consultant. They actually get something from brokers.

So while analysts exist to make money for their employers and their clients, they are there also as corporate critics?

Yes, that's right.

Do you think it's important to talk to the media?

Until recently, we had a policy where we just didn't do it and that was basically because some of the very big clients out there told us they didn't want us to do it. At the moment we are grappling with somehow trying to build a brand name, which probably means reversing some of that. Personally, I will talk to them and feed stories, but only after I've fed it to my client base. But my number one responsibility is to speak to my clients first.

So the average investor who reads something in the paper that a broker has said should treat it as fairly old data and realize that it's already in the stock price?

Yes.

How important is patience to the average investor?

I think it's a very sad thing, but I don't think many fund managers out there, with the way performance is, have really had the opportunity to be patient.

Because of quarterly performance and benchmarking?

Yes, and I think there is a big difference between trading and investing. And you're right, I think fund managers are increasingly being forced to be traders rather than investors, because of the constraints that are put on them.

It becomes very circular. You've got to market to get the money in, and therefore quarterly performance is a marketing tool. It becomes a very vicious circle.

It does, because it never catches the fact that capital gains tax is a big consideration in it.

What was your experience of October 1987?

I had been in the business for just a few weeks. It was the most amazing day I have ever experienced. I can remember quite specifically on that day, I heard the news coming in and I wandered down to the floor.

It was boards back then, wasn't it? It hadn't gone electronic?

Yes, that's right. It was just bedlam. It was absolutely incredible. It was amazing to see the reactions of some people, older people. I remember one older guy outside the stock exchange just crying. Then the next day to read in the paper about some guy who had made a squillion dollars over those two trading days — it was an incredible contrast.

Did you think that you were in the wrong business?

I can remember coming in every day for the next month and thinking, "The U.S. market *has* to go up, otherwise I won't have a job." I mean, it was *that* bad.

But did you think that you should get out and go back to the more stable world of accounting?

No, I knew that I would never go back to what I did before.

Why?

Because if you're in the accounting game, you are there either to learn something in order to go and do something else, or to become a partner. I don't think I ever really wanted to become a partner.

But in this business, a lot of people work in this business to get out of this business.

That's probably true in some instances, but I would also flag that one of the big drivers for me for many years was to aspire to do my job better. It's hard to say this without sounding arrogant, but it's satisfying to be noted for doing my job well.

Professional respect?

Yes, and to some extent that's the one thing I really love about my job at the moment. It has taken a long time to get here, but to be able to do it well now, and to have the opportunity to meet and speak with smart people, is one of the real pleasures of the job. I now have the opportunity to meet with people who are a lot smarter than I am and to have them listen to one — guys like Robert Maple Brown,[12] someone of that level of common sense, the Australian Warren Buffett — that's what I love about the job as well. And to have the opportunity to meet and speak with people like David Murray,[13] David Morgan,[14] and Don Argus[15] is a real privilege. And more to the point, it's a real privilege to have young assistants and to be able to introduce them to people like Don Argus. These people are the people making the news, and they are important. I really love that. There's one other thing I would add, and that's the importance of keeping things in perspective. It's often the little things that remind you not to get too carried away with your success or profile. For example, there is this great video from Cochlear, who make the bionic ear, and on it this little girl hears for the first time. Seeing that really brings home the fact that we can kid ourselves that what we do is important, but in the overall scheme of things it's not.

But you do play an important role in the market, which is part of the economy, and getting to number one in *any* pursuit isn't easy. But having said that, is there only one way from here — that is, down?

Well, you live in fear of it. We've got panel reviews. If I don't come in the top three, no-one comes up and hassles me, because I think it's perceived that I do a good job. But I spend more time worrying about accounts where I don't do well than about accounts where I do well. But that's my problem, not the firm's problem. One point I do want to make, though, is that being ranked number one is great. I can sit here and pretend, but really, I'm the brand name at the top. It's a combination of having great support and great salesmen who believe in you, and that's a very important thing. If I do well in a panel review, or if we get a big order or whatever, it's not just for me, it's for all the guys in the team. I believe that quite strongly. For example, I take my assistant to every marketing meeting, with the exception of my offshore trips because it doesn't make financial sense to do so then. He learns, and develops some personal rapport with the clients. He should have this opportunity, which is a very important component of the model I like to run. One of the things about this team approach is that I've just spent two weeks away. I would write morning meeting notes by remote control, but I've got a brand-new assistant and he did a sterling job while I was away. That's very important. This kind of team approach means that you can be in two places at one time. And that's a very important component.

What are the popular misconceptions out there about the stock market and investing in general?

I think there are a lot. The first thing, which I think we alluded to earlier, is that there is a big difference between investing and trading. And I think, unfortunately, quarterly performance sees a lot more trading coming through than true investing. The second big misconception is that it's easy, and it's not. I think there is a perception that we occasionally work very hard and that we play very hard a lot. And to be quite honest, I don't find a lot of time for playing. If you have a victory, you can't use that as an excuse to slacken off. You've just got to keep on driving forward.

You're only as good as your next call?

Yes, and you're only as good as your competition is at that time. The other thing is to have a healthy respect for what your competition is good at.

Do you change your calls very much?

No, not really, but there are subtle nuances in what clients demand.

For example?

I can ring them up and tell them that such-and-such a stock should be impacted by this on this day and that it will be bad news for it. Some people will say, "Well, would you sell out now?" while other people will say, "Well, would you add then?" So, it's just a matter of listening to what they would do.

Do you think people become overreliant on spreadsheets and think there is a Swiss watch-type precision about valuation and forecasting?

I've heard some analysts who just can't work out how their numbers could possibly be wrong. But I would suggest that there are very few times when the spreadsheets have spat out compositionally every number to give the right answer. I spend more time on results night immersed in the nuances of what the composition is than in the actual bottom-line numbers.

In summary, what would you say is the key to success as a sell-side analyst?

It's about surrounding yourself with good people. That's a very important part of it.

❋ ❋ ❋

According to Brian Johnson, going against the market and making a big call can reap big rewards; however, you have to make sure that you get it right. For example, Johnson's error on Westpac overshadowed one of his earliest and best calls, TNT. For a sell-side analyst, the lesson is that one bad call can undo all of the goodwill created by a good call, as the market tends to have a long memory for bad calls. Despite Johnson's obvious talent and skills as an analyst, by his own admission, his 1991 Westpac call probably labeled him (unfairly) as one of the worst analysts in the market for a number of years. But the lesson that Johnson learned was that if you're going to make a big call against the market, you have to make sure that your numbers are credible, so that if you don't get the call right, at least you have a credible second line of defense. Moreover, Johnson's early setback should be of some encouragement to those analysts who have made bad calls early on in their career, as it is still possible to recover from early mistakes. More importantly, Johnson's experience demonstrates that making mistakes is only fatal if you don't learn from them. Johnson's legendary attention to detail and incredible work ethic are arguably a legacy of his early mistake on Westpac.

Another aspect of Brian Johnson's approach that is interesting is that he believes equity analysis is widely viewed as arcane, or as "a black art." But the way he approaches analysis and valuation is very straightforward and very much based on common sense. Moreover, Johnson's view that price-to-book ratios are totally irrelevant and are an outcome is something that investors in bank stocks should reflect upon. His argument that banks really trade on earnings-based multiples and their yield on sustainable capital also helps to explain why a bank stock can be cheap at three times book and expensive at one times book. The other striking thing about Brian Johnson is his modesty and humility, insofar as he attributes a lot of his success to the people around him. However, perseverance, hard work, and an inquiring mind have also had a lot to do with his success.

---

[1]　TNT, a major Australian transport group that was acquired in 1996 by KPN Groep NV of the Netherlands.

[2]　Westpac Banking Corporation Limited provides general and savings banking, including lending, deposit taking and payment services. The company also provides investment portfolio management and advice, unit trust and superannuation fund management, nominee and custodian facilities, insurance services, consumer finance, leasing, general finance, foreign exchange dealing and money market services. At the time of writing the company had a stock-market capitalization of A\$22.9 billion.

[3]　Kerry Packer is Australia's wealthiest person and controls a vast television, newspaper, and publishing empire.

[4]　National Australia Bank Limited, Westpac Banking Corporation Limited, ANZ Banking Group Limited, and Commonwealth Bank of Australia Limited.

[5]　Return on equity.

[6] Price to earnings ratio (also referred to as price/earnings ratio).

[7] Australia & New Zealand Banking Group Limited is an international bank with activities in general banking, mortgage and installment lending, life insurance leasing, hire purchase and general finance. ANZ also provides international investment banking, investment and portfolio management and advisory services, nominee and custodian services, stockbroking and executor and trustee services. At the time of writing the company had a stock-market capitalization of A$18.4 billion.

[8] Commonwealth Bank of Australia Limited provides banking, life insurance and related services. The company also provides corporate and general banking, institutional banking and stockbroking and funds management products. At the time of writing the company had a stock-market capitalization of A$24.9 billion.

[9] Risk-adjusted return on capital.

[10] AMP Limited provides life insurance, superannuation, asset management products, pensions and other diviersifieid financial services throughout Australia, New Zealand and the United Kingdom. At the time of writing the company had a stock-market capitalization of A$17.8 billion.

[11] Bank Holding Company Capital Ratios and Shareholder Payouts. Federal Reserve Bank of New York, *Current Issues in Economics and Finance*, Vol. 4, No. 9, September 1998.

[12] Robert Maple-Brown is a principal of the highly respected $A11bn value-driven investment house of Maple-Brown Abbott.

[13] Managing director of Commonwealth Bank of Australia Limited.

[14] Managing director of Westpac Banking Corporation Limited.

[15] Former managing director of National Australia Bank Limited and now chairman of BHP Limited.

4

David Fisher:
The Holistic Approach

"If you wouldn't buy the whole company then you had better not buy 100,000 shares, 1000 shares, or 100 shares, because then it becomes a greater fool theory that somebody else is going to pay you more for a piece of paper, and that's not what we think investing is about."

David Fisher is chairman of the board of Capital Group International Inc., the institutional arm of The Capital Group Companies Inc., which he chaired for eight years. The Capital Group is an employee-owned organization founded in 1931 by Jonathan Bell Lovelace and which today has more than US$500 billion under management. Three things strike you about The Capital Group. The first is that, for such a large fund manager, the group maintains an extremely low profile, relying on its track record rather than publicity and promotion to attract new business. The group's flagship fund, The New Perspective Fund, which was established in 1973, has a twenty-five-year compound annual rate of return of 15% and has never returned less than 13.1% in any ten-year period in its lifetime. To put this in perspective, US$10,000 invested in The New Perspective Fund back in 1973 would have been worth US$367,691 at the end of 1998, which would have been 29.7% more than if the money had been invested in the S&P 500, 84.2% more than if invested in the MSCI World Index,[1] and 102.3% more than if invested in the MSCI EAFE Index.[2]

The second thing about Capital is its long-term perspective and long-term, value-orientated investment philosophy. The group is the very model of a patient investor, with the average holding period of its investments being nearly four years, compared to an industry average of just fifteen months. The third, and perhaps most important, aspect of Capital's success has been its relatively early recognition of the value of global investing and portfolio diversification, with the group's prospectuses highlighting that over the last twenty-five years, an internationally diversified portfolio would have generated almost the same returns as the U.S. stock market but for less risk. Consequently, something approaching US$200 billion of the group's funds are international or global in nature, of which about US$25 billion are invested in emerging markets. Another feature of the group is the longevity and experience of its employees, with the group's portfolio managers averaging twenty-two years' industry experience and David Fisher himself being one of the longer serving, having chalked up thirty years with the group. And despite being one of the longest-serving and most successful fund managers in the industry, Fisher's passion for his work and his continued drive to make Capital "the best investment management firm in the world" remains undiminished.

How did you get started in this business?

I just fell into it. It was just dumb luck.

A happy accident?

Yes, that's really true. When I was twenty-five I had no reason to believe I would be in this business. I was born in New York and was raised in a small town in California. I went to the University of California Berkeley, and went through the ROTC program where the military pay for your schooling. I put myself through college, but I had a two-year military obligation after I graduated and I ended up at Fort Leonard Wood, Missouri.

How did you manage to get from Fort Leonard Wood to the funds management industry?

I used to go to the University of Missouri for a social life because there was nothing to do at Fort Leonard Wood. I met a guy who was a professor at the business school there and he said that he would give me a job, and I'd be able to get out of the army three months early and get my MBA. So that's what I did, and around graduation time, the corporations interviewed on campus and I ended up going to work for General Electric.[3] Jack Welch[4] was, in fact, my first boss in the world, and so I traveled all around for a couple of years with General Electric. One day the phone rang and some guy at the other end said that he was in charge of Smith Barney in Chicago. Somehow they had heard about me and thought that I knew the electrical equipment industry because I worked for General Electric, and he asked if I would be interested in talking to Smith Barney about a job as a sell-side analyst. He asked me if I had heard of Smith Barney, and all I could think of was Barney's clothing in New York, and I knew that wasn't it, so I said no, I'd never heard of them, but they hired me anyway. God knows why! But I worked there for two years and I got to know Capital, as it was one of the first clients I ran into. They asked me to join them. I did, working in our New York office for a year, and then I moved back to California in 1970 and that was it. But at the time I was very happy working at General Electric and I didn't have any idea what a sell-side analyst did and knew nothing about investments. But thirty years later, here I am.

And what's your view of sell-side research?

Well, it's not a topic that I spend a lot of time thinking about, if the truth be known. I've been at Capital for thirty years and I've been both an analyst and a portfolio manager and I've always used our internal people. My exposure to the sell-side for the last fifteen years has probably been something close to zero, because I don't know where the people on the sell-side are going to be tomorrow. Moreover, they also have other motivations besides just being right, whereas there's a high probability that people with Capital *are* going to be here tomorrow. We've got 165 analysts around the world and that's who I listen to. And, yes, they should talk to the sell-side, because the sell-side does impact stock prices and they should be aware of what the sell-side are thinking, but we have never used the sell-side in my time at Capital for sources of recommendations. I mean, it's interesting how they approach things, how they look at valuations, what drives their decision processes, because they do move stock prices and in that sense it's interesting, but not because of their recommendations.

It's interesting that you say that, because Mark Mobius[5] made the same point in an interview for this book. He doesn't value the sell-side for their recommendations or their valuations either.

It's very funny — Mark and I, as it turns out, were born in the same small town on Long Island, and we only found this out about a year ago. He's the only person I've ever met who's from this small town. Talk about a coincidence.

You were recently quoted as saying, "The goal of Capital is to have our clients think of us as the best investment manager in the world." Was that an accurate statement?

Yes, it was. What I say all the time is that I want us to be known by our clients as the best investment management firm in the world. And those words were carefully chosen. I said the *best*, I didn't say the biggest, and I said known by *our clients*, not known by everyone, and that's what our objective or goal is.

And when you say to be the "best," what are the criteria that you are measuring that by?

The criteria are going to be determined by the client and not by us, because different people have different criteria. Some may focus simply on investment results and say that over long periods of time they have done the best. Others may look at the total service and investment results and think of it that way. Others may take into account some very subjective things, such as how do they feel about the people, do they like them, do they respect them, how do they feel about our role in the industry — do they like it, do they respect it? But different people are going to measure us in different ways, and I just want us to be known by our clients as the best investment management firm in the world.

Could we talk about the principles or your philosophy toward investing? Jonathan Bell Lovelace[6] laid out some important principles for good investing. First, buy securities at reasonable prices relative to their prospects and hold them for the long term. Second, do the research necessary to determine the actual worth of the investment. How do you determine what is a reasonable price, because, arguably, value is in the eye of the beholder? Some investors look at it in absolute terms, others in relative terms.

Well, the way you just quoted it is absolutely accurate. And I have said on a number of occasions that it's easy to say those words and what you are suggesting is that it's difficult to execute — and it is, because essentially what we adopt is the *whole company* approach. We look at the price of the stock and multiply it by the number of shares outstanding, and that tells us what the *market* thinks the company is worth. Then the question is, "What do *we* think the company is worth?" Now, as I said, that's an easy question to ask, but in order to answer that, you've got to be focused on the future. You've got to understand the competitive position of the company, its strengths, its weaknesses, its strategy, its regulatory environment, its labor environment — there are a whole series of issues that you have to address. Then, when you arrive at a value for the whole company, the question then is — and you're looking at three to five years down the track — how does that compare with what the market says it's worth? And I think it's more of an absolute rather than a relative valuation issue, because the world is full of things that you don't have to buy and so you had better find the company absolutely attractive if you're going to invest.

How do you determine the premium you are prepared to pay for growth, for example?

We don't have any formula that provides an answer regarding how much we would pay for, say, 25% growth. And by the way, what is your certainty of that 25% growth anyway? Is it a very uncertain 25% versus a relatively predictable 10%? But if you think of it as if you are a businessman with unlimited resources, the question you should really ask is, "Would I buy the *whole* company for this price?" And if you wouldn't buy the whole company, then you had better not buy 100,000 shares, 1000 shares, or 100 shares, because then it becomes a greater fool theory that somebody else is going to pay you more for a piece of paper, and that's not what we think investing is about.

That sounds similar to Warren Buffett's[7] approach of, "Is it fundamentally a good business and would I want to own it for keeps?"

Absolutely. In my responsibility I have companies that I've owned for twenty-five years and a lot for more than ten years, and for the most part these are probably names I will own for the rest of my career. But what's interesting is that they are great *companies* or *businesses*, but they haven't always been great *stocks* every year. But over long periods of time they have been terrific. And I think Warren Buffett has got it right. Moreover, I think he has said a number of things that are not only common sense but wise — for example, why don't you look to add to your large positions rather than your small positions, because they seem to represent your highest conviction so why wouldn't you buy more of your highest conviction, and things like that. That's common sense and very wise.

In the process of forming your conviction, how important is the company's management in the equation?

For a combination of reasons, probably number one, number two, number three, and number four. I prefer to invest in companies where people make a difference. I don't like investing in companies that are driven by macro things over which I have no control. For example, if it's the direction of interest rates or oil prices or whatever that's going to be the overriding influence as to whether the stock works out or not, it usually doesn't interest me. I love investing where people can really have an impact on the outcome, and if that's what you are going to invest in, then you'd better be right about the people. So, it's always interesting to me that when I look back over the big holdings in my responsibility at almost any time, in the vast majority of cases I have had a personal exposure to management. It may be an old impression or it may be a recent impression, but I have an impression based on a personal exposure. So, yes, I've always believed that good people tend to make good things happen, and if you can find good key people, and let them work for you — work for you in the sense that you invest in their company and your interests are aligned.

Are there any strong examples that come to mind?

I think Lend Lease[8] would be a good example in Australia. I think Johnson Electric[9] in Hong Kong would be a great example. Those are both companies where we have had exposure for what seems like forever. The people are just very talented, and what's interesting is they have been able to maintain it for more than a generation. It's not just one generation, it's a culture that they create. And there are a multitude of examples of companies in the United States and outside the United States where they have really done it differently.

Why doesn't the sell-side focus more on this as an investment parameter?

Well, they tend to get caught up with what's the consensus estimate. Are they going to beat the whisper number? The quarter is five cents light; therefore, sell the stock. That's not what investing is about, from my perspective. It never has been. And it's interesting because at the time people should be lengthening their time horizon, they are actually shortening it. I don't know why we would feel that we would have a competitive advantage over figuring out what this quarter's earnings are going to be versus anybody else. But where we *do* have a competitive advantage, however, is in putting a company in a global perspective and understanding how it fits in the long term. So, in my opinion, you should use the quarterly numbers to the extent that, when they drive stock prices down, they are opportunities, not risks.

Quarterly performance also applies to fund managers and, again, it's probably not the best measure to judge a fund manager by. What was behind your comment that the case for indexing tends to be the most compelling when it's the most dangerous to index?

I would say that, as a rule of thumb, any time the evidence to index is truly compelling, don't do it. I think that you would be happier in life and be a better investor if you follow that rule. There have been four times in my career when the case for indexing has been *absolutely* compelling. One was in the mid-1970s and the "nifty fifty," where active managers had underperformed for four years and everybody knew that active managers couldn't beat the index. So, all you had to do was own these great stocks and it didn't matter what their earnings were. Their stock prices were just driven to $150.

The second time was at the end of the 1970s and early 1980s when oil prices were supposed to go to US$100 a barrel and oil stocks — energy, broadly defined — became 40% of the S&P Index. I remember doing a client meeting, I guess it was 1980 or early 1981, when energy was 40% of the S&P and we had only 3% in energy and I felt really stupid. And everybody said, "Why don't we just index?" At that point, it would have been the worst thing you could possibly have done, because it was right before the crash in oil prices. It was the same thing for Japan for international investors in the 1980s. Japan was 65% of the Europe, Australian, and Far East Index and 40% of the World Index! But if you look back at our five-year record, or our eight-year record in 1988 or 1989, we did pretty well relative to most people, but we still trailed the index quite a bit over that time frame.

But what's more interesting is that recently I saw a consultant's universe that went through the ten-year performance of something like 140 to 150 fund managers for the period to June 30, 1999. And in this study they took out the top 5% and the bottom 5% performers, so it was actually possible to be outside the performance graph. Now it had a performance graph that showed the manager results for the ten years ending June 30, 1999, and yet the benchmark index was *outside* the performance chart on the low side. So, in 1999 more than 95% of the managers outperformed the index whereas in 1989, the opposite ws true.

And in terms of today, you could also say that the case for indexing in the U.S. market is quite compelling at the moment, because if you didn't own the twenty largest stocks in the U.S., you would have had a hard time beating the index over the last few years. So, guess what's happening? People are indexing because they can't select the good active managers! I think there are times when indexation makes sense, and I think if you have a hundred-billion-dollar pool of assets I can understand why you would index a portion of that. But make that decision *after* your active managers have beaten the index. There is nothing inherently smart about an index. Nothing inherently smart at all. So why you would believe that an index manager over a long period of time would do better than other managers, I don't know.

But *why* can't fund managers on average outperform the market?

What is implied by your question is that 77% *of the market* can't outperform the market, and by definition they can't. What's more, you're going to have transaction costs, so it's generally going to be a below-average outcome. The issue is really whether you can identify *some* managers that can outperform the index, and I think the answer to *that* question is "yes."

How do you go about doing that?

It's pretty much based on things we discussed earlier — you know, the way you look at companies, who are the people, what is the culture, what is the process, who are the people who brought you the investment record, are they still there? It's all about those issues; it's not that complicated.

If you have a strong indexing bias, does it mean that you are likely to miss out on golden opportunities?

More than likely. For example, I just wrote a letter to clients on benchmark risk and tracking error. Now, I was raised with the idea to be the best that you can be, so the idea of mediocrity as an objective just stuns me. But out there, there's this fear of failure, where some investors will say, "Well, as long as I don't deviate from the index too much then I won't be badly wrong and therefore I won't get fired either as an organization or as an individual." And that type of thinking drives me nuts, because frankly, the people who are going to spend their lives worrying about getting fired aren't the people who are likely to be good investors.

But ultimately, your performance is measured against a benchmark and that is what you are judged by.

Yes, you have to pay attention to the benchmarks, because you want to know what bets you are making. You should, for example, know that Microsoft[10] is 3½% of the S&P or whatever it is, and that if you only own 3½% of Microsoft you really aren't making a big bet on it. So, you ought to know that — but I don't think you should be driven by it. But what you see a lot of are people who own a bunch of stocks only because these stocks represent so much of the S&P and they don't want to deviate too much from that because, after all, you could be wrong.

Apart from the bias toward indexing, what are the other risks or trends that are affecting the nature of investing?

Globalization is the most important trend. That is true of the investment management business, and it's also true for the companies that the investors invest in. So, from both perspectives, globalization is the most important thing going on at the moment. And I think that a side effect from globalization is that you're getting flatter playing fields, more level playing fields. For example, it used to be that we, as an American-based firm, were significantly handicapped in Japan and the U.K., but it's pretty open to us now. It's not perfectly level, but it's a lot more level than it was, and that creates a different kind of competition and the competition is real now, and if we're good and we execute, we'll be successful. And if we're not, we won't be successful, and that's the way the world should work. I think aging populations are also clearly a significant trend that impacts the investment business as well. For example, what's going to happen to the populations in Japan and Germany? That dynamic has a lot of implications for this business, and for corporations as well. Another issue is the role of technology, in terms of the ability to do things at an individual level that you probably couldn't do before, is also quite profound. For example, there's a wonderful column I saw last week that put forward the notion of twenty-four-hour global trading of securities. The guy who wrote the article equated it to night baseball. Essentially what he said was that when night baseball started, it greatly expanded the number of people that went to baseball games because they could do it at night and not just during the day, and would twenty-four-hour trading mean the same thing? Would there be all these people who now had blocks of time that they could apply to investing? I thought that was pretty interesting and provocative. And while I thought it was pretty good, I'm not advocating that it's right, but it's something worth thinking about.

What are the implications of globalization for the skill sets required by investors and analysts?

Globalization is also creating the need for — and I know it's true at Capital and I think it's true in other organizations — greater diversity of people. And I'm not sure if everyone has caught on to this yet. If you look at Capital today, more than 40% of our analysts aren't Americans. I don't know what that number would have been ten or twenty years ago, but I know it would have been a lot lower. And you can look around this office, right on this floor, and if you went down the hall the order of people you'd meet are Canadian, Chilean, French, German, American, Brazilian, French, Chinese, Argentinean, Indian. We speak forty languages in this organization, and I think that if you are going to be a global organization and investor, you have to be multicultural and multilingual.

What skills can be taught and what can't?

Very few of the skills that are necessary to be successful can actually be taught. However, while I think you need a certain level of intelligence in order to be successful, because you've got to juggle a lot of variables in your head and that requires certainly some above-average level of intelligence, but once you get to that level I'm absolutely persuaded that there is no correlation between increased intelligence and increased success. From that point on, give me common sense, street smarts, all those types of qualities. That, I think, is incredibly more important.

Is a healthy degree of cynicism also required?

Cynicism is something I don't like. Skepticism is okay, but cynicism isn't, because cynics tend to believe nothing good can happen.

They smell flowers and look for a coffin?

Yes [*laughs*]. But I think some skepticism really helps in this business. I actually think the most important characteristic — if we assume we can find the right people with common sense and all the other qualities — I really believe what you want are people who are introspective and they have thought about themselves and they like themselves. It doesn't mean they have to have a certain personality — they can be shy *or* outgoing — but whoever they are, they have to have thought about themselves and like themselves. And the reason that ends up being so important is that this is a business in which you are going to be wrong a great deal, and you are going to be visibly wrong to yourself, to your associates, and to your clients. And people who aren't comfortable with themselves tend to freeze and they don't want to make another decision and therefore run the risk of being wrong again. And so it's only those people who actually have thought a lot about who they are, and who like who they are, that tend to be truly successful in this business.

So, you have to have humility?

Yes. I have said on many occasions that stock markets only exist to make money managers humble. We can talk about the capital-raising process and how important stock markets are in the broader scheme of the economy, but actually they only exist to make money managers humble.

So success has a lot to do with how well you handle failure?

Yes, I would agree with that, because you are going to make mistakes and you have to know how to deal with that.

What was your worst call, and what did you learn from it?

I would probably cite a couple. One worked out and the other didn't — it worked out eventually and it was an interesting one. I started out here as the media and consumer electronics and electrical equipment analyst in 1969. In 1972 I wrote a report that called Warner Communications[11] the communications company of the 1970s, and the stock was, I don't know, US$37–39 at the time. And I wrote this big report, obviously only for internal consumption, and on the back of that we bought a lot of stock. By the time it bottomed in 1974 it went to $7, and that was both the bad news and the good news, because we were able to continue to buy the stock and who knows what the average price was, US$18 or US$20, or some number like that, and subsequently by the late 1970s or early 1980s that stock was at US$200. The same stock. So, it had a happy ending, but that was after two years of real pain and the pain was really exacerbated by the fact that this was in the "nifty fifty" era, and at that time we had the reputation that if it didn't rust, we wouldn't own it, because we didn't like all the "nifty fifty" growth stocks. And so clients would fire us and then the new manager would take over the assets and sell the same Warner Communications stock out of the portfolio and that was very painful for us. I guess what I learned from it is that the last thing in the world you want is instant gratification in an investment, because the reason Warner worked out so well over the long term was because it did so poorly over the short term — short term being two years, which seemed like a lifetime at the time.

What attracted you to the stock in the first place? You spoke earlier about the importance of management. Was it that, or was it an industry thematic?

Steve Ross was running the company and he was one of the brightest people I have ever run into. He had all these assets to work with, and I thought they were going to pull it off. That's what attracted me, and I also happened to like media business back then, too.

What was the other call that you mentioned that didn't work out?

The other one — well, there were two others, actually. I had two disasters early in my career that didn't work out. One was Singer Manufacturing,[12] which hardly exists today, and the other was RCA. In RCA's case I initially missed that there was no place for the consumer electronics industry in the United States. It was gone. What's more, the company management didn't appreciate it either. And the big lesson for me was that I learned in the mid-1970s that American companies in general hadn't realized what had gone on in the world and they weren't really competitive on a global basis. It was a combination of arrogance and the size of the U.S. market. They didn't think they had to worry about it, because the U.S. market was big enough to have growth opportunities for them. But they didn't realize that all these other guys who came from smaller markets were going to come and attack here. And in Singer's case, I don't know why I ever thought that they could go from selling sewing machines to selling all kinds of other non-related goods and be successful at it, but they diversified into office products. They tried to do a range of other things and they were very bad at it. We ended up getting out of both of those stocks sometime in the later 1970s. But both were awful investments. And in fact, to this day, whenever I get cocky about something, one of my older associates will say, "Remember Singer." So, talk about humility!

What's the most common mistake you tend to see from the average analyst or investor?

There's a whole laundry list of mistakes that people make. Things I worry about are assuming that you know a lot more than the market does, and not asking yourself the question, "Could the market be right?" I think that's a very common mistake. Furthermore, and my young associates would hate to hear me say this, but I always worry about a guy who is two years out of business school and is absolutely sure he knows how to run the company better than the guy that's been at the company for forty years and who has been running the company for fifteen. I mean, you sort of want to say, "What qualifies you to say that?"

I can recall one CEO of a blue chip, a very successful company, who was reputed to have said to a business school graduate, "I'll offer you the job despite your handicap." What are the advantages of going to business school, and is it a prerequisite for success?

I think some people go to business school for the wrong reasons, as it's all about career and not necessarily about what they want to do. It's not about a passion. I think a lot of people go to business school because they are risk-averse and it's the safe thing to do, because if you have an MBA you'll probably get a job. By contrast, we instituted a program here about eighteen years ago where we hire people straight out of undergraduate courses. It's known as the TAP Program — The Associates Program. What we do is hire people who, for the most part, are liberal arts graduates — no business majors — and what they have in common is they're smart, they're creative, they're ambitious and very curious folk, with diversity from all over the world. They spend two years doing different things at Capital. During the program, we expose them to accounting and all the other technical stuff that they need to know. Many of the most important hires we have made over the last eighteen years have come from this program.

What advice would you give a novice analyst or someone who is thinking of coming into the business?

To figure out yourself and figure out what your competitive advantage is, because different people have different competitive advantages. Looking around our organization, there are people who can look at a balance sheet and it talks to them. There are other people whose competitive advantage is that they know the managements better than anyone else. A lot of people know products. So, figure out what your competitive advantage is and focus on that, and not on things where you don't have a competitive advantage. And I would recommend that they ask a lot of people how they have approached the process of how to analyze an industry and then take what feels right for you, because nobody has Truth. There isn't just one way to do this. So, talk to a lot of people and ask them how they did it, how they do it, and adapt that to what feels right for you. And work hard at it.

Should you be in a hurry?

Yes. If you aren't in a hurry, then you're probably not motivated enough, and this business attracts people who are in a hurry. But that doesn't mean you shouldn't take a deep breath before you say something or do something. I don't think you can suggest to people that they shouldn't be in a hurry. But that being said, it's also a journey.

Do you use charts at all?

I look at charts. I don't think it's sacrilegious to look at a chart. I'm interested in what a stock has done over time. Does it determine what companies I think are attractive? No. But I really think it's probably a mistake to be oblivious to charts.

Given that you take a very fundamental approach to investing, what do you think about the Internet and Internet stocks?

I believe that the Internet is an enormously powerful catalyst for change in the world. I think it's a big deal and you shouldn't underestimate the impact of it. On the other hand, I think most of the stocks aren't attractive, and I think I said it in March 1999 that of the Internet IPOs that come on from this point, I think it's predictable that 75% of them won't be around as companies in the next five to ten years. Now, some of them will be enormous successes, but the odds aren't on the side of success from here on in, because I think much of it has already happened. But notwithstanding that, I believe it's a real revolution that is meaningful and significant but most of the stocks at today's prices aren't attractive.

What is the best way for people to make money from the Internet?

I think the places you make money out of it are probably twofold. One is by investing in companies that are *not* considered Internet companies but that have an enormous capability and a strategy, and that are going to unlock that valuation at some time. The other is figuring out who is going to get hurt by all this and getting rid of the stocks you don't want to own. You will help your investment results a lot by identifying those sorts of companies.

Finally, how do you measure success in this business? What is success?

I've been at Capital for thirty years, so success for me is defined organizationally. I mean, it's about really contributing to Capital being regarded as, if not *the* best, then one of the best money management firms in the world. I have said for quite a while that I think I probably have the best job in the world, and there is no-one that I'm aware of who has a job I would trade for my own. I think it's been important that I've been able to involve the family, because this job isn't compartmentalized, it's really overlapping. And as my kids are fond of saying, they have never been on a normal vacation. For example, we have never been to Hawaii as a family, and yet we're only three hours away and all our friends go to Hawaii for their vacation. We have never done that, but as a family we've gone to Russia, China, Brazil, Turkey, Vietnam, and all those kinds of places, so I've been able to combine those things. And it's been great fun. I have never found any conflict between my fiduciary responsibility and laughing. I mean, those are not a conflict, as the people around here will tell you. I've been known to walk out there and bark, or to do something else outrageous, and so it's really important to me that the work is fun, and it is.

* * *

If there has been a recurring theme from both the buy- and sell-side through the course of all the interviews for this book, it has been that quality of management is a key investment criterion, and David Fisher's views on the subject are among the strongest. And while patience, self-confidence, humility, and passion are all essential ingredients for successful investing, the key elements of Fisher's philosophy and approach are:

- Management is perhaps *the* most important investment issue. Invest in companies where people make a difference, and be sure that you are right about the people. Moreover, try to understand the culture that is promoted within the company and avoid companies with a reputation for arrogance.
- Do your own research and be independent in your thinking, but don't forget to ask yourself the question, "Could the market be right?"
- Given unlimited resources, would you buy the *whole* company and is it an attractive *business* selling at an attractive price? Moreover, is the company *absolutely* attractive, because the world is full of things that you don't have to own. Furthermore, understand the difference between a great company and a great

stock. Sometimes companies may be doing very well, whereas their stock prices aren't (and vice versa).

- Focus on the future, especially on the strategic outlook for the company. Try to understand where the company will be in the next five years and where it will stand in a long-term global perspective. Warner Communications, Singer, and RCA were all examples of where an understanding of the strategic and global competitive outlook of a company was a key investment issue.

- Money management is important. Weight your portfolio by your degree of conviction. However, when the evidence to index your portfolio is overwhelming, don't do it.

- Don't be unduly influenced by short-term market sentiment, and be prepared to take advantage of short-term pessimism or disappointment.

- Stock markets only exist to make money managers humble, so don't be scared to fail, and know how to deal with your mistakes.

- Common sense and skepticism are important qualities, but remember that a cynic knows the price of everything but the value of nothing.

---

[1] Morgan Stanley Capital International World Index tracks the performance of twenty-two of the world's major stock markets.

[2] Morgan Stanley Capital International EAFE Index tracks the performance of the major stock markets of Europe, Australasia, and the Far East.

[3] General Electric Company had, at the time of writing, a stock-market capitalization of US$444.3 billion. The company develops, manufactures, and markets products for the generation, distribution, and utilization of electricity. Through General Electric Capital Services, Inc., the company also provides a variety of financial services including mutual fund management, financing, asset management, and insurance. General Electric also owns the National Broadcasting Company.

[4] Chairman and CEO of General Electric Company.

[5] See Chapter 2.

[6] Jonathan Bell Lovelace (1895–1979) was the founder of Capital Research and Management Company. He was almost unscathed by the 1929 crash and subsequent Depression, as his investment methods highlighted that by 1929 there was no relationship between stock-market prices and underlying value.

[7] Warren Buffett is chairman and CEO of Berkshire Hathaway and is widely regarded as one of the world's most astute investors. He is the third-wealthiest person in the United States, with an estimated net worth of US$31 billion.

[8] Lend Lease Corporation Limited, which at the time of writing had a stock-market capitalization of A$9.1 billion, provides real estate project management, project design, project financing, and construction services, along with property development. The company also manages REITs and provides funds management services including superannuation, unit trusts, life insurance, investment advice, asset management, and management of infrastructure assets.

[9] Johnson Electric Holdings Limited., which at the time of writing had a stock-market capitalization of HK$46.5 billion, designs, manufactures, and markets micromotors used in automobile components, home appliances, power tools, and personal care and business equipment.

[10] Microsoft Corporation develops, manufactures, licenses, sells, and supports software products. At the time of writing, the company had a stock-market capitalization of US$474.9 billion.

[11] Time Warner Inc. is a media and entertainment company with interests in cable television programming, magazine publishing, book publishing, direct marketing, filmed entertainment, television production, television broadcasting, recorded music, music publishing, and cable television systems. At the time of writing, the company had a stock-market capitalization of US$112.6 billion.

[12] The Singer Company retails and distributes consumer durable products in 150 countries. At the time of writing, the company's stock-market capitalization was US$48.6 million. The company's products include industrial and consumer sewing machines.

5

Lise Buyer: Keep your Eyelids up to See what you can See

"We are only on step two of this hundred-step staircase. We are in the midst of something that is truly profound. The Internet isn't going to change the way we get up in the morning, it's not going to change basic human needs or what people like and don't like, but it's going to change the way we all do most of the things that we do."

Based in Palo Alto in Silicon Valley, California, Lise Buyer is director and senior equity analyst at Credit Suisse First Boston and is one of the leading Internet analysts in the United States. With over fourteen years' equities markets experience on both the buy- and sell-side, Buyer was comfortably settled as an equity analyst and portfolio manager for T. Rowe Price Associates, a conservative US$130 billion mutual fund, until the summer of 1995 when she attended a conference at the Aspen Institute in Aspen, Colorado. At the conference, a group of companies were talking about how a communications mechanism called the Internet might change the way companies do business. Buyer was immediately struck by the enormous potential of the Internet and wanted to be part of it. However, the investment profile of Internet stocks did not fit with T. Rowe Price's (or, indeed, many other institutions') traditional stock selection criteria, and so Buyer had to go back to the sell-side to pursue her beliefs. What is interesting about Buyer's approach to Internet stocks is that, in a sector that is widely regarded as having no fundamental basis for valuation or analysis, Buyer finds reassurance in a quote taped to the wall in her office:

"Unseasoned companies in new fields of activity provide no sound basis for the determination of intrinsic value. The risks inherent in the business, an untested management, and uncertain access to additional capital combine to make an analytical determination of value unlikely if not impossible. Analysts serve their discipline best by identifying such companies as highly speculative and by not attempting to value them, even though we recognize that there will be pressure to make valuations for initial public offerings (IPOs) and other unseasoned issues. The buyer of such securities is not making an investment, but a bet on a new technology, a new market, and new service, or an innovation in established markets. Winning bets on such situations can choose very rich rewards, but they are in an odds setting rather than a valuation process."

Buyer points out that this piece of investment advice is reputedly from Benjamin Graham and David L. Dodd's *Security Analysis*[1] originally published in 1934, and has to some extent helped her to rationalize and cope with some of the incredible valuations the stock market has put on Internet or Internet-related companies. And while by her own admission "the hardest part with Internet stocks is that they don't behave rationally," there are some basic rules that investors should follow when looking to invest in the sector. Even if you don't hold or ever plan to own an Internet stock, Lise Buyer's views should be of interest if only to understand the potential impact of the Internet on traditional business models and company valuations.

How did you get into this business, and were you always attracted to it?

I was with T. Rowe Price before joining CSFB, and I had been on the sell-side for a number of years before that. I was originally attracted to this business because I really wanted to be a trader; I desperately wanted to sit on the equity-trading desk. But at the time, which was fourteen years ago, they didn't hire women for that job very frequently. So, although I had enough success in the interview process to make me think I could do it, at the end of the day I didn't get the job. But it was still pretty tempting, so I figured the real trick was to get into an investment bank by any means possible and then leverage whatever job I had over to being a trader.

How do you define trading? Day trading, arbitrage, sales trading, for example?

Institutional traders are responsible for fulfilling clients' buy and sell orders. They also trade for the firm, both to ensure liquidity and, hopefully, for profit. The key is that those traders have to make split-second decisions when only pieces of the relevant information are available. Mistakes can be very, very expensive. Therefore, the objective is to very rapidly process information from a variety of sources — from the newswires, incoming orders, the firm's position — and come up with a best guess as to how the overall market will react to an order to make a buy or sell decision. There's no long-term investment side to it at all.

What was the turning point in terms of moving away from that to doing a job where you have to have a longer-term perspective?

You're right, research is an entirely different job from trading. Trading is all about reacting when you have no news. So, in some ways it's the complete opposite of research where, in theory, you are supposed to analyze something before you make a decision. On the trading desk you have no time. It's, this is the piece of news — what do you buy and what do you sell? I took a research job because it was the only way that I could get in the door, and then, much to my surprise, I actually liked it. So, that was the initial turning point.

Was that with T. Rowe Price?

No, that was with Fred Alger Management, which was another buy-side shop based in New York. It was a hot shop at the time and is again, although there were a few tough years in the interim. I joined them, stayed for two years, and then was hired away by Prudential Bache to be a sell-side analyst. I didn't know very much about being a sell-side analyst, but what I did know certainly seemed interesting to me. I did that for about four years and eventually concluded that it's much more interesting to be in the front line of investing. It's much more challenging to actually have to commit, whereas sell-side analysts say "buy" one day and the next, "Oh, I'm changing my recommendation." Buy-side analysts/portfolio managers actually own the stock.

There's not the same degree of pain when you are on the sell-side.

Right — there's no real pain. You may be embarrassed, or people may yell at you, but you never go to sleep at night having lost somebody $60 million. On the buy-side you have to deal with those sorts of challenges. I really liked the buy-side because it required commitment — it's about putting your money where your mouth is. And I was really enjoying things at T. Rowe Price and would have stayed if the Internet hadn't come along. But I could see that this was going to be something massive and yet no-one had any answers, and that was a challenge too interesting to let pass.

What made you think that the Internet was going to be massive?

I whittled my way into a conference at the Aspen Institute in Aspen,

Colorado, where a group of companies were talking about how this communications mechanism might change things. I think that was pivotal. I heard someone say something that absolutely stuck with me, which was that the world changed when we first developed written language. It used to be that you and I could talk, but we couldn't record anything. When someone learned how to write, they could pass on the idea to several people. So, suddenly there was a reason to be educated, because people needed to be able to read and write. When you had people who needed to be educated, that changed the world. First, we had one-to-one communication (conversations) and then, with the advent of written language, we could communicate on a one-to-some basis. Then, many years later, there was Gutenberg, who came up with movable type, and Aldus Manutiuns, who developed different fonts and created the publishing industry. Suddenly, we could produce books. People then had the written word on something besides handwriting on parchment, and that gave people outside of the monasteries a reason to learn. Publishing created a need for education for the masses. This major communications change fundamentally changed the entire fabric of society.

Now, if we fast-forward many years, we hit radio and television, and that meant we didn't have to live in the same community anymore to get the news or keep informed. While people talk about the automobile as having enabled the suburbs, I would argue that broadcast mechanisms — that is, the means by which one person could talk to many people concurrently — once again completely changed the social fabric. For example, we could suddenly communicate with people in Europe on a real-time basis, or with people in New York. That connection/communication link changed how and where we could live. So, we had one-to-one, one-to-some, one-to-many communications breakthroughs, and each time the human experience underwent a tremendous change. Now we have the Internet, which, for the first time, enables many people to communicate simultaneously with many others — many-to-many communications. I don't know what the resulting massive social change will be, but I do know changes are coming. We're not there yet; in fact, we're not even close. We are only on step two of this hundred-step staircase. We are in the midst of something that is truly profound. The Internet isn't going to change the way we get up in the morning, it's not going to change basic human needs or what people like and don't like, but it's going to change the way we all do most of the things that we do. Whether it's banking or communications, whether it's the way we buy our cars, whatever it is, it will be changed by the Internet.

What is the best way to go about investing in this phenomenon?

The hardest part with Internet stocks is that they don't behave rationally, which is evidenced by the fact that the valuations don't correlate with the underlying fundamentals. And it's a situation that will be maintained for some time. However, there will be a reckoning, because at the end of the proverbial day, all stock prices must reflect the discounted stream of future earnings. But today we have a total disconnect in the sector between fundamentals and valuation. So for the average person on the street, in many ways, investing in Internet stocks is just like going to Las Vegas; there is no legal way of knowing the real value of what you are buying or the odds of success. One can certainly make some bets that are smarter than others. Every week that passes, we learn a little more about the prospects of success for different companies and I think there are companies with distinguishing characteristics that seem to position them for success, but the best way for the person on the street to invest in Internet stocks is arguably the *best way for them to invest in any stocks*.

Which is?

Well, I keep in my office a Dr. Seuss book titled *To Think That I Saw it on Mulberry Street*. The opening line of that book is, "When I set off for school each day my father says to me, 'Marco, keep your eyelids up to see what you can see.'" That is the answer for *all* of investing. Don't invest in things you don't understand. If you happen to see something that you and all of your friends are using or doing, or some new product that you are all buying, think about it. It's certainly not a guarantee that it's going to be a successful investment, but it's a place to start.

You have to be able to relate to it.

Yes. You have to relate to it. For example, there were a lot of people suddenly using AOL[2] three or four years ago and during the Internet access crisis no-one was turning it off. Everyone said, "I hate this service." But if you asked, "Well, have you dropped out?" the answer was, "Well, no." There was a powerful message there.

Is there such a thing as a blue-chip Internet stock?

There are some Internet stocks that are the blue chips of the group, but even these carry the caveats inherent in all Internet stocks. There is no Internet stock that is as stable as some of the traditional blue chips. But even then, history is full of blue-chip companies that had their fair share of problems. Within the Internet universe, there are companies that have distinguished themselves by growing sales significantly more rapidly than others. The biggest difference between these and their more slower-growing competitors is superior management. Moreover, it's not just about having one smart person at the farm; it isn't just about Jeff Bezos,[3] or Tim Koogle,[4] or Scott Cook;[5] it's about the people with whom *those* people have surrounded themselves. It's about having management that is as deep as it is talented; one person doesn't run a company. A *team* makes a company work. I am biased in my investment recommendations toward those organizations that are led by an incredibly talented team.

What are the things you look for in management?

It isn't experience, interestingly enough. A lot of people say, "Oh, I want an experienced management team." Bill Gates[6] didn't have experience running a software business. Jeff Bezos hadn't run any business at all, but he'd been a Wall Streeter. Yet, both of them founded and now run incredibly savvy organizations. The one member of management for whom experience is critical is the chief financial officer. Investors need to know that the CFO knows the rules and knows the details. It doesn't matter if the details are particularly relevant to me building my model or not, but I want to be very sure that, if they are running promotion X, someone has worked it all the way through to figure out all the intricacies of what promotion X really means in terms of costs, expected returns, and opportunity costs. However, with the CEO, I look for someone who makes me think in new ways — somebody who is visionary and creative and has likely done something that a hundred people denounced as "the stupidest thing I've ever heard of." The really successful companies — in technology, anyway — more often than not are those that no-one wanted to fund.

For example?

Intel[7] was funded by its founders. Compaq[8] worked hard to find Ben Rosen. The general reaction was, "How could you possibly think that you could compete with IBM[9] in the PC space?" Intuit couldn't get funded. Amazon.com *did* get funded, but people thought Bezos was crazy. And his initial venture investors weren't any of the big names. Kleiner[10] came along later, but they weren't there in the beginning and the general attitude was, "You want to sell books online — what's that?" The real entrepreneurs are those who continued to believe in what they were doing when all of the "smart people" told them it was going to be a failure. So, that's part of it, actually — have you failed? Or, who has hated this business? Because if everyone loved the business from the beginning, you probably haven't learned enough to be running it. To the best of my knowledge, there has never been a business that didn't run into a wall at some point. I have never seen a company that hasn't hit some sort of a wall at some point. Look at Dell Computer.[11] Dell was a disaster. But it came out of that disaster and is living proof of the cliché, "If it doesn't kill you, it makes you much, much stronger."

Is Bill Gates right, though, in saying that bankers are dinosaurs and an endangered species, and that hard-copy books are probably going to disappear?

Bill Gates has spent a lot of time backtracking on that dinosaur comment. I would say that businesses as we know them today, as they are structured today, are an endangered species. I mean, look at the insurance companies who cross their arms in front of their chests and say, "We'll never sell policies online." That's great for their competitors, because those who think the Internet won't affect their businesses will undoubtedly go into negative growth mode within a few years. Another example that comes up a lot is automatic teller machines. Automatic teller machines used to be built into the walls of banks, yet it took people ten years to want to use them. That tells us that we don't change our habits very quickly. However, when someone offers me a compelling solution to a real problem, then I'll pay attention. For instance, what does Amazon.com do for me? I'll tell you — they wrap and ship presents at Christmas when I can't fold corners correctly or take the time to stand in line at the post office. I can call them and say, "Wrap it and send it." That's a wonderful thing. Obviously, there's more to it than that, but I understand why people would want to use that type of business. More often than not, when I see Internet companies, I say, "Explain to me who needs your products." But coming back to the issue of banking, I wouldn't say that banks are dinosaurs. I would say they are closer to early primates. Now is the time when they are either going to have to learn to stand up and walk on two feet, or forever accept a smaller and less profitable position in the social hierarchy.

Or, alternatively put, can elephants tap dance?

Yes, some of them can. Look at Charles Schwab.[12] A brilliant company. The company saw the Internet and seized it as a tool. The smartest companies are recognizing that the Internet isn't some weird new animal; it's a *tool,* and it's a tool that will help them to reach more customers, more effectively, and more efficiently.

One of the biggest problems for the banking industry, though, appears to be the melding of the old and the new. It's very difficult to marry new and emerging technologies and business plans into an entity with a long history, particularly if that history was successful.

The world is changing, and that can be difficult. It's much easier for the companies that started with a clean slate than for those that are trying to evolve. Human nature is particularly hard to change; employees don't always like to change what they're doing, either. We all know the attitude, "I know what I'm doing, I know my job, I'm good at my job, don't ask me to change." So there is undoubtedly going to be stress as these conversions take place. There was tremendous social stress during the industrial revolution, and there has been and will be huge stress during this entire communications revolution. This stuff is hard to do.

While we're discussing stress, what is the hardest part of your job?

The hardest part of the job of the Internet sell-side analyst in this environment is time management. The amount of pressure from the investment banking side to be focused on investment banking deals is immense, and that's incredibly time-consuming. If you're spending your time working on deals, then you're not spending your time doing fundamental research. The second thing that I think is very difficult, from the Internet analyst's perspective, is the huge lack of tangible information. When I followed personal computers I could go to the distributors and to the stores and count boxes at the end of the quarter and tell who was stuffing the channel. There is no way to do that in this sector. There is no third-party source of information. There are a couple of people who publish the number of page views and time spent online, but that information doesn't tell me very much. Its only tells me that in the summer those numbers go down, because people on college campuses go home. That tells me nothing about the Internet's intrinsic growth or lack thereof. So, I think the second most difficult part is the lack of alternative sources of information other than the company itself — and you never get the unexpected insights from the company; you get that from suppliers or distributors. Objective third parties — that's really where the best calls come from.

You've got to be a detective?

Yes, you have to be a detective, but unfortunately there's nothing tangible to detect!

Is it at all possible to measure the operational efficiency of an Internet company?

Yes, but it's very hard. You can certainly look at gross margins,[13] because it's in the cost of goods sold where they put much of the technology that runs the store. How do you measure operational efficiency at Yahoo!, for example? On a quarterly basis I can measure revenue per employee, and operating expenses per employee, and I can do that for the entire base of Internet companies. In fact, every month I measure a basket of these companies on a range of different measures which will tell me the *relative* performance, but this work doesn't tell me the *base-level* performance. For example, I look at the revenues generated per customer who visits the site. I'm not interested in page views, and don't tell me about customers. I'm interested in how you *monetize* those customers. So, revenue per customer is important. I also want to look at sales and marketing expense per customer as a proxy for the cost of customer acquisition. It's also kind of nice to look at gross profit per customer versus sales and marketing expense — that is, what you are paying to get them, versus what you are generating from them before overheads. In most cases, that's still negative for these companies — most companies spend more to attract a customer than they generate in gross margin dollars from that customer. Notwithstanding that, I can certainly watch the trends; if they're getting worse, I know the company's basically at the mercy of the capital markets. As long as the market is willing to take endless secondary issues, these companies are fine. However, the minute the market tightens up, some of these companies, which are losing $100 a customer before accounting for overhead, will be in very difficult straits. Many of them have models that I believe are unsustainable.

You mentioned customer acquisition costs – banks pay anywhere from $1000 to $5000 to acquire customers. But it's interesting that the market has difficulty coming to grips with Internet companies paying similar premiums.

Well, at the end of the day — at least for the consumer Internet companies, not the business-to-business ones — valuation and long-term economic viability will be about how many customers you have and how profitable each one is. It's just like the cable TV business and, as you mentioned, banking.

So it's about customer acquisition, customer management, and customer retention. For the average investor, is it better not only to look at a portfolio of shares but also to think in terms of relative value?

Correct, but it's very hard for the average investor on the street. I get to sit here once a month and crank through the numbers, but if you're working your job as an auto salesman, do you come home at night and try to determine the revenue per customer? I don't think you can.

Are the day traders causing a lot of the volatility in your sector?

Absolutely. And they are causing a disconnect between the fundamentals and reality, the fundamentals and the stock prices. But are they a bane of my existence? No. They are part of the game. Now, what's interesting is that the institutional investors, including me when I was one of them, all turned up their noses at these Internet stocks when they first emerged in 1995 and 1996 because the business models looked so ridiculous. But retail investors bought them up and up and up. The difference? Those folks were using Yahoo! and AOL — although AOL probably isn't a good example, because that stock always had strong institutional ownership. But they were using Yahoo!, they were using Excite,[14] and they were using Lycos,[15] and they subsequently bid those stocks up. But the institutions didn't want to play. Then, in the summer and spring of 1998, Compaq, Intel, and Motorola[16] in short order all missed their quarters due to problems in Asia and problems with demand. Their stock prices got hammered. But what then happened was that investors who had money that had to be invested in technology, because that was their mandate, had nowhere to go except companies that weren't going to miss their quarter because they didn't have any quarter in the first place! That was the first time the Internet stocks really started to find their way into institutional portfolios in any meaningful way. That summer the trends continued, and even into the next year the stocks kept going up. I believe that was due to a bit of a spiraling issue insofar as individuals bought the stocks and then institutions bought them. When the institutions bought them, there was more momentum than when individuals bought them, and so it continued that way with a couple of ups and downs until the first quarter of 1998. Thanks to those dynamics, the Internet stocks had performed outrageously — up 200% and 300% during the year *on average*. Another contributing factor emerged in the fourth quarter. That's the time when institutions have to publish their year-end holdings list. None of them wanted to stand up and say, "We have no exposure to the Internet." So, in the fourth quarter, they went on a wild buying spree, bidding up stocks like AOL, Amazon.com, Yahoo!, etc., just to be able to list them among their holdings.

In view of the fact that prices were driven more by liquidity flows and a supply and demand imbalance, would charts or technical analysis be a more useful tool for understanding where the prices are likely to go compared to, say, fundamental analysis?

Well, in this sort of environment, it's as helpful as anything else. I look at them, but I can't say I actually use them. For example, I'll look at charts if I want to see what a price has done — has it rebounded as aggressively as it has in the past, for example — but I don't actually draw a line from charts. I would add no value if all I did was chart.

The other thing that strikes me about the Internet companies is the debtor–creditor cycle, where you actually have a cash surplus for, say, a period of thirty days. Does that mean that interest rates are also going to be an important driver of share prices, and are the stocks, ironically, going to become very interest rate-sensitive?

Absolutely. They're very interest rate-sensitive for two reasons. First, they do all have this negative cash cycle that you mentioned, where they get paid well before they have to pay out, so interest income is a significant part of income. Second, because the real returns are so far in the future, that slight change in interest rates on the discount rate makes a huge difference to valuation. So, I would say the Internet stocks are *very* interest rate-sensitive.

How tough is it keeping up with all the technology changes?

It's impossible to keep up with everything that's going on. To help cope with that, we at CSFB have split the Internet into various subgroups. For instance, there's another member of our group who is purely responsible for the back-end infrastructure. I need to have *some* idea of what's going on, but mostly I just need to know that my companies' sites are up and running. So, do I need to know what DSL[17] is? Do I need to know what XML[18] is? Do I need to know what technology changes are on the horizon? Certainly I do, but do I need to know the intricacies of those technologies? No, I'm leaving that for somebody else.

Within the broad Internet competitive landscape, how big a threat is Microsoft[19] to AOL, for example?

I think that will be a very interesting story over the next year. I think Microsoft always has that weapon of price. For example, Microsoft understood that they were way behind in spreadsheets, word processors, and database products, and when they finally had a product that was ready, they jumped in the market and cut the price in half. We see AOL sitting out there with a US$21.95 access fee. I think that $21.95 is in significant danger. Having said that, I think Microsoft can probably continue to issue provocative press releases and they can cut some prices, but whether or not Microsoft can execute and deliver the service is much less certain. People need to understand that it's phenomenally challenging to do what AOL does, which is to serve nineteen million customers. That's an issue with which eBay[20] is quite familiar. Is the issue that management doesn't care? No. Management cares a ton, but no-one has had to handle that kind of interactive traffic before. In technology terms, eBay is going where no company has gone before. As the pioneer, you do tend to get the proverbial arrow in the back.

Can we talk about valuation? I saw something recently where you raised Intuit as a strong buy with a target at US$115.

Could you walk us through how you arrived at that target price and the risks to that.

Intuit, AOL, and Electronic Arts[21] are the three companies in my universe where I can actually do some fundamental valuations. Intuit has a number of different businesses; a personal finance business divided into Quicken, their flagship product, and Quicken.com, their Internet business. Then there is their tax division, which is broken into a consumer tax division which has Turbo Tax and a professional tax division. The third major business they have is the small business opportunity, based on Quickbooks with associated products and supplies. For example, if you buy Quickbooks (a small business accounting package), chances are that you're also going to buy invoices. And if you do that, you're probably also going to buy envelopes. The supplies business is small, but quite profitable. The fourth part of their business is their international operation. I can take the business apart and say, "Wait a minute, Intuit isn't a software company and it's not an Internet company — it's a combination of the two." We try to value each part depending on what it is. Take Intuit's Quicken business, for example — it's a consumer software company. How do I value a consumer software company? These businesses used to sell for as much as six times revenue — they certainly don't do that now, but even a second-rate consumer software company trades for a multiple of two to three times revenue. Now, Quicken has 75% market share and a high rate of returning customers, so you ask, "Why do you think theirs is a reasonably good software business?" It isn't growing very fast. On a unit share basis it's growing, but on a dollar basis it's shrinking. The market for people who want to buy personal finance software is pretty much tapped out. It isn't growing, but it has a big market share, so what is a reasonable multiple to put on that? Well, if a second-rate consumer software company can trade for two to three times revenue, maybe a first-rate company with that kind of dominance in the market can trade for four times revenue. So, I put a multiple of four on that piece of the business.

Moving down to the consumer tax business, again it's a consumer software product, but it's one where the customer *has* to come back every single year because the tax laws always change and therefore you can't use the same product twice. It has a very high repeat customer rate and, what's more, the business is growing. Not only is the business growing, but the economics of the business are getting better as the company moves much of the business to the Web. For example, think of the savings as they move the support function to the Web. Many products used to ship with an instruction book that had over 150 pages — which meant printing costs and shipping costs. Now, most of the information is online, so you have costs coming out of the product. Given those improvements, I put a revenue multiple of five times on that business. Moreover, to help justify that, note that Intuit bought a large professional tax software business company to combine with their own for which they paid five times revenue. If they paid five times revenue for a business they bought and have combined it with the other business that they originally had, they now have a much bigger, more important player that they can leverage off to other parts of their business. Ultimately, I put a multiple of five-and-a-half times on that, which could still be conservative. Now, moving on, their international business hasn't been growing at all, it's been having a difficult time, so I put a multiple of one times revenue on that business.

What's most interesting is the Quickbooks business which is right now the most compelling part of the story. Sales to small businesses are booming. The unit sales and the dollar sales are up impressively this past six months. For example, for the first six months of 1998 the average selling price on Quickbooks was US$130, whereas in the first six months of 1999 the average selling price was US$162. That price increase reflects the fact that the customer base is upgrading and buying the professional version rather than the basic version, or the multi-user version rather than the single-user version. Here's a product that (a) is gaining users and (b) gathering incremental dollars from each user that it gets. Now, that's a wonderful thing. I think you can put a multiple of five times on that business.

The final part is the supplies business, which is little envelopes and paper, but it's actually a large, tangible part of the revenue stream. I looked at some acquisitions of office supplies products companies and they appeared to have been acquired for roughly three times revenues when they weren't growing very fast. By comparison, this one is growing rapidly along with Quickbooks, but I left the multiple at three times revenues. So, you add all of those up, add in a discounted value of the cash and short-term securities, and then divide by the number of shares outstanding. That math results in a projected price of US$115 per share.

And what about their investment portfolio?

Intuit has done a remarkable job in investing. They're not an investment company, but if you look at where they have strategically invested with partners, they bought shares of Excite at US$3.50 and they sold them at a little more than US$100. They bought shares of CheckFree[22] at US$10, and the stock at this moment is trading at US$41. They have been early investors in VeriSign[23] and they've done tremendously well. So, they have quite a bit of cash in their short-term security portfolio — at the end of last quarter it was worth US$1.2 billion — so, I took that and immediately took 20% off it assuming volatility.

So, basically it's a sum of the parts based on relative valuation?

Yes, a total sum of the parts and then aggressively discounted. First, I just counted the cash, then I put the whole thing together and discounted the whole thing, so the cash gets discounted twice.

Do you find that generally the buy-side have no problem with that logic?

To be honest, I find they're delighted that there's actually some fundamental analysis going on. But sometimes there's a question over the Internet revenues segment of the analysis, because I put a multiple of twenty-five times on those; the appropriate multiple is certainly subject to debate.

How did you arrive at twenty-five times?

I picked that number by looking at a group of comparable companies. But why isn't it thirty times? Why isn't it twenty times? There's always going to be some debate about the multiple.

How much pressure are these stock-market valuations putting on company managements?

It's putting pressure on them in terms of hiring new people, and in terms of where stock options are priced. But does management feel a responsibility to keep the price at US$200 a share? I don't think so. Amazon.com has been the one to clearly demonstrate that. They make the announcements that are right for their business, and if it halves the stock price, it halves the stock price. This doesn't mean that the employees aren't a little grouchy over the fact that they all used to be worth X and now they're worth 0.5 X. They're probably quite unhappy about that, but the companies really don't feel a responsibility, and rightly so. Yahoo! had days when the stock was up US$70, and that was completely out of management's control. I think there's been so much volatility that the smart managements are the ones that have sort of thrown in the towel and said, "I'm going to run the business, and the stock is going to do what the stock is going to do. I can't control it. At some point in the future, maybe volatility will calm down and maybe then I can work toward a more rational price. For now, the best that I can do is hold an analysts meeting once a year, go visit fund managers, and hold quarterly conference calls."

Is the supply–demand imbalance in some of the stocks a major factor in these stock prices?

Yes, but the industry is addressing that issue by bringing out what seems like thousands of IPOs and through the expirations of lock-up periods on those companies that went public six months ago. The supply–demand issue isn't today what it was six months ago, and six months from now it will be even less of an issue.

As a sell-side analyst, we all bring something different to the market and perhaps Internet analysts are in a different category of analyst to anyone else. As an Internet analyst, where do you think you add the most value? Some people would argue that Internet analysts add value not so much from their binary call or their valuation, but by increasing the supply of stock by bringing new companies to the market.

Yes, I'd agree that it certainly isn't the buy or sell recommendations. For example, you can come up with a buy recommendation and it's on CNBC and the stock is up US$10 but your institutional clients really don't care. I try to use strong buys very sparingly so that if I *do* use that rating, people know I *really* mean it. There is also merit in the point you just made about the value added in bringing new deals out and bringing some stability to the market. I think that's true, but I don't think the sector lends itself to great fundamental analysis. Notwithstanding that, I do think periodically one can learn some incremental that will affect a stock's price. For example, Yahoo! recently raised its advertising rates; the buy-side wants to hear that — it's incremental news. When I was on the buy-side, I couldn't have cared less what the sell-side's stock recommendations were. I cared about the incremental bit of information that the sell-side could get that I couldn't get, because I was responsible for a hundred companies and the sell-side was responsible for ten.

It sounds like the sell-side is perhaps focusing on the wrong things?

Well, that was certainly one of the main reasons why I came back to the sell-side. The main one was that I was attracted by the Internet. However, it's intriguing to note that there was a clear disconnect between what the buy-side wanted and what the sell-side offered. When I was on the buy-side, I had the luxury of working for a firm where we had a big staff of analysts, so I didn't need the sell-side to do analysis for me; I had the time and the mandate to do that myself. What I *did* need from the sell-side was incremental information — the things that I couldn't get because I was in the office more. Little things might not mean anything to the sell-side analyst, a tidbit might mean nothing to them, but might, in conjunction with tidbits from other sell-side analysts, be the last piece of an important puzzle.

Like, for example, "I saw Bill Gates and Jeff Bezos having lunch"?

Yes. Another example would be, and I don't really know yet what it means, but I noticed that Preview Travel[24] just canceled a bunch of its ads out of *Ad Week*. Maybe that does mean something, or maybe they just moved to a different magazine. I don't know. But when I was on the buy-side, that's the sort of thing I really wanted to hear. I didn't want the phone call after the quarterly analyst's report summing up what I'd already heard. If I cared about the stock, I was on that call too.

But maybe the value added on that sort of phone call is, "Look, there's a very subtle thing here that might have gone unnoticed. There's a wrinkle in the tax note that shows XYZ and we think the market might have missed this."

Yes, that sort of thing is very helpful, but spitting back what the company said on the conference call is irrelevant. If a sell-sider can do some analysis on something that wasn't as evident, that's tremendously helpful. It helps me to synthesize what I've just heard. Or if I'm a buy-sider and I've had six conference calls all in the same afternoon, can somebody please shrink each of them down to the high points. What are the three things I need to know about the Compaq or the Yahoo! conference call? One of my hopes in coming back to the sell-side was to get information out to investors in a more timely and effective manner. Sadly, however, it's more difficult to do that than it initially seems, because of the SEC's regulations regarding insider information and unequal dissemination. Wouldn't it be great if I could put all the information I've collected and then blast it out in a timely email once a week? It seems easy, but in reality it's almost impossible.

Because of compliance issues, like not favoring one set of investors and making sure that data or information is widely dispersed?

Yes. You've got information and you can't get it out because, by the time it goes through compliance and gets approved, it's no longer interesting.

So from the sell-side, there's probably too much emphasis on the binary call, on regurgitating publicly available information, and on making junk phone calls, rather than on getting into the industry issues and passing this information on?

Yes, and there has been too much of an assumption from the sell-side that it knows much more than the buy-side. In my experience, at least at the big buy-side accounts, it's actually the other way around. The buy-side knows more, because companies have more of a vested interest in helping their shareholders to understand the business than they do in helping the mouthpiece.

What's the future for sell-side research?

I think there is great value that the sell-side *can* add. But are any of us really doing that right now? Nope, not many at all. We're all too busy being involved in investment banking transactions. Conceptually, there is value that the sell-side can add; theoretically, we get to focus and there is something to be said for focusing. But at the same time, there's something to be said for having a broad technology overview. There is also merit to the argument that says being completely focused on an area brings an advantage, because that way it's easier to notice the subtleties. Unfortunately, the wild IPO environment that we're in right now makes it very challenging to deliver that sort of real analysis.

How do you balance those demands? On the sell-side, you're either working for the buyers of equity or the sellers of equity, and occasionally you're going to run into conflict. What advice would you give about handling that conflict?

That's a very good question. I think that at the end of the day, nothing as a sell-side analyst is more important than your analytical integrity and credibility. Sometimes, you have to find a way to subtly say, "I'm supposed to call you to tell you that I really like this stock, but let me tell you that I *really* like this IPO for at least the first twenty minutes." You need to find a way to do that. At any time, I will likely have a couple of companies that I work with where I'm less enthusiastic about the stocks, but there's pressure from the investment banking side to be friendly. So, it comes down to the subtlety in the tone of the writing and the hope that investors will be able to read the differences in the research notes. That can be quite a challenge, because you do need friends on both sides.

What advice would you give to the novice analyst coming into the industry?

Number one, there are fourteen people following your space already, so figure out what you're going to do differently. Don't be the fourteenth person saying the same thing. If you can find an angle, exploit it. For example, I was a Toys "Я" Us analyst many years ago and I guess I didn't look like the standard analyst because one Thanksgiving weekend I got in my car and drove to fifteen malls and stood in line to talk to Santa. I wanted to know what people wanted from Santa. That call caught everybody's attention, because no-one else was standing in line to sit on Santa's lap. It's fundamental analysis. However, in the Internet sector it's difficult, because there aren't third parties. Still, in most businesses there is some other way you can get the information. So, I guess the number one piece of advice is to find a way to differentiate yourself based on the information you're gathering. Either analyze it a different way, or use alternative — even, perhaps, some surprising — sources, because you can learn from them. I think I became a very good PC analyst because I spent all my time with the distributors and none of my time with Apple,[25] Compaq, and IBM. The distributors know things, so go up or down the food chain — that's where you can really learn about the business. I also have some advice that says, use the stronger stock recommendations ratings sparingly. If you're trying to make a statement, keep your powder dry.

Is Wall Street a great place for information but a relatively poor place for investment advice?

The buy-siders who have been in the business understand that the sell-side can't put a sell on most things, because if you put a sell on a stock, (a) the management of that company never talks to you again, and (b) all of the shareholders who own it blame you for the fall in share price. And by the way, the people who don't own it don't care. So, you've infuriated both constituencies and helped no-one, including yourself.

So it's easier to be popular than contrarian?

Yes. It's easier, and that's the nature of the game. What's more, it's smarter, which is a shame, but that's the way it works. People don't want to hear buy and sell. They want to hear buy on what they own, and sell on what their competitors own. You have to be subtle with negative recommendations unless there is something really very wrong. When the downgrade is based on a changing opinion, it can be appropriate to communicate the message by saying, "This is not my favorite stock at this point in time."

In a very commercial and at times opaque industry, how do you judge success?

I think it goes back to the question of credibility. I want to be able to look myself straight in the eye in the mirror every night and every morning and be able to say I didn't try to shove some stock I don't believe in down my clients' throat just to get a banking deal done. That's number one. Number two is the type of people who call me. I don't need 5000 people to be listening to me. I need the key people to be listening to me. Analyst polls are purely popularity contests. That's great, and I'm happy for those people who do well in them. However, those results are often based on how many phone calls an analyst makes, not on the quality of the research. Playing that game strikes me as a waste of time. I guess what's relevant to me is that the people I respect, respect me back. That's how I measure success. I feel good about the fact that I'll go in to meet a company and they'll say, "Oh, we've heard you do good work." I like that — professional respect. Professional respect ought to translate into winning some investment banking deals when you really want them. So, there are tangible ways to measure success; it isn't all ethereal. The best days in this business are the days when you're right about a stock for the right reasons. You made the stock call, and other people didn't see it. The stock went up and you made people money. The folks who said, "Buy Amazon.com. at $40" made a wonderful CNBC call, a wonderful retail call. The stock went up, names went in the headlines, and stars were born. But there was no fundamental analysis there. That strategy may be a great success for those who choose to employ it, but it's a toss of a coin. In my book, real success is when you go to the store, for example, and count Apple computer boxes and you work out that there is way too much Apple merchandise in the store. It's particularly interesting if it's March 23. You've discovered that somebody is stuffing the channel. A good sell-sider will use that information to convince some investors to get out of the stock. If three weeks later Apple announces that it missed its quarter, then that call was a success.

How hard is it to maintain a balanced life? This industry is notorious for burnout.

I think right now it's impossible — which is pathetic, but true. One of the great challenges of this business is, how do you get away? I tried to take four days over Labor day — four days over a holiday weekend. Two-and-a-half days in I was getting urgent phone calls: "You must call so-and-so right away." I think another way of measuring success — and it's something I haven't mastered yet — is being able to say, "I'm sorry, I'm away." Just learning to say no. It's absolutely critical if you're going to survive. I've learned to say no sometimes, but not often enough. Still, I'm making progress. I went away recently and left my pager on my desk where my coworkers could easily see it and note that *it* was there, while *I* wasn't.

Do you have any major principles about how you approach company analysis?

Ask yourself four questions about every company you run into. How big is the market? What is this company's proprietary or sustainable advantage? Why is this company going to capitalize on it? Who are the people who are running it who are going to get it there? If there's a big market, and if this company can capitalize on it, is there a compelling business model that will actually throw off profitability at some point? That's it. That's all you need to know about any company.

Which sounds a little like your Graham and Dodd quote, which is ironical because you're talking about investment principles enunciated in 1934. Sixty-five years later, nothing has really changed?

That's dead right. I quote that all the time.

What constitutes a safe Internet stock? Is there such a thing?

I think Intuit and Electronic Arts are safe Internet stocks, because they have real underlying fundamental businesses that are generating real profits. These businesses are supplemented by a call option on the Internet. I think that's relatively safe.

What about the AOL versus Yahoo! comparison?

AOL has nineteen million customers, who pay them US$21.95 a month, and that's pretty compelling. Quarter in, quarter out, and that's very compelling. Yahoo! has no tie into physical infrastructure other than the servers they're running the sites from. They can change with the technology — broadband, narrowband — so it's very interesting.

It's unsafe to compare the two?

No. I think that Yahoo! may be structurally better positioned for the long term, but I would never underestimate the value of nineteen million customers who don't want to change.

Are they truly customers or subscribers, or people who have just visited the portal?

For AOL, they are real, honest-to-goodness customers. They pay up every month. But for Yahoo!, they're not. For Yahoo! they drift in and you sure hope they'll look at an advertisement. I don't actually recommend one over the other. I would argue that there are at least three of these general service providers that will thrive. One is AOL, one is Yahoo!, and I suspect the third one will be Microsoft. But we'll see. Microsoft has been stunningly slow here, and for all their sabre rattling they're still not there yet.

Is the Internet sector an emerging market in view of the fact that it is typified by volatility, poor information, strong growth expectations, and is very sensitive to interest rates?

That's a really accurate assessment.

Finally, why aren't Internet spin-offs such a good idea for those companies that have Internet subsidiaries?

There are some companies where the Internet business is totally separate from the main business. Maybe those companies can rightfully do a spin-off. But, generally speaking, the Internet is a communications tool and companies should no more be spinning off their communications tool than spinning off their telephone infrastructure. Again, the smart companies are those who are recognizing that this is something that can *change* their business. It's not a separate animal. It's a mechanism by which to make the current business more efficient and more effective. I realize that lots of companies are looking at the multiples on Internet stocks and saying, "Let's spin one off." There is also pressure from the employee base that wants to own a snazzy Internet stock. Then there is pressure from the board of directors. Basically, there is all kinds of pressure, but the question that any company that's considering a spin-off should ask themselves is, "Where are we going to be in two years?" If you are a retailer and you spin off your Internet division, you're going to be at a tremendous disadvantage in two years' time compared to those companies that have both a physical store and an Internet presence. And if you spin off a division and for some reason the stock price doesn't go straight through the roof, what have you achieved except dilution of your ownership and infrastructure? What's more, eventually you're going to have conflicts of interest. The spin-off company is going to want to do different things. Why should I, the investor, want to own the old company if the growth vehicle has been spun off? For most companies, I would argue that spin-offs are only a short-term solution that may lead to increased liquidity and a near-term increased valuation, but could also result in major headaches in the long term.

✳ ✳ ✳

Despite the fact that Lise Buyer is working in one of the toughest and most volatile sectors of the stock market, her approach to analysis remains very pragmatic and fundamentally driven. Buyer's experience in having worked on both the buy-side and the sell-side, together with her original strong interest in trading, is a relatively unique combination among sell-side analysts and has arguably equipped her to deal with the tough challenge of following Internet stocks.

The key aspects of Buyer's approach, which may be difficult for the average investor to emulate given their lack of access to company management, are:

- Understand the difference between trading and investing. In Buyer's view, trading is all about reacting when you have no news. In many ways, it's quite the opposite of investing, which requires patience, commitment, and courage.
- The Internet is going to continue to have a massive impact on our lives, but no-one knows yet the full extent of it or has all of the answers. Consequently, while there may be potentially very high rewards, the risks still remain significant. And in view of the disconnect between stock-market valuations and the underlying

fundamentals of Internet companies, for the average person in the street, investing in Internet stocks is akin to betting in a casino. However, for those investors with a higher tolerance for risk, the best way to invest is to buy stocks where you understand their products or services. Moreover, in view of the tremendous volatility in Internet stock prices, dollar cost averaging would be a sensible strategy for the average investor to adopt.

- Try to understand and distinguish between company managements. Companies that have distinguished themselves are not only those that have grown sales at a relatively higher rate than their competitors, but more importantly, they have strong management teams. Look beyond the chief executive, and try to understand the depth of talent that exists in the company.

- Even if you will never invest in an Internet company, try to understand how the Internet will affect the business of the stocks that you are currently invested in. In Buyer's view, companies whose management think that the Internet won't affect their business are in danger of going into negative growth mode. This is especially true of financial stocks such as insurance companies and banks. The winners will be those companies who recognize that the Internet is a tool that will help them to reach customers more effectively. Moreover, companies that are starting with a clean technology slate will, in certain areas, be a major competitive threat to companies that have large, inflexible technology infrastructures.

- One of the biggest problems for an Internet stock investor (and analyst) is the lack of tangible information and reliable third-party sources of information. But despite this, there are ways of getting a handle on operational performance. Statistics like revenue per employee and operating expenses per employee are useful proxies for operational efficiency. Moreover, performance should be monitored on a quarterly basis, and investors should be aware that Wall Street will punish stock prices of companies that disappoint. More importantly, though, while the absolute base level of performance can be hard to measure, relative performance is probably the best way of identifying potential winners and losers. Furthermore, watch the broad trends for these headline performance statistics.

- The capital markets will be critical in determining which Internet companies survive, and as long as the markets are content to continue to fund loss-making start-up technology companies, those companies are fine. Investors, however, should be aware that the moment sentiment turns, those companies that are losing money will be questioned. Ultimately, the market's confidence will be based on the number of customers that the company controls and how profitable each one is.

- Internet stocks will continue to be extremely volatile for three reasons. First is the high degree of forecasting risk that comes with the sector, combined with extraordinarily high valuation multiples and market expectations. Therefore, the scope for earnings or operational disappointment is high. Second, due to their negative cash cycle, where interest income is a high proportion of total income, they are very sensitive to interest rates. Moreover, due to the fact that the real rates of return are so far into the future, a small change in the discount rate will have a significant impact on valuation. Third, liquidity flows and a chronic supply–demand imbalance, as well as day traders, are a significant contributor to short-term volatility in the sector.

- Despite the sector's reputation for being beyond any reasonable basis for valuation, there are some companies where it is possible to undertake a fundamental valuation. Intuit, AOL, and Electronic Arts fall into this category.

- Be very cautious about companies that are spinning off their Internet operations. Companies that float their growth vehicles run the risk of losing control of one of the most important parts of their business infrastructure.

Having worked on both the buy-side and the sell-side, Buyer's views

of what the buy-side generally wants and what the sell-side offers
should be of interest to anyone just starting out in their careers as a
sell-side analyst:

- The buy or sell recommendation isn't where you are likely to add
  the greatest value. Incremental information or analysis is often of
  more value to a fund manager than a binary stock view.
- A common error made by the sell-side is that they assume they
  know more about the company and its prospects than the buy-
  side.
- Be focused, and figure out where your competitive advantage is.
  Don't be the fourteenth person to say the same thing. Find an
  angle or a niche and exploit it. Try to differentiate yourself based
  on either your sources of information or the way you analyze it.
- Use strong stock ratings very sparingly. That way, people will know
  when you are really making a statement with conviction.
- It's easy to be popular, but very hard to be contrarian. Find ways to
  communicate negative views in a way that doesn't alienate clients
  or companies.
- You will have conflicts from time to time; learn how to deal with
  them and at the same time understand that nothing is more
  important than your analytical integrity and credibility.
- In looking at any company, but especially technology-based
  companies, ask four key questions. How big is the market? What is
  this company's proprietary or sustainable advantage? Why is this
  company going to capitalize on it? Who are the people who are
  running the company and how are they going to get it there?

---

[1]   Benjamin Graham and David L. Dodd, *Security Analysis* (New York: McGraw-Hill,
      1934).
[2]   America Online, Inc. provides interactive communications and services. At the
      time of writing, the company's stock-market capitalization was US$148.4 billion.
[3]   CEO and founder of Amazon.com, Inc., an online retailer that sells books, music,
      videotapes, audiotapes, and other products. The company offers a catalog of

approximately three million titles, search and browse features, email services, personalized shopping services, Web-based credit card payment, and direct shipping to customers. At the time of writing, the company had a stock-market capitalization of US$23.3 billion.

4 CEO and chairman of Yahoo! Inc., a global Internet media company that offers an online guide to Web navigation, communication services, and commerce. The company's site includes a hierarchical, subject-based directory of websites that enables users to locate and access information and services through hypertext links. At the time of writing, the company had a stock-market capitalization of US$46.7 billion.

5 Chairman and founder of Intuit Inc., which develops and markets software products and related services that allow households and small businesses to automate financial tasks, including accounting and personal finances. Intuit also offers supplies, checks and invoices, and financial services. At the time of writing, the company had a stock-market capitalization of US$5.7 billion.

6 William H. Gates III, the chairman and founder of Microsoft Corporation.

7 Intel Corporation designs and manufactures computer components and related products. Intel's product range includes microprocessors, chipsets, embedded processors and microcontrollers, flash memory products, graphics products, network and communications products, systems management software, conferencing products, and digital imaging products. At the time of writing, the company had a stock-market capitalization of US$274.8 billion.

8 Compaq Computer Corporation develops, manufactures, and distributes networking and communication products, commercial desktop and portable products, and consumer personal computers. At the time of writing, the company's stock-market capitalization was US$32 billion.

9 International Business Machines Corporation (IBM) provides advanced information technology services and products, including mainframe, desktop, and laptop computers. At the time of writing, the company had a stock-market capitalization of US$169.9 billion.

10 Eugene Kleiner, who in 1972 cofounded Kleiner Perkins Caufield & Byers, a venture capital firm. The Kleiner Perkins partnership has provided seed-capital for some of America's most innovative new companies. Investments include: @Home Network, Amazon.com, America Online, CBS SportsLine, and Netscape Communications.

11 Dell Computer Corporation designs, develops, manufactures, and directly sells standard and custom-specified computer systems that include desktop computer systems, notebook computers, workstations, and network server and storage products. At the time of writing, the company had a stock-market capitalization of US$105.5 billion.

12 The Charles Schwab Corporation provides financial services to individual investors, independent investment managers, retirement plans, and institutions through multiple service channels, including the Internet, branch offices, telephone, and multilingual technologies. At the time of writing, the company had a stock-market capitalization of US$38.1 billion.

13 The gross margin is calculated by dividing gross profit (i.e., sales less cost of goods sold) by total sales revenue.

14 Excite, Inc. is an Internet media company that provides Internet navigation services. The company was acquired by @Home Corp. in January 1999 in an all-stock deal valued at US$6.7 billion.

15 Lycos, Inc. develops and provides guides to online content, third-party content Web search, and directory services. At the time of writing, the company's stock-market capitalization was US$5.3 billion.

16 Motorola, Inc. provides integrated communications and embedded electronic products. The company offers software-enhanced wireless telephones, two-way radios, messaging and satellite communications products and systems, as well as networking and Internet-access products. At the time of writing, the company had a stock-market capitalization of US$62.9 billion.

17 Digital Subscriber Line.

18 eXtensible Markup Language (XML) — the emerging core Web language.

19 Microsoft Corporation develops, manufactures, licenses, sells, and supports software products. The company offers operating system software, server application software, business and consumer applications software, software development tools, and Internet and Intranet software. Microsoft also develops the MSN network of Internet products and services. At the time of writing, the company's stock-market capitalization was US$473 billion.

20 eBay Inc. is a person-to-person trading community on the Internet. The company's service is used by buyers and sellers for the exchange of personal items such as coins, collectibles, computers, memorabilia, stamps, and toys. At the time of writing, the company's stock-market capitalization was US$16.3 billion.

21 Electronic Arts (Nasdaq: ERTS) is the world's largest interactive entertainment software company. At the time of writing, the company had a stock-market capitalization of US$4.8 billion.

22 CheckFree Corporation designs and develops software and services for electronic payments and collections, and secure transactions on the Internet. At the time of writing, the company's stock-market capitalization was US$2 billion.

23 VeriSign, Inc. provides Internet-based trust services needed by websites, enterprises, and individuals to conduct secure electronic commerce and communications over the Internet. At the time of writing, the company's stock-market capitalization was US$8.1 billion.

24 Preview Travel, Inc. provides online travel services for holiday and small business travelers. The company's services include reservation services, real-time schedule access, pricing, and availability information for airlines, hotels, and major car rental companies. At the time of writing, the company had a stock-market capitalization of US$471.6 million.

25 Apple Computer, Inc. designs, manufactures, and markets personal computers and related personal computing and communications products. At the time of writing, the company had a stock-market capitalization of US$15.5 billion.

6

Tim Jensen: Nothing is Forever Right or Forever Wrong

"The wonderful opportunities are when the perception of a company changes. That's a wonderful chance for outperformance."

Tim Jensen is the co-portfolio manager of the Oaktree Capital Management Emerging Markets Funds; part of Oaktree Capital LLC, a US$16 billion fund manager. Prior to joining Oaktree, Jensen was the chief investment officer for Morgan Stanley Dean Witter Investment Management Company (MSDW) based in Singapore, and oversaw the management of over US$6 billion in Asia-Pacific equities. A commercial banker by training, Jensen has been involved in equity investing for ten years and has specialized in emerging markets, specifically Eastern Europe, Latin America, and Asia. Perhaps reflecting his background in commercial banking, where bankers live with their decisions for a long time, Jensen's approach to investing is very fundamentally driven. This is no better illustrated than by the fact that he cites the quality of management as a key investment criterion. Jensen's early experiences in emerging market investing involved working with hedge funds, where absolute returns were important and the supply of investment capital was limited. In that environment volatility was his friend. Jensen has also operated in a "relative world" and, in line with most money managers, his performance was judged relative to a benchmark index where volatility was something to be minimized and returns maximized. This underscores Jensen's view that any investment philosophy or approach must be relative to the criteria against which performance is measured. In addition, understanding how perceptions about stocks are fashioned, and what may cause them to change, is an important part of Jensen's approach to investment.

How did you get into this business?

I came into listed equities in a very indirect way. I started out after college as a commercial banker, went through bank credit training, went to business school — it was the late 1980s and leverage buyouts were hot — and I ended up taking a job with a leveraged buyout firm in Los Angeles and worked there for three years. Then we ran into the Drexel bankruptcy, which had quite an impact on a number of sources of our money. So, 1990 was tough, and I was looking around for what to do next. I was asked by a family based in Switzerland if I would be interested in doing more direct investments in mainly emerging markets. So, in July of 1990, three weeks ahead of the Gulf War, I moved to Budapest and was trying to do direct investments in Hungary, which, as it turned out, was about three to four years too early.

How long were you there?

I stayed there for about six months, but the people I worked for got impatient and moved me to Bangkok, and that's when I started working in listed emerging market equities. In late 1990, early 1991, I started working on emerging markets equities full-time. I was moved around a lot, as I was doing the big analysis on block deals.

What were some of your first investments?

Back then we bought 10% of Shinawatra Computer[1] in Thailand, and

4% of Land and Houses.[2] We went to Mexico and bought big blocks of a bunch of different Mexican names — Cemex,[3] Bancomer[4] — and then they started to move me around the world. I would spend, say, two to six months in a given city and look through potential stocks that we would invest in and try to make hits on a few big ones. However, I was getting a bit tired of all the moving around. I wanted to move back to the States, so I took a job doing Latin American equities. Mostly what I had done for the family was Asian equities, but I had spent some time in Latin America, and in 1993, to move back to the States, it was easier to get a job covering Latin American stocks. I then spent the next three-and-a-half years or so working purely on Latin equities.

Was that a different ball game?

It was, because the cycles were so sharp in Latin America. Shortly after, I went to work for a hedge fund where I could short stocks and long stocks and take more advantage of the volatility.

Did that require a different skill set?

Not really, because the critical thing in the way that I have always tried to approach stocks is just to use common sense.

What constitutes common sense?

You start with the core things, like what does the analyst community think about a stock, for example. However, in the early 1990s there wasn't much of an analyst community in some of these markets. If you went to Mexico in 1991, for example, the research was very thin. There were some Mexican brokers, and Barings were involved pretty early, but basically it was very thin. The research wasn't very good either, so what I would do was just my normal work on a company. I'd get the financials, I'd meet with managers, try to understand what drove their business, and I'd meet their competitors. I like to meet managers in order to make an assessment of whether I like the way they approach the business and the way they approach the use of my capital. That's very important to me. I want to make sure they're not going to waste it. Then I always cross-check, as I'm a skeptical guy. I've been told things in the past that weren't true, and that's always an occupational hazard. I cross-check with as many competitors as possible to see if the story is reasonable. I like to do cross-border valuation checks as well.

For example?

The cement industry is a classic example. It can be a really interesting business to invest in if it has a tight oligopoly structure. But if you have an oligopoly, you're also going to have periodic breakdowns if conditions get weak. For example, seven or eight years ago, Mexican cement companies were out of favor. Then people suddenly realized there was a construction boom going on, and so prices went up, margins went up, and the volumes got very attractive. But then prices overreached themselves. In Mexico in early 1994, for example, you had cement companies that were trading at three to three-and-a-half times the replacement value of their plants. It was alchemy!

Cemex, for example, would announce that they were going to build a new plant and the sell-side would then put it in their models on the basis that the company could sell all the cement they could ever produce without any limits! So, the dynamic and the type of thinking that was driving the market was that Cemex could construct a plant for US$120 a ton, the market would then put a US$325–350 per ton valuation on it, and the stock price would go up and Cemex would raise more capital. So, pretty soon, you had an overbuilt industry. And you find yourself asking in those situations, "What's the test of reasonableness here? How much cement do people consume? What's the most cement-intensive country in the world? What's the least cement-intensive? Where are we in the economic cycle? Are people raising money that doesn't make sense?" So, one of the biggest early investments I worked on was to buy Cemex stock. But even more interesting is the fact that one of my most successful shorts when I worked at hedge funds years later was also Cemex, because it had just gotten carried away and didn't hold together.

How do you approach the issue of valuation?

I look at it a few different ways, and I have to say up front that valuation can be very difficult in Asia, because the economies are at different stages of development and the accounting varies by country. I tend to start on companies where there is something like a tangible factory or some hard assets. Then, I like to compare the enterprise value[5] to replacement cost of the assets. I never look at market capitalization alone; I always look at the total capital structure. So, that's the first thing. I then look at enterprise value to capacity and I also look at enterprise value to gross cash flow. And by the way, I think EBIT[6] and EBITDA[7] multiples are probably some of the most misused concepts in investing because it's a return *of* capital and not a return *on* capital.

So, I'll look at a range of benchmarks, and then I'll look at what are the capex needs. I tend to like companies that I can buy for attractive valuation multiples that aren't hogs for additional capital. What I want is something that I can get at an attractive multiple, that has growth prospects, but where the *cost* to grow isn't too high. People often overlook the capital intensity of a business. For example, they'll look at a company and say, "Ah, the EBIT or EBITDA multiple is only X," but they don't look at what the company has to reinvest to stay in business. So, it's just nonsense. The other concept that has crept into sell-side analysis is enterprise value to EBITDA to growth rate. I don't know what that means!

It's probably just another reason for brokers to come up with new buy and sell recommendations.

That's probably right, but all the same, I went back to my Gordon growth model[8] and all the stuff I learned in business school and I couldn't find anything theoretical that would underpin that ratio. But one good thing I'll say about EBITDA is that it's the one measure of earnings that is least susceptible to different accounting treatments. But even then, you have to be careful not to capitalize expenses.

And depreciation policies can be different too.

That's right. So, then you have to work your way around the balance sheet. In addition, I'm a little bit more *value*-orientated, whereas some fund managers are very *growth*-orientated and don't seem to care as much about value. I care about value and valuation. I think it matters in the long run, particularly when you are in emerging markets which are highly volatile. And when things get tough, you have to have something to fall back on. So, as I'm value-orientated, I look at measures of enterprise value to cash flow, and enterprise value to replacement value, and then I'll look at things like PERs,[9] but I'll adjust that if a company has a very long depreciation policy compared to one with a very short depreciation policy.

Are there any companies that come to mind?

A classic example would be Advanced Info Service[10] in Thailand, because it's a company that has a very slow depreciation policy. If you look at a PER only, you wind up paying too much for that company. The other thing about how to look at stocks is that I always want to find something where there are multiple ways for a stock to work, because you're not always going to be right. You're going to make mistakes. If you can construct a thesis where, for example, you think the earnings growth is going to be better than the street is expecting, because you've done good work on the comparisons in the industry and you have a good relationship with the management and you are convinced that they'll do better, then that's one thing that might drive the stock price. But it's really nice if, on top of that, you can find a company that is turning free cash flow positive, and can buy back shares or do something with their excess capital. Or there might be some sort of potential strategic investor that could enter the company. I like to have stocks where there are three or four ways to make money out of them.

Three or four angles?

Yes, three or four angles. Because any one angle isn't always going to work. For example, with the steel companies in Asia, it might be a commodity story. Posco[11] is a good example. If you looked at that stock in December 1998, no-one wanted to touch it, and I was wondering if it was ever going to work out. It was lagging the Korean market and, as I was a relative investor back then and some of the more speculative stocks had been moving, I thought that Posco looked interesting. We bought some stock, because I thought steel consumption was going to surprise on the upside. The investment case was that you were buying a steel company when steel prices were very low and there was a potential upside. Moreover, the prices of a couple of key raw materials, coking coal and iron ore, had just been reset down in contracts with their suppliers. So, there was cost cutting on the horizon, and those costs were going to flow through cheaper for the next twelve months. Lower costs were therefore locked in. Furthermore, the company wasn't going to build a new plant, so they could turn free cash flow positive and start to pay down debt and become more efficient in their balance sheet structure. So, while it was a fundamentally boring story — that is, a steel company and a cyclical — there were four or five interesting ways that the stock could work for me. And that's basically what we try to do, get something with a reasonable valuation with multiple ways to make money. If, by contrast, you're going to play a stock that's a high multiple stock, like technology or Internet stocks, the one thing that is absolutely critical is that you know how the business is going. When you buy a high multiple stock, you've got to be sure that the company isn't going to miss the numbers and that the stock can continue to compound. But when you have something that's a cheap stock with some sort of catalyst that could push the stock price up, you can make a lot of money at perhaps lower risk.

So, basically what you are emphasizing is looking at situations where there is a large difference between price and value, together with three or four ways for potential catalysts to drive the stock price?

Yes, that's right. And perhaps an even better example than Posco was Thai Airways.[12] At the beginning of 1999, Thai Airways was highly indebted and barely paying its debt. I was wondering how it was going to finance its new aircraft. I looked at the numbers for the company, and the stock had been a strong performer. I also took a look at Qantas[13] in Australia. Now, as a business and an operator, I like Qantas a lot, and as I'd flown both airlines, I decided to look at what was going on with Qantas's numbers. They were making a lot more money than Thai Airways; they had a wonderful balance sheet; they had a great management team, and it was by far the cheaper airline. And when I looked at any kind of enterprise value to replacement value comparison, Thai Airways was trading on substantially higher multiples than Qantas. So I looked at it upside, downside, and I thought, "Qantas is in a developed market. It's less sexy than Thai Airways from the growth angle, but fundamentally it's a wonderful story." Both countries had undervalued currencies and were very attractive tourist destinations. But on top of that, Qantas had a strong domestic market in Australia. I wondered, then, why Thai Airways was at a higher multiple than Qantas. It was just a commonsense thing that jumped out at me and said, "Why is this one so expensive and this one so cheap?"

The dollar of value that you could buy for 50 cents?

Yes, or maybe that the Thai dollar of value was too expensive, but relative performance said that Qantas was still cheap. In relative terms, it was just outlandish where Thai Airways was priced in mid-January 1999 compared to Qantas. The comparison was straightforward: "I can buy Qantas's airline fleet so much cheaper, and it's got many of the same business drivers that make Thai Airways attractive. What's more, I'd have a more solid company that pays its debts, as well as great management, as opposed to a highly leveraged state-run company with a very heavy forward capex program and that's probably going to have a problem paying for all its ordered aircraft." Now, you don't want something that is ex-growth, but you do want something that can either grow at a reasonable rate or that at least has the flexibility to do something with its cash flow. Qantas could do that, whereas Thai Airways couldn't.

Do you think that a lot of people are impatient when it comes to equity investing?

Yes, no doubt about it. You can get impatient. I had a stock in Latin America — YPF,[14] a big oil company — that I thought was really, really inexpensive. It was cheap on assets, it was *relatively* cheap on cash flow, and it was cheap on EBITDA. It wasn't *really* cheap on cash flow, because the management team that was in place right after it was privatized was still investing heavily in capex and making investments. Consequently, they weren't really getting a kicker on making their investment dollar, and then, tragically, the CEO died in a plane crash and the company went through a search for a new management team. The stock underperformed for a long time. But still, it was fundamentally a cheap asset. So I was working on it and searching for the catalyst that would make the price perform. And ultimately I found that there were multiple ways to make money on the stock.

First was the potential impact of a new management team. The previous CEO had been sold very strongly to the market when the company was privatized, and the previous management had spent a lot of money trying to generate growth, which ultimately didn't flow through to the bottom line. They cut costs a bit, but not as aggressively as they could have. Furthermore, the stock consistently missed earnings estimates, because they didn't prepare Wall Street very well. Another contribution to that was that they just weren't getting the bang for their buck on their investment budget. So, when the CEO passed away, the company went through a strategic review on what to do next.

The new management cut the capex budget and brought in a very sensible manager, but not as CEO immediately. We met with him, and it became very clear that we had a cheap asset staring us in the face. This new guy, who was likely to become the CEO, was much tighter on his capex budget than his predecessor had been, and he subsequently tightened up the budget and raised the return parameters. Second, we had a company that was very sensitive to improving oil prices. It's a little bit like what happened at BHP[15] in Australia, which you're probably aware of. So, with YPF, we had a couple of things that could move the stock price. The first was a management team that had been hailed as strong but which significantly underperformed. The new manager was more sensible. Second, we had a company that then took control of its capital budget. Third, the commodity price went in favor of the company, whose stock had been a long-term laggard and the market viewed it as a boring stock. People didn't want to talk about it. But over the last four years it has been one of the top performers. It was later sold to a Spanish company, so it no longer trades. But this was a stock that you could have bought in 1995, when it was in the mid-teens and paid a dividend of about 80 cents and got out of at $42! There aren't too many things in Argentina over that time span where you could have made almost three times your money.

But you had to be patient.

Yes, you had to be patient. And it was one of those things where you couldn't get in too early on value alone. You had to see the catalysts developing, and the new management team brought them. Once they brought the capital budget under control, generated free cash flow, and worked on their balance sheet, it all clicked. Oil went up, there was a perception that there was a management improvement, and there was a capital budgeting improvement. So it ended up being a commodity price play, a management play, and a balance sheet restructuring play.

That comes back to your three or four angles argument.

Yes, there were three ways to make money on that stock.

You touched on an interesting point when you spoke about perceptions. It's probably a common misperception by the average person in the street that this is a very *exact* business, whereas in reality it's a very *inexact* business and one mainly shaped by perceptions, sentiment, and emotion.

Yes, that's probably right. BHP is probably a good example of that in action. For many, many years, BHP was one of the dominant companies in Australia. When I was covering Latin America, I remember when they paid a lot of money to buy copper assets. And that looked kind of crazy to me at that time, because I knew how much capacity was coming on in Chile. So by overpaying for those assets, we've seen a company that has gone from being a highly touted powerhouse to one having discredited management. By the end of 1998, no-one in Australia had any time for the stock, as far as I could tell. The whole world was underweight the stock for a number of reasons, especially as commodities were in the toilet. So, basically, BHP lined up a lot like YPF. There was a sense of déjà vu, as it looked like YPF all over again — a commodity price-sensitive stock, very poor management reputation, and a new management team yet to come in. When the new CEO came in, he promised to sell assets and to turn the company from being a capital guzzler to a more efficient investor of capital. So, there were multiple ways that you could have made money on BHP, but the investment community in Australia had a stubborn negative perception of the company and everyone was as underweight as they could be. But I thought that it was a really attractive risk/reward proposition to step up and buy it in November 1998, as it was one of those situations where, again, multiple things lined up. Since then, new management has come in and changed perceptions, the stock has performed, and commodities have gone up as well. Now the management has to deliver. Perversely, it's a much riskier stock at A$18 than it was at A$12. But I think management will do a pretty good job. They've already done a lot, but there's a lot more to do. That would justify A$18. The stock had been at a high of A$20 when it was well-liked, but there's a lot more debt in the company now. So, on an enterprise value it's at an all-time high, at least in Australian dollar terms. But it's interesting how quickly perceptions of the company changed — it went from being regarded as a down-and-out stock at A$12 that no-one wanted to hold, to an A$18 stock with a lot of expectations.

To be fair, while companies make mistakes and hopefully learn from them, so does the buy-side and the sell-side. What was your worst call, and what did you learn from it?

Oh boy, there were so many! Let's see, what would be my worst? I tend to sell things too early. Here's an interesting one. I had a little bit of success in 1994 when Mexico was in trouble. There were so many imbalances in the Mexican economy and there was real risk for the peso. I thought it wise to minimize my exposure to Mexico, if not go a bit short. That actually worked out reasonably well. But it ended up causing me some problems because it encouraged me to spend too much time on macro issues when my forte is micro. And I spent the next year or two looking for the next big macro trade that I could make money on, and the result was that I consistently lost money on Brazilian real put options. It's one of those things that when you have had some success at one thing that isn't really your forte, you get a little carried away with your success. And even in the Mexico success, I got short the market four months too early and that sort of mistiming can really hurt when you're taking a short position. Basically, the direction was right and it worked out okay in the end, but the mistake was trying to be a macro guy when I'm really a micro guy. Interestingly, Brazil eventually devalued its currency, but my timing was wrong and it cost a lot of money. But the lesson, quite clearly, is: understand your strengths and play to them. Don't get distracted.

Is it important to be right for the right reasons?

The worst thing that I could do is try to be right all the time. If you're stubborn and wait to be right in the market, you can look awful for a long time. What you have to be, however, is prudent, and understand the risks and the opportunities. With Brazil, I was trying to make a big macro call way too early. I strayed from my expertise. Ultimately, the real was devalued two years later, after I had wasted a lot of money on put options. But the critical lesson is, if you dig in and say, "I want to be right on this one," you'll just end up getting killed.

So you have to keep an open mind, not hold stubborn views about companies, and be flexible in your thinking.

Yes, absolutely. You have to be flexible because the facts change. And like Keynes said, when the facts change, you have to consider changing your mind. One thing you see, particularly out here in Asia, is that certain companies have entrenched reputations that aren't deserved. But don't go by the reputation. When there is a reputation, good *or* bad, respect the fact that it exists, but then test it and see if it's still correct. The wonderful opportunities are when the perception of a company changes. That's a wonderful chance for outperformance. Alternatively, when a group has a great reputation and starts to do funny things, you've got to back away from it. My point is, if you get too entrenched in a viewpoint or an approach, you'll lose. I missed opportunities in Brazil on the real and I didn't make nearly as much money as I could have, because I was stubborn. The currency was overvalued, but the current account and the debt situation weren't at a level that was going to blow up the currency — the catalyst wasn't there to make the thing blow up.

Why were you right about Mexico?

Mexico was different, because the catalyst was there and they had a much larger current account deficit. They also had more short-term dollar debt. They were out of dollars, and they had two political shocks in a year, which drove money offshore. So, there were all the right conditions. Whereas in Brazil, sure, you had an overvalued currency, but it wasn't my area of expertise. Just stick with what you do right and what you do well.

What batting average is required to be successful?

If I can get the majority — 65-70% — of my binary calls right and I weight them properly, then I'm a genius. It's all about risk management. I have a motto that says, "Weight your bet on your position accompanied by your conviction." If I have a lot of conviction, I'll take a big position. If I don't have much conviction, I have no business taking a really extreme position. And in this business you're going to make mistakes, so you have to learn from them. When you're wrong, you try to make it up on the next round.

Do you see similar patterns across different markets and stocks?

Yes, very much so. The interesting thing about this business is that, from one market to another, there are lots of parallels. It's never going to work exactly the same way, but the YPF/BHP comparison is a good example of that. You'll see things that are an opportunity in one market that may come around a little bit later in another market. And you just have to learn that if you missed it last time, you've got to be open-minded the next time it pops up.

What does the buy-side really value from the sell-side?

Part of it depends on the kind of money that I'm involved with. When I was working at a smaller fund, I had a different set of requirements from today. At Morgan Stanley we were relatively large in these markets and we couldn't be that nimble due to liquidity issues. For example, if I got past the first list of top stocks in the market, I had to go into smaller-sized companies and that would take me a month of buying as well as introduce new risks.

Like not moving the price too much?

Yes, and if the stock just doesn't trade — if I'm wrong — it's going to take me a lot longer than a month to get out of it. So, the last thing I want is some analyst who is whipping around recommendations quickly. I'm not a fan of analysts who put a buy at the bottom of the trading range and, when it's up by 20%, move it to a hold. Sure, they generate commission by doing that. There are a few houses out there that I think are short-term orientated like that and who push their analysts far too much to take a short-term view. The ideal analyst, to me, is someone who knows their industry well and is sufficiently skeptical not simply to transmit management's message, and yet who isn't going to come out and be super-negative and get shut out from information flows. I don't expect a sell-side analyst to come out and slam a management if they don't like one particular move. But I want someone with a reasonable degree of skepticism, and I want someone who is going to study the industry and competitors and really give me a fundamental view of what's going on in the business. I also want someone who keeps current with what's happening in the industry.

Are there any examples that come to mind?

A good example is the telecommunications industry. It's changing so rapidly that some people who were very good analysts five or six years ago, if they haven't kept current, are missing out now. They've got to keep current with the trends and technology in telecommunications. Moreover, the convergence is happening at such a staggering pace that I look at some of the analysis that I did five or six years ago and I think it's archaic already. So, what I need is someone who is adaptable. One of the beautiful things about doing emerging markets is that companies don't have to reinvent the wheel here. All you need to do is find something that works well elsewhere and implement it with a reasonable degree of competence. If the economy is okay, you're going to look like a hero.

Like HSBC[16] — they're not number one in everything they do, but what they do they do solidly and well.

Exactly. So if you can get an analyst who is alert to what trends are happening in industry, that's valuable. For example, there is a management team in Hong Kong telecommunications — which is an extremely tough industry — in a company called SmartTone.[17] They're in the cellular phone business, which on fundamentals is an overcrowded market that is too penetrated. But I really like the way their management studies what's going on elsewhere in the world. Now, being the best-studied management in a really tough industry isn't necessarily going to make them the most money, but if they weren't well-studied and well-researched managers, they'd be out of business. So what I need is an analyst who can keep up with what's changing around them and who can understand how opportunities in more developed markets have transformed industries. There are a significant number of analysts in Asia who I don't think have ever looked outside of Asia. But there were a couple of analysts who caught on that the global cement business was consolidating, and they went and studied the global trends — you know, who were the consolidators, and who looked like they were going to be bought up. So when the crisis hit Asia in 1997, the local oligopoly was vulnerable. And we made a fair amount of money by identifying the most likely targets that the consolidators were going to buy. Now, if I had had an analyst who only looked at their little patch, they would have missed what was coming. This consolidation wave has totally transformed the cement business, and there were natural stocks that were going to outperform but which, on their own, weren't good companies. So, you need an analyst who is going to do good industry work, not try to be a wheeler-dealer trader type, who will study trends, and who will try to identify managements that can implement things that have been implemented elsewhere. Companies don't have to reinvent that much; they just need to execute well. So, if an analyst studies their sector and knows what needs to be executed, that's very valuable. For example, it's much more important to me to have a bank analyst who can tell me what the benefits of an in-market merger could be in a place like Singapore, than it is for me to hear some little spin like …

… X is going to merge with Y Bank?

Exactly. I don't care. What I care about is if two banks merge here, what will the resulting bank look like? And someone who has studied what an in-market merger looks like and can tell me, "Hey, these are relatively efficient banks on cost to income, but this is the kind of cost reduction you *could* see" — well, that's a good research report.

But that's not exactly a popular or common approach. Is it easier to be contrary or popular?

Popular, but the nice thing about being a contrarian is that when it works, it feels great.

You get an intellectual resonance from the fact that you've made money from a tough call?

Yes. And it feels wonderful! But it's hard, particularly if you are an index-based manager. However, if it's an absolute-return fund, that's different. Now I just have to make money. And I don't have an unlimited supply of capital. But all I have to do is make money over time, and that's a different game from having to beat the index. We are in a business where people do look at shorter-term relative performance, so for me to be a contrarian, I need to see some sort of catalyst. It's not easy to say, "You should buy Posco, because hot roll coil prices are in the low $200 range and they'll go to the low $400 range when the cycle turns." For me to be able to make that bet, I have to see two or three other ways that could work out. I can tell you, it didn't feel good being overweight Posco in December 1998 when everything else in Korea was outperforming. There were really highly geared stocks that were just flying at that point, so I was kind of stuck with it, but it worked out pretty well in the end. So, yes, it's hard to be contrarian in a relative world, but it feels great when it works. But it also feels *really* bad when it's not working, because you see the numbers every day when you sit down at your desk. You want to do well, ideally each quarter, and I love the contrarian calls, but you have to be very careful. What's more, you can be contrarian too early and look foolish for quite a while.

What are the misperceptions the average person in the street has about this business?

Probably that we have a lot of information and are in a privileged position, but a lot of the information is just white noise. In reality, there is *too much* information and, consequently, data overload.

Disinformation?

Yes. And what's more, this job isn't an exact science. Here is a classic example. When I was at MSDW we were involved in Korea, and in line with a lot of fund managers, over the past couple of years, Korea had gone from being a tiny part of our index to a huge part of our index. This was due to market outperformance and changes in the country's relative weighting. And so you had to try to determine what could go right and what could go wrong. And Korea was a very cyclical story, with both high financial and operating leverage.

So, with leverage, if it goes right, it can go *very* right. And we were in Singapore looking at how to deal with Korea, and I thought to myself, "Anyone who has followed Korea closely knows that the Daewoo[18] Group has too much debt." I *just knew* that that was going to affect the market at some point in time. Furthermore, this was something we had been highlighting as a risk factor in all our internal memos for quite some time. So I spent a week in Korea at the beginning of July 1999, and we met over thirty companies and spent the majority of our time talking about the implications of what would happen if something went wrong with Daewoo. We left with a lot of useful information, but we had absolutely no sense that, five days after we got off the plane back in Singapore, the Daewoo debt problem would hit. We had done an awful lot of work, we knew that there were problems, but we had painted it in big block letters that this is a major risk, and despite all of that, as an investor, you will never know when the perceptions will change and that the risk is *now*. And as it's not going to be over for quite a while, the market will continue to ebb and flow as perceptions change. But the irony is that every analyst knew that there was a problem, but none, including us, could tell that it was going to really hit in the third week of July.

So, timing is probably the hardest part of the job?

Yes, it's a huge challenge for fund managers. As we previously discussed, my classic case of mistiming was the Brazilian real put trade. I knew that the real was overvalued, but there was nothing to force it to change at that time. There was no catalyst, which made timing very problematical. But coming back to Korea, I knew

Daewoo was a major problem and we had very limited exposure to the Daewoo group of companies, but when we started to peel the onion, we found that Daewoo exposure was enormous throughout the whole financial system. Yet, nothing we heard signaled that the storm would hit five days after we returned from our visit to Korea. So, timing is very difficult. You just have to try and balance the risks. If you know it's a risk and the prices are getting ahead of themselves, you just try to manage risk a little better. That might result in tending to get in too early, and even getting out too early, but that's one of the costs of risk management.

Do you find charts useful in helping with timing?

A litte bit. I always refer to them as cartoons! I really didn't think there was much to them at all, but I'll say that in a market that's running in one direction or another, or when perceptions are so heated that you can lose a little bit of connection with reality, I have found on a number of occasions that those charts can be pretty darned accurate! It's scary [*laughs*]. I hate to admit it, but for short-term trading in particular, they can be very useful. Morever, when I have concerns about the market or some other fundamental issue, or I've had the benefit of a good run and it hits a level on a chart that looks fairly extended, I'll tend to lighten up. Alternatively, when a market is getting hit and I like some stocks, I'll try to use charts a little to time some buys. But they probably only work because other guys look at them as well, so there must be a lot of people looking at them [*laughs*]!

So, it's just another piece of data or information that you can't ignore?

That's right. But I wouldn't use them for a big, dramatic call. However, for example, my index at MSDW was the MSCI Far East ex-Japan,[19] and the core index fell almost 70% during the Asian crisis. The index then rallied sharply in late 1998 and early 1999, until it reached the U.S. dollar levels that used to mark the bottom of a pre-crisis three-year trading range for the index. What's interesting is that that was exactly where the Mexican rally had stalled when Mexico recovered from its crisis — that is, when it reached the bottom of the pre-crisis trading range of the index. The Asian markets had rallied into the same chart levels that Mexico had stalled at during its recovery. Therefore, we thought the markets might have trouble moving higher. So, I incrementally reduced risk in the fund. Nothing dramatic, but the markets corrected for the next six weeks!

On the technical side, charts are useful in flagging changes and highlighting extremes. The chart for the Asian index suggested we could run into the same sort of roadblock we saw in Latin America and I thought we were going to have a tough time. There were lots of other fundamental reasons why the Asian markets should have stalled when they did — whether it was supply of new stock, or unresolved issues like Daewoo, or whatever — but coincidentally we rallied back to the level where Latin America had a tough time too, so I thought it was time to take stock and accept that we had had a good run.

So, charts can be like the third or clinching point in an argument?

Exactly. It's just one more data point that says, "This is something to watch out for." We also look at the occasional money flows charts to see what's working and what isn't working by sector or stock, and they can sometimes highlight something you might otherwise miss, some sort of trend or an inflection point.

While we are talking about technical issues, can we talk a little about econometrics? I don't find econometrics very useful at all, but some people are very keen on regression analysis, for example, and other statistical methods. What is your view on that?

I don't think much of them either. We like to focus on fundamentals, and regressions can be just like a fishing expedition. But the one area where we used quantitative methods at MSDW was when we used risk packages that evaluated the riskiness of our portfolio versus the benchmark we had to track. They were based on the arbitrage pricing theory model[20]. We used them to assess how much risk we were taking and to do a reality check. They could tell us that a portfolio was very risky or not very risky, say.

If an analyst came to you with a regression model and argued that you should buy a stock based either on the predictive value of that model's output or on a causal relationship with another variable, would you act on that?

No. It doesn't do that much for us because, in the markets that we are dealing with, a lot of the data isn't that good. I'm not going to buy off an econometric model or statistical argument.

At the other end of the technology curve, what do you think is the likely impact of the Internet on investing?

There will be a number of impacts. First, it makes information so much more available, but that just adds to information overload to a certain extent. Second, I think that it's going to have a negative impact on commission spreads in your business and probably on fees in my business, because the value we add from traveling and gathering information will be less, as the information flow will be much better. In terms of the impact on corporations, I'm of the belief that every company will have to have some sort of strategy to deal with the Internet. The impact of the Internet will be like the impact of the telephone or something similar. Would you invest in a company that doesn't use telephones? Of course not, but at the same time, having an Internet strategy doesn't necessarily make a company a more profitable business. So, companies must have some strategy for addressing how to deal with the Internet. It may not add to profits at all, or be a key success factor, but it's going to be an infrastructure requirement. The Internet will enable certain businesses — for instance, some outsourcers — to run with, at least theoretically, much leaner inventory levels, and their customers to keep a closer watch on their orders and follow their product through the various supply/distribution channels. There are a couple of people that I talk to who are trying to get to that level. But notwithstanding this, I'm not a big fan of some of the Internet-related concept stocks.

However, I think that everyone is going to have an Internet strategy, and the more money that is raised and the more e-commerce models that evolve that focus on specific industries, the more pressure there is going to be on the margins of the organic or fundamental businesses. For example, the Internet has targeted booksellers. If you have a generic product that is easily sold over the Internet, your margins will be pressured for as long as e-commerce companies can raise cheap capital.

We're not heavily invested in the dot.com companies, but it's nice to have a fundamental company that has an Internet sideline to it, or alternatively has a product that can be sold over the Internet. We were speaking recently with a CEO of a Hong Kong outsourcing company about how the Internet was affecting his relationships with some of his key clients. He mentioned that Toys "Я" Us were going to try to supply more private-label toys, because they are getting killed by people going direct over the Internet for branded products. So, it's really having an impact in some areas. The CEO was talking about how his customers are changing their buying patterns. Consequently, his profit structure is changing. He sees the move to private-labeling as a net positive for companies who can source private-label products. He is also working on it from the other angle, efficiency. People can track their orders more efficiently using the Internet than by sending faxes and making telephone calls. This Hong Kong company thus has a couple of different strategies to deal with the Internet, and clearly it's having an impact on the way people do business. If you have a product that doesn't have a high degree of sales educational component to it — for example, if it's a generic product like a best-selling book, or a video, or a CD, or something like that — it may be more efficient to sell it over the Internet.

So, commodity-style products and services will be disintermediated?

Yes, disintermediation is the right word. Basically, as investors, that's what we have to watch out for. The Hong Kong CEO I mentioned thinks that disintermediation will impact on his customer lists. If he can deliver a unique product, then he benefits from disintermediation

How do you judge success?

Well, it depends. In my current job, I have to make absolute returns. But at MSDW, success was defined as beating an index consistently over time and without getting blown up relative to the index. So, in view of that, I think the critical success factor is longevity or sustainability of performance. I think those guys who can beat markets or make absolute money over a long period of time are amazing and should be respected for that. There's some question about whether the guys who have short track records can really be considered successful. We should all take out hats off to those people who build an approach, run things for a long period of time, and do it well. That's success.

Like Warren Buffett?

Yes. It's the guys who just bang out the numbers year in and year out. They are the ones we should all try to emulate.

What's an appropriate period over which to evaluate or judge success. Five years?

Yes, that's about right. Anything less than three is just the entry ticket. After that, it's a matter of who can bang it out over time. They are the ones who matter to me.

What advice would you give someone just coming into the buy-side?

I would say, first off, be very thorough in your work and in how you approach companies. Also, be flexible in your views on an industry or a stock. Things change over time, so don't lock yourself into categorizing companies. Do your homework on the industry and on the stocks. Get to know management and preferably do it in one place. If you can stay in one position and build institutional credibility within one firm and look at your stocks, sectors, and markets over a longer period of time, it will help you to develop consistency in your approach, build up your reputation in the industry, and develop the weight of your opinions. So, be thorough, be consistent, don't chase tips, and be adaptive when something new comes along. And another thing, there is no question that the Internet is for real and will impact all our businesses, so you can't dismiss it. You have to think how it will affect your stocks and be able to adapt to changes like that. But that aside, if you build up your track record, then opportunities will come your way. If you've done thorough work and people recognize that you're consistent and credible, then you'll have many opportunities presented to you.

Finally, what advice would you give to someone going into the sell-side for the first time?

I think the first and most important thing is to understand the company, the industry, and then the dynamics — the short-term dynamics of how a stock will trade. The most frustrating thing to me is analysts who change their ratings on a stock all the time in order to catch every zig and zag on a chart. What I need is an analyst who will tell me, "Look, this deal or this announcement is significant because of the impact it's going to have on the profitability of the company or the standing of the company within the industry, and these are the long-term effects of it." I don't want a guy who is going to look at a chart, see something that has outperformed, and look for an excuse to downgrade. I don't want an analyst who is too flighty, and any analyst who is going to put a trading buy or a trading sell on a stock isn't doing his job. The analyst's job is to get good information about the fundamentals of the company and how they are changing. I can subsequently make the decision on whether or not the stock should be bought or sold. So, you have to really think about what you are adding to the client from the sell-side. I want to have a couple of analysts in every sector that I can go to when there is a merger or an announcement or a regulatory change or something and get a good, reasoned opinion. I don't need an analyst to say "buy on this" because the stock will jump short-term, or "sell on this" because a short-term dip is coming up. I need an analyst who is thinking through the implications longer-term.

✳ ✳ ✳

Tim Jensen's approach to investing will appeal to those investors who are fundamentally driven and value-orientated. While his principles are relatively straightforward, they nevertheless require patience, diligence, and hard work to implement successfully. The key principles of Jensen's approach are:

- Value is important. This is especially true in the emerging markets, which are highly volatile. In Jensen's view, "When things get tough, you have to have something to fall back on."
- While growth is important, it is also important that the cost of growth (i.e., additional debt or equity) isn't too demanding or dilutive. Jensen says, "What I want is something that I can get at an attractive multiple, that has growth prospects, but where the cost to grow isn't too high." Internal capital generation is therefore an

important (and often overlooked) investment parameter.

- Relativity is important. The relative comparison of Qantas against Thai Airways is a good example of how to identify mispriced or undervalued securities.
- When focusing on out-of-favor stocks, don't rely on just one factor to drive the stock price. Identify three or four potential angles that could work in your favor. The way Jensen approached his investments in Posco, YFP, and BHP are all good examples of this principle in action.
- Patience is important, but don't get in too early on value (price) alone, otherwise your patience could be tested over an extended period. Make sure that you can see three or four potential catalysts developing that could move the share price in your favor.
- Don't stray from your area of competence and don't get distracted. Stick to what you know and play to your strengths. Jensen's experience with Brazilian real puts brought home to him that his strengths and skills were in micro, not macro, analysis.
- Be flexible and keep an open mind. One of the toughest challenges for both the buy- and the sell-side is not to hold entrenched views about a company, its management, or its prospects. As the facts change, you have to consider changing your view.
- Lightning does strike twice and history does repeat itself. Look out for similar trends or patterns across countries, sectors, or companies. Jensen's YPF and BHP trades are good examples of how investors can profit from cross-market comparisons.
- If you invest in high-growth, expensive stocks, you have to be very confident that they will meet expectations and that management will deliver. These are stocks whose prices are generally driven by strong sentiment and high expectations. Any disappointment in the numbers can mean an extended period of underperformance. A portfolio approach to investing in these types of stocks is usually best.
- Stock prices are primarily driven by perceptions, and perceptions

can change for the worse or better very quickly. Respect that and take advantage of situations where perceptions have become too negative in what are fundamentally sound businesses. In Tim Jensen's words, "The wonderful opportunities are when the perception of a company changes. That's a wonderful chance for outperformance." Turnaround situations are excellent candidates, and BHP and YPF are two examples of just how quickly perceptions can change with the introduction of new management, for example. But as previously mentioned, don't get in too early on value (price) alone, and make sure that you can see three or four potential catalysts that could move the share price.

- Don't chase tips, and be thorough and flexible in your work. Make as strong an effort as possible to understand management and the way they think about the business.
- You are going to make mistakes, but make sure you learn from them. Moreover, it's possible to be very successful even if you're wrong three or four times out of ten. Money management and weighting your investments carefully is an important and often overlooked part of successful investing.

---

[1]   Shinawatra Computer and Communications Group.
[2]   Land and House Public Company Limited. is a Thai company that develops real estate projects including single-detached homes, townhouses, and condominiums. At the time of writing, the company had a stock-market capitalization of THB 9.3 billion.
[3]   Cemex S.A. de C.V. is the world's third-largest cement company. At the time of writing, the company had a stock-market capitalization of US$5.9 billion.
[4]   Bancomer S.A. is a subsidiary of Grupo Financiero Bancomer, which is a commercial bank providing services in Mexico. At the time of writing, the parent company had a stock-market capitalization of MXM 23.6 billion.
[5]   Enterprise value is defined as a company's market capitalization plus the market value of its debt less cash plus long-term liabilities plus deferred tax plus minority interests.
[6]   Earnings before interest expense and taxes.
[7]   Earnings before interest expense, taxes, depreciation, and amortization.
[8]   The Gordon growth model is a dividend discount valuation model, where the

value of a firm is equal to the forecast dividend per share for next year divided by the required rate of return less the growth rate in dividends in perpetuity. It is a useful way of valuing companies that are growing at a stable rate.

9 Price earnings ratios.

10 Advanced Info Service Public Company Limited is a Thai cellular cell phone company. At the time of writing, the company had a stock-market capitalization of THB 100.9 billion.

11 Pohang Iron & Steel Company Limited manufactures hot and cold rolled steel products, heavy plate, and other steel products. At the time of writing, the company had a stock-market capitalization of KRW 8.4 trillion.

12 Thai Airways is a state-enterprise which is 93%-owned by the Thai government and the balance by the public. At the time of writing, the company had a stock-market capitalization of THB 56 billion.

13 Qantas Airways Limited is 25%-owned by British Airways Plc.

14 YPF S.A. is an integrated oil company.

15 Broken Hill Proprietary Company Limited is an Australian-based international resources company whose principal business lines are steel production, minerals exploration and production (coal, iron ore, gold, copper concentrate), and petroleum exploration, production, and refining. At the time of writing the company had a stock-market capitalization of A$32.4 billion.

16 HSBC Holdings plc is the holding company for the HSBC Group, one of the largest financial services and banking groups in the world. At the time of writing, the company had a stock-market capitalization of £60.5 billion.

17 SmartTone Telecommunications Holdings Limited is an investment holding company whose subsidiaries provide cellular communication services and sell cellular handsets in Hong Kong. At the time of writing the company had a stock-market capitalization of HK$15.6 billion.

18 Daewoo is a major South Korean conglomerate and one of the country's largest *chaebol*.

19 Morgan Stanley Capital International Index (MSCI) all-country indices represent both the developed and the emerging markets for a particular region.

20 The arbitrage pricing model is similar to the CAPM insofar as its premise is that investors will be rewarded for taking nondiversifiable risk.

7

Pierre Prentice: Patience is a Virtue

"The mindset has to be one of getting rich slowly."

Pierre Prentice is one of Australia's most respected and experienced industrial analysts. After a twelve-year career as a stockbroking analyst with Bankers Trust Australia Limited, where he was an executive vice president and formerly head of industrial research, he has recently taken a position on the buy-side with Jardine Fleming Capital Partners. At JFCP, Prentice manages the financial forecasting and analysis functions that form part of their stock selection and valuation process. Prentice originally qualified as a chartered accountant and finished his accounting career as a manager and partner of Arthur Andersen and KPMG, respectively, in their audit/business advisory divisions. With twelve years' experience as a sell-side analyst, Prentice has a remarkable track record insofar as he has never been rated outside the top five in his sectors — the top three for his core sectors — over a nine-year stretch. For sheer persistence and consistency, Prentice's track record is hard to match. An excellent reader of financial statements, with a legendary eye for detail, Prentice is widely regarded as "an analyst's analyst" as he combines strategic analysis with outstanding analytical, forecasting, and valuation skills. Prentice's technical skills are no more evident than in the fact that he was widely consulted on the drafting of the Australian Accounting Standard for Earnings per Share. Prentice's experiences and views should be of especial interest to sell-side analysts who are just starting out on their careers.

How did you get into the business?

That happened because, when I came back to Australia from a stint overseas, I rejoined my old accounting firm. That wasn't a particularly happy experience, because they were under pressure from so much new work that they were unable to carve out the new position that we had agreed on. So, I made the decision to leave. As I had reached the level of partner in an international accounting firm, I had the opportunity to get two careers into one lifetime. I looked for something completely different. It boiled down to a choice between going to Mildura (340 miles north of Melbourne where by wife Kym comes from) to work as a financial controller for the Dried Fruits Co-operative, or stockbroking.

Why did you go for stockbroking?

I felt that the other option wasn't really the best use of my talents. I did a bit of a stocktake of my strengths and weaknesses, and I thought that to be a good financial analyst you had to be a good accountant. What I subsequently found fascinating once I got into the stockbroking industry was that very few people had any accounting knowledge.

Does that still hold?

To a large degree it does, but there are a lot more people with financial accounting backgrounds in the business now. When I entered the industry there wasn't, and that gave me quite a large competitive advantage for a very long time, especially when the 1987 crash hit and people were running around trying to get back to basics and analyze financial statements. I felt — perhaps naively at the time — that you had to be a good accountant and have a good understanding of financial reporting. My other strengths were my verbal and especially written communication skills, and they would be very important in the stockbroking business — which I perceived as primarily consisting of writing reports. And one of my other criteria was to get a job that would interest me.

So, stockbroking was the clear choice?

Yes, it was. I had been investing in the market over quite a number of years as well. I remember sitting on the steps at university poring over the quotes, the buys and sells, and playing the stock market from that age. So, it's something that I've always done and my objective was to get paid for doing a hobby. And in the early days, it really was like that. It was just wonderful in those really early Bankers Trust days.

How did your perceptions of the business compare to the reality of the business as you became more immersed in it?

It actually took a long time to get face-to-face with the reality of being a stockbroker.

Which was?

The reality of being a broker is that there is tremendous pressure to generate business.

Commission.

Yes, commission — or brokerage, if you prefer. Pressure to generate stock turnover and therefore commission. I would say tremendous pressure, but I think you can withstand it. My view has been — and this is what I tried to inculcate in other team members — you are the agent of the investor. After all, that's why it's sometimes referred to as the agency business.

A professional advisor to the owners of the business?

Yes, their professional advisor. You're going out trying to find what's good for them in the context of their investment objectives. That should be the basis of any professional relationship. That's how I tried to run our part of the business — as a professional advisor. Stockbroking is called a profession. It could be one, but in reality, I don't think it is.

Why?

Not enough is done with the client's objectives and interests as the driver of effort. I suppose the reality is that there isn't enough brokerage to go around to support one-on-one professional relationships. They get homogenized as a result, and broking analysts are often motivated by what the average client might want.

Earlier you mentioned the 1987 crash. What was your experience of the crash?

It was fantastic. It was the cheapest lesson that you could possibly get in a career. I joined the industry in May 1987 and the crash was five months later. So it was very early on in my career. It was a wonderful example, a wonderful reminder of how irrational markets can get in the short term. And I had actually joined the industry at the beginning of a very irrational phase. With that experience under my belt, it just made it so much easier to be alert to markets getting irrational and the opportunities that come with it. It underscored the need to always get back to basics, regardless of what the stock price is doing, and to ask yourself, "Is the company or, more specifically, management adding any value regardless of the stock's price performance?"

Price is what you pay, but value is what you get?

Beautifully put.

How do you define the basics? The value part of the argument, for example?

The basics are completely independent of the share price. They really are addressing the question of whether the company is doing what it is supposed to do. All companies or, specifically, managements have a role, which is to manage the capital that shareholders entrust to them in a way that augments the original capital and thereby adds value. That is the essential starting point. But notwithstanding some of the dogma, the shorter the period, the less the connection there will be between what the share price is doing — market value-added, as it is called — and what economic value[1] is being added. Now, in the long run, of course, they should converge. But what we have to realize as analysts is that, in the short term, they can head in different directions because of sentiment or money flows, but they should ultimately converge. So the focus of the basics of analysis is on *economic* value-added, or shareholder value creation, which is really about ensuring that the company is positioning itself in a manner that enables it to find opportunities to earn more than the return that equity investors expect from money put into the stock market as a whole.

In terms of a valuation approach, no one method necessarily works all the time. What are your preferred approaches to looking at valuation?

In recent years, toward the end of my career as a stockbroking analyst, I became more and more convinced of the virtues of discounted cash flow and/or economic valued-added, which amount to the same thing. They present the same information in a different way. I suppose if I had to pick one, I'd pick economic value-added because it's just a little more transparent and you can see the returns on capital versus the cost of capital better. You can make judgments more readily — especially when you are forecasting about how realistic the results of your forecasting are.

Do you think price/earnings ratios[2] and price-to-book ratios[3] are still relevant today?

Price-to-book ratios are just junk insofar as nonfinancial stocks are concerned. But I think things like PERs[4] and EBIT[5] multiple ratios are useful shortcuts for stockbroking analysts. They have to form part of the vocabulary, because so many people still use them.

The grammar and syntax used by the broader market, if you like?

Exactly. When I started, PERs were all the rage and EBIT multiples didn't exist. But ten years later, EBIT multiples were the common currency. Now EBITDA[6] disease is taking hold. I say "disease" because, by leaving depreciation out of the calculation, multiples based on using EBITDA as a denominator implies that the capital intensity of the stocks being compared is identical, and in many cases this is just not the case. So, it's very dangerous and can lead to errors.

So valuation methodology and methods aren't static — they evolve, and you have to be aware of their shortcomings?

Certainly.

When you were a stockbroker, what was the hardest part of your job — valuation or marketing?

The hardest part was just withstanding the demands of the job, because it's all-encompassing. As a stockbroking analyst, you are packaging so many things. It's a complete business — you're a self-contained business. You are responsible for the origination. You are responsible for the processing of the data that you originate, and that involves financial forecasting. You come to a conclusion after having done a valuation, and then you have to communicate the conclusion in written form. That's your product. You've got two products I suppose: the valuation, and you draw a conclusion on the share price by comparing it with the valuation. Your other product is the report, which describes how you arrived at that valuation and conclusion. Then there is the marketing, which is taking the report and communicating it to your clients. So, the role encompasses an enormous array of activity. Coming back to one of your earlier questions though, about the difference between my preconceptions of the job and what it actually turned out to be, for me, one was the extraordinary amount of time that you spent marketing. I had always perceived the job as being one in which you wrote a report and then got right on to the next one. In many ways the job hadn't started until you did the marketing. My teammate, Martin Yule (now with Morgan Stanley in Sydney), and I had a motto: "A report not marketed is a report not done." It's that important to market from a commercial sense as a stockbroker.

Can an average report be made into a good report with good marketing?

Nothing will save a bad report, but an ineffective report could be made into an effective one simply by marketing. What you don't realize as an outsider is how much your clients are bombarded with written material. The only way that you can really stand out and have your message heard is by getting their ear. And that means telephone marketing or, even better, face-to-face marketing.

Does that create problems, since the supply of research is increasing but demand is actually falling away due, in part, to the fact that the quality of research is diminishing as greater effort is being put into marketing than into writing good research?

Yes. There is an element of that emerging, but I don't think it's out of control. It will eventually find a balance, because if the demands for marketing are too high, then taking the phenomenon to its conclusion, clients will end up getting packaged air, nothing more. So, it's a matter of finding a balance between the two. The key to it is rationalization of industry participants. We have seen quite a number of stockbrokers just rationalized out of business, and that has certainly helped to address the imbalance that you are talking about. We have now got a reduced number of stockbrokers and, if anything, an increased number of fund managers.

What is the worst stock call you ever made, and what were the lessons that you learned from it?

In some ways, there is no such thing as a mistake — unless you don't learn from it. That said, I think my worst call would have to be Brash's.[7]

Brash Holdings Ltd?

Brash Holdings, yes.

Could you walk us through that?

Well, it was a retailing stock that sold recorded music, musical and sound equipment, and was beginning to move into household appliances. I had been following retailing for quite some time, and there weren't that many retail stocks on the main board. Woolworth's was about to list, and I thought I might be able to carve out a bit of a specialty in retailing as I could see the retail sector developing a bit. Brash's was unloved at the time, and I knew it was on dangerous ground because it was a company that was going through the wringer, but I felt that it was oversold and fundamentally undervalued. After gradually going backwards it showed signs of stabilizing, but all of a sudden it produced a very bad result. I think it was in the second half of the 1993 financial year, and I remember doing a complete reassessment at that point — a real inventory of where we were at — and giving myself an opportunity to back down on my earlier positive view. I came out with the view that it was a speculative buy. For the next nine months or so, I retained that stance of it being a speculative buy and constantly reminded people that this was a risky proposition. And even though I left the door open, I have to admit that I was a whiter shade of pale on the day the company announced that an administrator had been appointed. Everyone was just stunned that this could happen to a national household name.

Was it life-threatening?

No, it wasn't. First, it was a small stock. By the time I started covering the stock it was so small that few major institutions could be represented in a meaningful way. So it had a very small following. Second, a lot of investors had already voted with their feet, and really my role was to identify whether it was time for them to get back in. And clearly, anything with a speculative tag isn't an aggressive invitation to get back in. But the fact is, I had a buy recommendation on a company that went under.

How did you manage that? What did you learn?

One lesson was the benefit of risk management — labeling the stock as speculative was preemptive and contained the damage. So, it didn't really turn out to be as embarrassing a situation as it could have been had I been following the stock with just a buy recommendation on it long before it started down the slippery slope. No-one was really relying on my work to have invested in the first place. My clients were all institutional and were grown up and consenting adults and going in with their eyes wide open. They had formed their own views, and those investors who had made the decision to stay were using me more as a source of information. Still, it's damaging from a reputation point of view to have had a buy recommendation on a stock that went belly-up. There was some consolation from the fact that the administrator came very close to suing the auditors, because the prior year accounts gave no clue of the pending demise. The carrying value of inventories on the balance sheet, for example, was a problematic issue.

Inventories are usually a key area.

Yes, that really was a lesson for me as far as retailers were concerned: keep a very close eye on inventory levels, because even though they took a big write-down at the end of the previous financial year, it wasn't enough. The other false signal that occurred was after a really bad result for the second half of the 1993 financial year. There was a change of management and initially the directors were very coy about making any prognostications about the future. And then at the next annual general meeting, in a pretty considered fashion, they said that the worm had turned and they were seeing good times ahead. That's why people were so surprised.

At the other end of the spectrum, what was your *best* call? Is it more satisfying to have a sell on a stock that really does tumble, or a buy on a stock that makes people money?

It's very satisfying to have a good sell recommendation, because it takes courage to come up with a good, aggressive sell recommendation. For commercial reasons, sell recommendations aren't common, but as part of our agency philosophy we always tried to have as many sell recommendations as buy recommendations. The fact is that as sure as the sun comes over the horizon every morning, there will always be roughly 50% of the stocks that underperform and 50% that outperform. So, we felt we had to reflect that in our calls. And what's more, if we were truly to be the agents of the investor, rather than short-term generators of business, we had to be guided by that. But notwithstanding that, it's still hard, especially when the market is against you and your more memorable calls tend to be made against the market. Pacific Dunlop[8] was one of those.

Can you walk us through that and the things you saw there?

Pacific Dunlop was one where I intuitively knew that management couldn't manage all their businesses well at the same time. They had about nine businesses then, and even before the anti-conglomerate theme really got into full swing, I realized that management couldn't really be above-average in most of their diverse collection of businesses. I formed a firm view that management wasn't up to delivering the sorts of returns they were promising. They were perennial disappointers — the Royal Artillery, as one of our guys used to call them. "We're gunner do this, and we're gunner do that ..." But they seldom delivered at the end of the year when it counted. They had a fabulous PR machine and they marketed the company very, very well, but, having followed them for several years, I worked out the system. They used to manage up expectations over the course of the half-year and then, just before the results were due, they would manage them down. So for five months out of six, the investment community was very happy with Pacific Dunlop. I thought that this eventually had to catch up with the stock. Even though it picked up, as they did deliver one good result, I stuck to my fundamental view that the management challenge was beyond them. So I called it against the market, on the basis that they would be unable to deliver the year's profit expectation.

The fundamental call was based on your perception of management?

Yes. But there was also another interesting little twist as well.

The financials?

Yes, there was a little thing in the financials. People said, "Prentice, you've got it wrong. Look at the cash flow. Add back depreciation to profit and look at the cash flow they're generating." Back in those days, what they used to do, and some analysts still do this today, was take price and divide it by the cash flow, crudely defined as profit after tax plus depreciation expense. Of course, what they were overlooking was that, just to stay afloat, Pacific Dunlop had to spend much more in capital expenditure than their depreciation expense. Sure, you had a wonderful and very alluring statistic, but the fact of the matter was that it was an irrelevant statistic, because the company didn't have any *free* cash flow, which is what it's all about at the end of the day.

I used to find that the most sensitive variable in forecasting earnings and growth was capital expenditure, and that was especially the case with Brambles[9] for example.

That's an interesting comparison, as both Brambles and Pacific Dunlop operate in fairly capital-intensive industries, especially Pacific Dunlop as it was back then. And it was the relative effectiveness or ineffectiveness of their capital expenditure programs that made the two companies diverge.

So, they would be two good case studies to look at?

Excellent case studies. Pacific Dunlop squandered its capital expenditure by throwing good money after bad, and Brambles has used it very, very well.

The other critical variable is management, which is an area that's often overlooked in equity analysis. You made a very good point earlier about getting to know management well. How did you do that?

I tried to talk to as much of the management as possible, down to the divisional head level. I used to attend all of their presentations. I never missed one of those. I also used to go to the annual general meetings and bail management up afterwards.

Did you interview over the phone?

The executives I talked to in the companies I followed were all very busy men and running very big businesses, many of them multinational. In fact, most of them were multinational. That was rather unusual. For example, Pacific Dunlop was an Australian-based conglomerate of multinationals, which, on its own, tells you that it was a company out to achieve objectives that in reality were probably never achievable. So, these guys were very busy and often I couldn't meet them face-to-face. It had to be mainly by telephone, and it had to be in pretty short bites of ten to fifteen minutes.

So, in short, it's easy to overlook the fact that management is a key variable, and that in many instances it is qualitative rather than quantitative variables that determine whether or not a stock will be a successful investment?

Yes. What you have to get a feel for as well is the culture of the company. What does the culture promote? There are many little signs that can demonstrate that: how people behave, the related party notes in the annual report, the stories you hear on the street. Arrogance levels are a very important negative indicator as well.

BHP[10] is probably going to be viewed as a classic case.

It could well be seen as one. They thought they were untouchable. The cultural thing is very important, because if they are a badly performing company and they've got a bad culture, it's going to perpetuate underperformance.

The buy-side tends to highlight that the one area where the sell-side is quite poor, is talking about management. After all, it's people who run the businesses, and that's what they really want to know more about.

But there's an obvious risk there. If you write anything negative, not only will you soon find yourself without anything to write, you might also find yourself in court. So you have to be fairly careful about that. Practically speaking, it's difficult.

What eventually happened to Pacific Dunlop's share price?

It was over A$5 when I called it a sell. It went to A$5.92 and then experienced a long and steady decline over several years down to around A$2.50.

And where is the stock now?

Around the A$2.60 mark.

What was your best buy call?

On the buy-side, the one I'm most happy with would be Mildara.[11] It was only a small company when I picked it up. I had been interested in developments in the wine industry in Australia, and I had a good feeling about where those industry developments could lead. I'm fairly passionate about wine, and many people would say that I just lucked into Mildara by speaking with my heart and not my head. But I like to think there was more to it than that. However, I couldn't really express my view off a commercial platform or in a professional capacity until we had a company that was big enough for institutional investors to hold. And that occurred when Mildara made a bid for Wolf Blass.[12] After that, we had something big enough for institutional investors to get into.

Despite its relatively small size, on what criteria did it strike you as being undervalued?

Primarily because of the growth prospects of both the industry and the company, together with the fact that I thought management were the smartest in the industry, and that wasn't fully appreciated by the market either.

Was that due to the fact that people weren't looking at it because it was small?

Yes, that was part of the reason. But another part of the reason was that the industry had changed, but people hadn't yet cottoned on to the depth and ramifications of the change. One of the lessons that I got out of this was that you can't assume that things are always going to be the same. I remember taking the Mildara story to some institutions and they said, "Ah, no. We've seen it all before — boom, bust, etc., etc., etc." Indeed, that *had* been the history of the Australian wine industry. But what had changed was that we were now making wines with new technology which was also being applied in the vineyard because the Australian wine industry had restructured itself under Brian Croser as president of the Wine Makers Federation. Australia was producing remarkably good wines and, thanks to technology, consistently good, flavorsome, easy-to-drink wines that couldn't help but appeal to overseas drinkers. Therefore, the shores of Australia were no longer the limits to our market. The world was our oyster. All we needed was the marketing ability to project the message that we were now making consistently good, low-priced wines for the world.

A message in a bottle that ended up giving the French a bit of a shake?

Yes. It gave *everyone* one hell of a shake. The fact that the Australian industry was so concentrated, with something like 80% of the industry in the hands of four companies, meant that it was very easy for the industry to organize itself and promote itself in a rational manner overseas, compared to the extremely fragmented French or Italian industries, and that was a big advantage.

It was a combination of macro issues and micro issues then?

Yes. But really, it was all about Australia having an international, competitive advantage, and this was the first work where I had actually enunciated that, because it was so obvious to me as a consumer and a relatively serious student of the product.

So, understanding or relating to the product was an important part of it?

Yes. Knowing the product and having drunk wine overseas and being an informed consumer.

Which is like Warren Buffett[13] never having bought Microsoft. He only buys stocks that he can relate to or where he understands the product well. It can be as simple as that.

You could say that. Having a good understanding of the industry, it was clear to us what the potential was and I made a long-term industry call in about June 1991 when Mildara was A\$2.50. In February 1996, Mildara was taken out by Foster's Brewing[14] at A\$7.75 per share.

You've touched on a good point there with Mildara about the issue of having entrenched perceptions and prejudices against certain stocks or industries. How hard is it not to have too fixed an idea of a particular stock or industry?

That's a real dilemma.

How hard is it to keep an open mind?

In stockbroking, in some ways, you're not encouraged to keep an open mind, because you've got to succeed in your marketing, and therefore you have to be very forceful and that means you have to be consistent and unequivocal.

And opinionated?

That's right. It looks insincere if you change your mind. It calls your label into question. So any changes tend to be gradual, and you have to manage the change over a period of time. You have to condition your clients for your change in view, emphasizing the underlying background changes that gave you no choice but to change your view.

Is it easier to be contrarian or popular?

It's very easy to be popular. It's hard to be contrarian.

Why is it hard to be contrarian?

There are disincentives to that, because you get yourself offside with company management and that's an important source of information. You have to consider that very carefully before you become too contrarian on a stock.

Can we talk about marketing a bit more? What does it take to be an effective marketer? Is it 100 phone calls a week, or is it ten? Is it the number of face-to-face presentations, the amount of column inches in a paper, and getting your face on TV, for example?

The most important thing is to make sure that you are producing work that looks at the problem or the issue from the perspective of as many clients as you can. I mentioned earlier that in some ways this is a profession and in other ways it isn't. One of the ways it's not a profession is you have an incredibly wide range of clients for whom you produce, generally speaking, non exclusive work. The flip side to that, however, is that you — not they — usually initiate the work, and you end up essentially peddling the same work to many clients who share in the results of your work. You are therefore more akin to a mass marketer than a professional. That said, I think one of the real keys to success in stockbroking is to break your clientele down into a number of different categories, each category consisting of people who are investing in a similar way. Then, having carved your clientele up into a manageable number of stereotypes, make sure that when you are writing, you are catering to each of those stereotypes. Make sure there is something in your product for each of these groups, and emphasize those aspects of your research that will interest them when making your phone calls or personal presentations.

Not quite the McDonald's approach, but it's close.

That's right, it's somewhere in between. If, for example, I only did a DCF[15] valuation on stocks, I would limit myself to an unconventional minority. So I have to do a PE-based valuation and an EBIT multiple valuation as well.

And have a yield story as well.

If you cover banks, you would have to do that. So, it's horses for courses. The other thing is to know what buttons to press with your client. There are some clients who like up-to-date gossip or rumors; others literally don't have the time of day for that sort of stuff.

So, you really have got to know your clients?

Absolutely, and when you get something that is potentially marketable, don't assume that you can market it to the entire client base.

Do you think the segmentation that you're talking about is the way of the future?

I think what I'm talking about is just the beginning, as far as domestic clients are concerned. The international clients, because they have time constraints in looking at a small market like Australia, tend to need most of what's on the smorgasbord — company and industry updates, estimates, valuations, and recommendations — and I think for some time they are going to accept and pay for the full shooting box. But domestic clients are getting sophisticated and selective — the consultants who advise the superannuation trustees are seeing to that. Australian clients are shifting into the domain of brokers. For example, once upon a time, domestic institutions would never have contemplated building serious models of companies. It's still rare, but it's happening. For example, at JFCP — a bit of an extreme case, maybe — we have built models that are quite a bit more sophisticated than those we had at BT. And, as you know, the BT team's models were, on average, up there with the best in the market. So, it's a matter of tailoring the service even more than before — getting really intimate with your client's process and working out how you can mesh in; what you can outsource for a client. Obviously, it's difficult to manage. It requires a change in mindset from both the head of research and, especially, the dealing desk. They have to shake off what I call the "publish or perish" syndrome, because the analyst of the future will be subcontracting more and more of his time to projects for clients. As an aside, I also think the days of the old-fashioned dealer are numbered too. The desk will break into three types. There'll be genuine advisors— ex-analysts, maybe — who sell the detail of the analyst's work to overseas and smaller institutions, freeing up the analyst for tailored production. There'll be order-executors (until institutions get the right to deal directly with one another). And there'll be client service personnel who keep the wheels of the relationship turning freely.

What do you think are the common misperceptions about stockbroking, and what are the common mistakes people make when it comes to investing?

I think that the average person thinks we have a tremendous knowledge about the market. But, of course, it's impossible to know with any meaningful certainty when the market is going to go up and when it's going to go down.

They think that we have a third eye?

Yes, that we are all-seeing and all-knowing. If we knew those sorts of things — that is, when stocks will go up or down — the markets wouldn't be doing their job. Perfectly informed markets would mean that gaps between price and true value would close as soon as we saw them. By poring over the market, analysts help to identify and close those gaps. And when it comes to forecasting profits and calling individual stocks, it's like a game of cards, but you've only got one-third of the deck. You don't have all the information necessary to make perfect judgments, and this handicap is something that is really underestimated by many of those who make disparaging jokes about stockbroking analysts. What people don't realize is just how difficult the job is. How difficult it is to beat the market, especially when you don't have all of the information necessary to make a call. That's one of the big misconceptions out there — that we have a lot more information than we actually do.

What are the common mistakes that you see from the average person in the street when it comes to investing?

Undoubtedly, it's getting caught up in sentiment.

Popularism?

Yes, riding popular waves that are often fueled by the press. The press jumps on a bandwagon and just takes the person in the street along with them.

So, patience and an independent mind are very important qualities when it comes to investing in the stock market?

Absolutely. I can't remember who said it, but never a truer word was said: "It's a matter of getting rich slowly."

Yes. They say that it's not your timing *of* the market, it's your time *in* the market.

Time in the market can be a two-edged sword, though. If, for example, you had spent a lot of time in the market with a stock like

Pacific Dunlop, you wouldn't be looking very good at the moment. So that in itself doesn't always work. Time is your best friend if you're on a stock that creates economic value. It's your enemy if you're on a value-destroyer. But the mindset has to be one of getting rich slowly, not quickly, because it's when you set out to get rich quickly that you start grasping at straws and start investing on momentum and sentiment rather than on value creation.

Do you have to be a good reader of balance sheets? Do you think someone can make a lot of money and still not know their way around a set of financial accounts?

I think that would be hard, but not impossible, because to really understand whether economic value has been created, not only do you have to understand financial statements as they are produced today, but you also need to understand how to adjust financial statements to get you to economic reality. You even have to make adjustments to the statement of cash flow to come up with free cash flow. Someone who didn't know their way around financial statements may think a balance sheet is a valuation statement, but under historical cost accounting, which still dominates financial reporting, assets, for example, are just costs that haven't yet gone through the profit and loss account. So, you've got to be able to take those balances and convert them into something that reflects economic reality. If you don't know how the balance sheet is put together in the first place, it's very difficult to make the necessary adjustments to it. Financial statements are a great starting point, but that's really all they are.

Do you need four balance sheets a year — that is, quarterly — or is one each year enough?

You don't really need four, but I think you would struggle with just one. It's not impossible, but you would open yourself up to a greater degree of risk if you relied on just one set of accounts, because there are things that happen during the year. I think two — every half-year — is adequate.

How do you judge success in this business?

There are a number of ways, but the extent of your credibility is one measure. For example, one of my criteria is how I'm regarded by my target clients and the esteem in which I'm held by the companies that I follow. Ultimately, you can't be much use to your clients if you're not well-respected by the companies that you follow. It's not impossible, but you're likely to be a lot more effective if you have the ear of the companies that you follow. For long-term success with your clientele, trust is paramount. You must avoid getting into a position where your motives are being questioned. It gets in the way of delivery of the message. In my opinion, to avoid such situations and to build trust or credibility, you should simply always go about your business as an agent of the investor. That was always my mind-set, and to be successful as a broking analyst you have to satisfy as many clients as you economically can by producing a product that has a little bit in it for everyone. That's important, because the reality is that you're not going to be able to provide everyone with a tailored, personalized, and exclusive product. Like all businesses, you need to focus your efforts, and minimize that expended on clients where there are cultural or personal issues that may get in the way of you being remunerated fairly. At a personal level, I think that the issue of balance is very important. That is linked to the other yardsticks of success — longevity and sustainability, which are areas people in this industry (myself included) have difficulty with. In other words, you need to remain balanced. A lot of people burn out of this industry very early, or if they don't burn themselves out, they burn out their wife or their family. I've never been number one, but I take pride from having been in the top three or five as internally measured amongst my clientele for the last nine or so years I was in the business, after I'd worked out what it involved.

Your batting average has always been high?

Yes — the long-term average. Another measure is the external ratings systems for analysts. Sadly, they are often methodologically flawed. There is also the accuracy of your calls. If you are an investment analyst on the buy-side, success is very easy for you to see. That's measured by your investment track record, which is meticulously measured. But, unfortunately, in stockbroking, investment performance in the form of accuracy of calls is very seldom measured. Everyone talks about measuring analysts' calls, but they don't invest time in doing it.

But it's not as simple as it sounds.

No, but it's not impossible. All you need is to record the calls and the stock prices at the time.

But do you measure it against the sector, the index, or just absolute returns?

That's a fair point, but you can measure it against any relevant index. I would say it should be *relative* performance that's measured, not absolute, given that we are pitching to investors who have already made their decision about how much money to put into stocks.

How important are recommendations and the valuations that back them?

This is a really interesting question, because, as broking analysts, we probably overestimate the importance of both to clients and over-emphasize them in our marketing. The reality is that most institutions make up their own mind on how a stock is likely to perform. If you take that away from them, what's left for them to do, some cynics on the sell-side would say. So, there's no point in ramming your recommendations down your clients' throats. If you're fortunate enough to be a leading analyst — a market opinion former — you can take some license and dwell on your recommendations a bit more, but few are in that position. Perhaps surprisingly, this applies a bit to valuations, too. As institutions become more sophisticated, they're getting more involved in valuations — rightly so, in many ways, because the more popular valuation methods, such as earnings multiples and that sort of thing, are very subjective. The takeout in all of this is that selling the componentry of your valuation is going to get a much better hearing from your client than thumping the table and saying, "This stock's worth $5 and it's selling for $4 — and you've gotta buy it!" Examples of the componentry are the rigor and depth of your forecasts, the analysis of the company's competitive position that went into the choice of earnings multiple premium or discount, why you chose a ten-year competitive advantage period or 4% residual growth in your DCF, and so on. Having said all that, I think it's very important for analysts — if they're going to call themselves professionals — to put the work into valuations and recommendations and to believe in them. I used to live and die by them. I suppose it all comes back to my belief that you're out there as the agent of the investor. If you put yourself in the shoes of your client and set yourself the same objective of beating the market without taking huge risks, then, obvious though that may sound, I think you're starting with a big disadvantage. It's about helping your clients arrive at the same destination, even though some of them may take credit for the last couple of steps of the journey.

What skills in this business can be taught and what skills can't be taught?

I think most of them can be taught.

Do you need any special talent?

Insightfulness, high energy levels, attention to detail, and persistence are very important qualities. Obviously, you can't take a deep introvert and turn him into a great stockbroking analyst because the fact is that, between the input and output ends of the business, there is a huge amount of social interaction required. Even in the middle — that is, within the firm — there's a lot. There are also a lot of politics in stockbroking firms, so you need some talent or skills in that area as well.

You work closely with people, so people skills are important.

Yes. You work very closely with people, both in the firm and outside. Both internally and externally, you've got to be able to develop respect, because if you haven't got respect, you're not going to get information from the input side of your business. Nor are you going to get a hearing on the output side. And given that stockbroking firms are a bit of a shark tank, you'll be kneecapped if you don't get on well with the people inside the firm, especially the sales desk.

What advice would you give to a novice analyst or someone just starting out?

You don't get paid for going out on a limb early, that's for sure. My advice is to take it one step at a time and pace yourself. It's like the unforgettable story I heard in my New Zealand childhood of the old bull and the young bull. They are standing on top of a hill overlooking a paddock that's full of cows, and the young bull says, "Gee, look at all those cows. Let's race down and get one of them." To which the old bull replies, "No, son, we'll walk down and get the lot." The thing about this business is there are very few moves, career-wise, open to you, and it's one of the reasons why stockbroking analysts are relatively well-paid. But it's a dead-end career. That's what I tell people who are contemplating it.

There's no next step.

There are only perhaps one or two next steps. Where can you go? Analyst to head of research, and maybe over to the other side as a fund manager.

Or investor relations?

There are different skills required there, but yes, you could go to investor relations. You might also go into the corporate finance area. Some go into equity underwriting, that sort of thing. But you are limited and there is no clear path, so you're not getting on a ladder that will take you somewhere. So, given that there are very few moves, you've got to space them out. And anyone who comes to me for advice on that score gets told, "Make sure you enjoy it on the way through. Don't try to get up there in lights in your first few years. Those that do inevitably come a cropper."

But there's no reason why you can't still be an analyst at the age of fifty, if you've got the energy and the drive.

I agree. But the big rider is whether you've got the energy. From my experience, once you get to the other side of forty, just finding the energy to efficiently and effectively discharge what is a massive role is very tough. You can bring other people in to help you, and that gives you a bit of longevity, but there are some things that you just can't delegate. We all have a use-by date, and I felt that last year I reached my use-by date as a sell-side analyst. The principal issues there were energy levels and balance — wanting to spend more time with my family. Most of the people that I was competing with were ten to fifteen years younger than me. Many of them weren't married, or if they were married they had no children. And that means they had more time to devote to work.

But to compensate for that, you've got more experience.

True, but one thing that negates that apparent advantage to some extent is the quality and practical nature of business studies nowadays. Graduates are so much better prepared than we were. We came out lightly armed with a very general business degree and then learned about its application to business finance and strategy on the run. The graduates coming out of university now, aged in their early twenties, are armed to the hilt with the latest thinking in highly relevant subjects like business strategy and valuations — subjects that didn't exist when we went to university.

What do you think is the ratio of sheer hard work and talent, and how hard is dealing with the repetition or grind aspect of the job?

Both are prerequisites. There's no escaping the hard work, though. One of the reasons I left is that I was starting to find that the job was becoming a little repetitive. However, one of the things that kept me in the industry so long, and why I think it's such a great industry, is that no two days are alike. It's fabulous. In my new job I get that as well. But after twelve years, there was an element of repetition building up. The other thing was that I found myself focusing more and more on valuation and strategy, which is something that isn't always rewarded on the sell-side.

Do you ever look at charts?

No, I never look at charts. I have no time for charts.

So, you are very much a fundamentally driven analyst?

Absolutely.

In view of the fact that you are very fundamentally driven, have you ever looked back and said, "The way I looked at that probably wasn't the best way — there was a better way of looking it"?

Yes. I learned pretty early on that for industrial stocks, dividend yield is pretty useless. We had a number of good examples. The first one was the Adsteam Group[16] where it was being promoted as a yield play with a fully franked dividend that was approaching 10%. Shortly

after, the company went belly-up. A more recent reminder of that sort
of flawed thinking was Burns Philp,[17] where people were once again
saying that it was a really good yield story as the stock was yielding
substantially more than the going rate for industrial stocks at the
time. So, my first reaction on seeing a high yield now is to ask, "Is this
a danger sign?" On the other hand, it could be that it's just a stock
with limited growth prospects giving cash back by way of dividend.
So, yield isn't really a valuation tool.

What about price/earnings ratios?

PERs are a favorite in the market and they are still a reasonable short-
cut valuation tool. But really, PERs are just a shorthand, discounted
cash flow arrangement with a lot of very important steps and
variables all combined into one statistic.

And EBIT multiples?

You could say the same about EBIT and EBITDA multiples. I still like
EBIT multiples, but they're not universally applicable. For example,
you can't use an EBIT multiple with a retailer, because so much
interest expense is included in operating lease rentals in respect of
the properties the retailer occupies. To illustrate the point a bit
further, if a company owns buildings, rather than leases them, it
would be incurring a combination of depreciation and interest
expense. But if it chose to lease them, it has operating lease expense
or rentals which are 90% interest expense in economic reality.
Company 1 will have higher EBIT and lower debt than Company 2.
But basic math means that they will have different enterprise value/
EBIT multiples despite having identical economics. So, no two
companies are really comparable on an EBIT multiple basis unless
they have identical asset financing policies.

And depreciation policies can also muddy the water?

Yes, they can, and in those situations, there's a case for using EBITDA multiples. But I'm generally very much against their use in a smaller market like Australia and have made a bit of a crusade against them. If you are comparing a whole lot of companies across the market based on EBITDA multiples, you are effectively saying, "Well, we can ignore depreciation on the grounds that it's not a cash expense." Sure, it's not a cash expense, but it's matched closely by capital expenditure, which *is* a cash drain and varies enormously from one company to another. And because it's often capital intensity that sets a good company apart from a bad one, using EBITDA multiples to identify value amongst companies not in identical businesses misses the whole point.

So, capital expenditure needs to be divided into maintenance and growth capex, and both are a cash expense as well as a major valuation issue?

Yes. It's a genuine expense, and it has got to be taken into account in the valuation process. EBITDA multiples do have some validity if you are comparing companies within an industry which has fairly homogenous capital intensity. And because of the bias toward industry or sector research in North America, EBITDA multiples are used a lot. But what you find is that the branch offices or subsidiaries of the U.S. stockbrokers in places like Australia say, "They are using EBITDA multiples in the U.S. We'd better start using them here." They then use EBITDA multiples to compare across the market. But because the difference in capital intensity between, for example, Skilled Engineering[18] and Pacific Dunlop is enormous — that is, one has negligible capital requirements, while the other has significant capital requirements — the implicit assumption in using an EBITDA multiple to compare pricing is that capital intensity is equal all round. It's not — you're comparing apples with oranges.

You mentioned two very different stocks, Skilled Engineering and Pacific Dunlop. Do you think that the average investor

can make more money by following the smaller stocks rather than the big stocks?

Most definitely they can. But the information is harder to obtain and the risk is higher with smaller companies. So, there is a trade-off there, and in view of that, it's costlier to participate and play the game. But, generally speaking, the smaller the stock, the less researched it is, the less information that is available, and the less perfect the market is. So, opportunities appear that you can take advantage of.

Could you walk us through your call on Skilled Engineering?

I can remember one morning meeting, when all the analysts around the table were asked by the head of sales to nominate their best growth stock, their best income stock, and their best combination of growth and income. When it was my turn, I said my best growth stock was Skilled Engineering, my best income stock was Skilled Engineering, and my best growth/income stock was also Skilled Engineering. The reason for that was that the market hadn't woken up to the implications of the fact that it was one of the first service companies — a new breed of company to come on to the market. And I remember when we did the analysis we looked very hard at the cash flow, and the tremendous thing was that the company's profit was almost cash flow, because it had to invest so little in capex in order to maintain its productive capacity.

What happened to the stock price?

It went from A$1 on listing in September 1994 to over A$4.50 in late 1996 before it had that hiccup with the Communications Division after I stopped following it. But Skilled Engineering was a good example of a stock that was what I would call a new breed of stock. I remember talking to one major institutional investor here who, at the time of the float, said: "Oh no, we couldn't invest in that. It's got negative tangible assets."

So has News Corporation.[19]

Yes. If you take out the revaluation reserves and intangible assets, you're right. That would have been an interesting one to throw back at him.

Did the Skilled Engineering call have much in common with Mildara?

Well, yes and no. With Skilled, I managed to identify well before the market the huge economic value that could be generated by the company, thanks to its low capital expenditure requirements. Moreover, it was a dominant company in a newly emerging growth industry. The Mildara call was, by contrast, based on Australia's competitive advantage in the worldwide market and the company's brand management and marketing skills. But, in contrast to Skilled, the wine industry is very capital-intensive, so the two companies are at opposite ends of the scale in that regard.

As a former head of industrial research and now a fund manager, what qualities do you look for in an analyst?

From a technical point of view, I look for the ability of the analyst to perform sound strategic analysis in order to identify a company's capability of adding value, whether it comes from being in the right industry, or from having a particularly strong competitive position in an industry. That kind of strategic analysis is very, very important. The other requirement is to mesh in with our process of converting past and future financial performance into economic value-added, cash flow, and ultimately valuation. We do that by taking financial statements, past and present, analyzing them, converting them into cash flow, and arriving at a value. That, in turn, depends on analysts with good forecasting skills and the ability to get good information through having very strong relationships with companies — being respected by company management, having their ear, and making them want to talk to you as a sort of a peer. If the analyst can share things with management or give them an insight into the business that they haven't got, that creates a two-way street.

You didn't mention credit skills. One thing that has always struck me in the equity markets is that the credit skills are generally speaking quite poor. It's quite amazing the number of analysts who have had buy recommendations on companies that have gone bust or gone close to going bust.

Like Brash Holdings!

Yes, have you reflected on that?

I have, and I've come to the view that beyond a certain point of financial strength, there isn't a lot of commonality of interest between the debt holders and the equity holders. In fact, they're almost opposed. The ideal company for the debt holder has no gearing apart from his own and loads of equity. Whereas for the equity holder, the ideal is to have quite a bit of gearing, or at least enough gearing to keep the company on its toes and enhance returns to shareholders. So, a prudent shareholder's perspective is very different from that of a prudent debt holder.

Maybe it's also partly due to the fact that bankers live with their decisions for a very long time, whereas investors can come and go as they please. But it's always something that I have found interesting.

I agree. That stands to reason.

You have sat on both sides of the table, as a broker and a fund manager. What are you finding different in the way you approach equity investing compared to when you were a broker?

Well, one of the things you learn is that you can make just as much money by being inactive as you can by being active.

You can make money from hold recommendations?

Yes. You can make money by doing nothing. Just being with the right stocks longer-term can be very profitable. There's no need to do something every day, whereas with broking, you've got to do something every day to justify your existence. That can lead to output of dubious value at the margin.

Does that imply that brokers and investors have a natural conflict, because brokers make money out of generating turnover, whereas people build wealth out of patience and, as you say, possibly being inactive.

Well, in theory, but not necessarily. A good analyst can constantly add to their clients' store of knowledge on stocks and industries with regular reports. But in practice, the demand for frequency probably leads to a short-term focus. The more short-term the focus, the greater the likelihood of conflict. I think a key to success as a broking analyst is being able to recognize and avoid that situation.

Now that you're on the other side, do you think the criticism of broking analysts by the institutions is valid?

That's a tough one — I suppose because the answer is both yes and no. It's fashionable to criticize analysts for doing commodity-style research — that is, research of a *reporting* nature as opposed to *analysis*. But frankly, I don't know how I'd do without it. I know how much time I used to put into reporting on an event so that my clients could get everything they needed to know about a transaction, say, in a tight package of readily digestible words. That included discussing the transaction with the company, assessing all the strategic angles, and rerunning numbers for the financial impact. Institutions underestimate the time saving in all of this and the value that's added. But, the point that broking houses aren't responding to is that we don't need fifteen reports on the same transaction. Someone's got to break from the pack, dare to be different, and spend their time adding value in different ways. But institutions are to blame here, too. They say they'll reward original research, but when the chips are down, they often reward the noisiest, and that used to really get my back up. So, the analysts — spurred on by the sales desk — are drawn back on to the well-worn path of frequent, but often superficial, reports. Then they compound the problem by spending a huge amount of time marketing the content of those reports by phone or face-to-face to something like twenty domestic institutions — for fear of being forgotten when it comes to the institutions' votes for their broker panel. I think that time would be much better spent doing original research — the point you raised earlier.

Or crunching better-quality numbers.

You're not wrong there. I think there's a real opportunity here for broking analysts: making numbers your niche, especially now that much of the reporting side of the role — being the first to the market with news — runs the risk of being considered inside information. The full impact of the present crusade by financial market regulators, especially in the United States, against so-called selective briefings is yet to be felt. It may well redefine the role of the stockbroking analyst when it has run its course. Some analysts will be disenfranchised as a result. The time and effort previously spent sourcing hot news will have to be redirected. Forecasting is one area that it could be channeled into — it certainly could do with a lot more attention.

With the benefit of hindsight, would you have preferred to have gone to the buy-side much earlier in your career, or do

you think broking is a good way to start off and then move across to the buy-side?

I would work on the sell-side first, if for no other reason than, as I said earlier, there are only so many moves that you can make in this industry, and one of the biggest moves is to work on the other side of the fence. Moreover, I think it would be hard to start on the buy-side and then go to the sell-side because of the additional energy required. The other important benefit of working on the sell-side is developing the skills and acquaintances necessary to source information. Should I have waited twelve years? It's taken me that long to understand what investment is all about. Those twelve years leave me feeling totally confident about managing other people's money — something that I think the true professionals amongst broking analysts will always want to end up doing.

❋ ❋ ❋

While enjoying a reputation as a highly numerate and analytical analyst, the key to Pierre Prentice's success has in fact been due to a combination of paying close attention to both macro and micro issues — or, in other words, combining a bottom-up and top-down approach to investing. For example, Prentice's success with Mildara was due to a combination of factors — that is, undertaking a strategic analysis of an industry and concluding that the companies in that industry were fundamentally undervalued. Moreover, Prentice's appreciation that management is also a key investment and valuation issue largely underscored his against-the-market call on Pacific Dunlop. In other words, qualitative analysis is just as important as quantitative analysis, if not more so. The key principles of Prentice's approach are:

• You need to be able to read and understand financial statements and balance sheets.

- Price is what you pay, but value is what you get, and investors should always try to understand that company fundamentals and prospects are independent of the share price. Sometimes they converge, and sometimes they diverge. Be ready to take advantage of that, especially with small, under-researched companies that are in a new fields of endeavor or are a new breed of company. Skilled Engineering is a good example of how it is possible to make abnormal returns by investing in under-researched, cash-flow free and rich, undervalued companies.
- Valuation is important, and don't get caught up in sentiment or popularism. While EBIT and PER multiples are useful yardsticks, they are shortcuts and should only be used as screening devices. Moreover, popular headline pricing multiples are prone to distortion due to different accounting policies and can be misleading especially in cross-border pricing comparisons. DCF and EVA analysis are viewed by Prentice as being superior valuation or investment tools.
- There's no such thing as a mistake unless you don't learn from it. Prentice's call on Brash Holdings taught him two things. First, as a sell-side analyst, when going out on a limb, understand the importance of risk management and the cost of being wrong. Labeling Brash's as a speculative buy, and understanding that the cost of being wrong wouldn't be fatal (as the major institutions were no longer in the stock), gave him some downside protection. While he was ultimately wrong in his call, if Prentice had approached the recommendation in a more aggressive way it could have been fatal to his reputation. Second, the failure of Brash's also drove home to him the importance of monitoring the level and carrying value of the inventory of retailers. This was an area that he subsequently paid greater attention to in his analysis of the sector.
- Be wary of stocks that trade at high yields (except for banks), as this can indicate that they are either ex-growth or companies that are potentially in difficulty and are trying to support their share

price through unsustainable dividend payouts.

- Understand the difference between gross cash flow and free cash flow, and don't invest in a company only because it is inexpensive on cash flow multiples. Capital expenditure requirements are a major determinant of growth and, ultimately, valuation. Pacific Dunlop and Brambles are excellent examples of how capital management or mismanagement can deliver significant share price outperformance or underperformance.
- Management is an important investment parameter, so try to understand the culture of a company. Avoid companies that have a reputation for arrogance, as pride usually comes before a fall.
- Good investing is also about being patient. Don't be in a hurry. Prentice believes that not only should the mindset be one of *getting rich slowly*, but investors can also do very well by adopting a buy-and-hold strategy. However, in taking this approach, you must still monitor your investments closely, as there is no such thing as a "forever" stock.

---

[1] Economic value added, or EVA as it is often referred to, differs from most other measures of corporate performance by charging profit for the cost of all the capital a company employs — debt as well as equity. Capital is also adjusted to reflect economic reality by taking into account off-balance-sheet debt and adding back unwarranted write-offs against equity. The result is better information and insight about a company for its managers, which enables them to make better decisions. EVA is not particularly new, as the concept, a registered trademark of Stern Stewart & Co., was first written about by Alfred Marshall, the English economist, in 1890.

[2] Also referred to as PE ratios and PERs.

[3] The stock's price divided by the stock's per share value of its equity or shareholders' funds.

[4] Price/earnings ratios.

[5] Earnings before interest expense and taxes.

[6] Earnings before interest expense, depreciation, amortization, and taxes.

[7] Brash Holdings Limited was an Australian retailer that failed in 1993.

[8] Pacific Dunlop Limited is an Australian-based international conglomerate. At the time of writing, the company had a stock-market capitalization of A$1.5 billion.

9   Brambles Industries Limited is an Australian-based transport, waste management, and industrial services company. At the time of writing, the company had a stock-market capitalization of A$11.0 billion.

10 Broken Hill Proprietary Company Limited is an Australian-based international resources company whose principal business lines are steel production, minerals exploration and production (coal, iron ore, gold, copper concentrate), and petroleum exploration, production, and refining. At the time of writing, the company had a stock-market capitalization of A$32.4 billion.

11 Mildara Blass Limited manufactures and markets wines throughout Australia. Mildara's subsidiaries operate in New Zealand, Europe, and the United States. In December 1995, Foster's Brewing Group Limited, Australia's largest brewer, made an A$842 million (US$540.7 million) takeover bid for Mildara Blass Limited.

12 Mildara Wines Limited merged with Wolf Blass Wines Limited in April 1991. The share-only offer valued Wolf Blass shares at A$1.04 each and the company at A$55.8 million. Mildara was valued at the time by the stock market at A$62.82 million.

13 Warren Buffett is the third-richest person in the United States and founder of Berkshire Hathaway.

14 Foster's Brewing Group Limited manufactures and markets alcoholic and non-alcoholic beverages and has a major investment in licensed properties. At the time of writing, the company had a stock-market capitalization of A$7.5 billion.

15 Discounted cash flow.

16 Adelaide Steamship Company Limited collapsed in 1990 with A$1.3 billion in debts.

17 Burns Philp & Company Limited processes, through fermentation, food products and ingredients, including bakers' yeast, vinegar, bacterial products, and consumer foods. The company operates worldwide, including Australia, North America, South America, and Europe. At the time of writing, the company had a stock-market capitalization of A$226 million.

18 Skilled Engineering Limited provides contract labor services to various industries, commerce, and government agencies. The company supplies skilled tradesmen and professionals in industries including engineering, drafting, maintenance, and communications. The company's employees are supplied to clients for hourly hire or for contract fees. At the time of writing, the company had a stock-market capitalization of A$168 million.

19 News Corporation Limited is an international media company. The company's operations include the production and distribution of motion pictures and television programming; television, satellite, and cable broadcasting; and the publication of newspapers, magazines, books, and promotional inserts. At the time of writing, the company had a stock-market capitalization of A$82.9 billion.

8

Murdoch Murchison: Buying Pessimism and Selling Optimism

"Markets tend to be obsessed with particular issues at particular points in time, and they tend to ignore other issues for better or for worse. Consequently, that drives excessive optimism or excessive pessimism. My job is to use those periods of excessive optimism or excessive pessimism to generate buy or sell decisions."

Murdoch Murchison originally trained as a lawyer in the United Kingdom and began his investment career as an oil analyst in the City of London with Schroders. He is now the global banking and global mining analyst for the Templeton Funds Group, which has US$90 billion under management. As globalization of markets and economies continues to increase, Murchison is one of a growing group of analysts who look at stocks on a global basis. What also distinguishes his approach from that of other analysts and fund managers is the strong value bias[1] that overlies his global approach to analysis and investing. This bias reflects, in part, the legacy and investment philosophy of Sir John Templeton,[2] who outlined sixteen rules for investment success, which are set out at the end of this chapter. Despite the fact that Sir John Templeton has retired and no longer has an association with Templeton Funds Group, these sixteen principles still form the foundation of Templeton's investment philosophy.

How did you get started in this industry?

By accident, rather than design. I studied law and considered working as a lawyer in the City of London. This offered long hours, more study, and a tortuous career structure. The unexpected opportunity arose to join Schroders. I knew little about finance or equity markets, but it was an easy choice to leave behind statutes and case law and try something very different.

Did you ever think about joining the sell-side?

At one point I nearly became a sell-side analyst. But for a couple of reasons I chose not to.

Why was that?

First, the position would have been in the U.K. market and the idea of making daily telephone calls to people about a 1% or 2% price movement in BP[3] or Shell,[4] and finding reasons to explain it, didn't really appeal. The second reason was I felt that, at that point in my working life, there was a danger of my becoming too specialized and too narrow.

In what sense?

On the buy-side I think you've got a bit more freedom to move about in terms of location and career development. A sell-side analyst is expected to know everything about a small number of stocks, so it can be difficult to switch tracks or keep the job stimulating. I think that once you've been through one or two investment cycles in the same industry, covering the same stocks, it becomes pretty difficult to generate the enthusiasm.

And how did you end up covering global banking?

A bit of background first. I joined Templeton in 1993, and we have a very clear goal of not wanting to produce "industry gurus"; you know, the sort of people whose views are never questioned because they are regarded as "Mr. Banks," or "Mr. Insurance", or "Mr. Retailing," or whatever. At Templeton we look at the investment world by global sector, so we all run global portfolios and every portfolio manager has responsibility for one or two global sectors. So, how did I end up looking at banks? Well, it was pretty simple insofar as I was asked to take over coverage of the banking sector when someone else left. It's a large sector undergoing a lot of change, so I was keen to take up the challenge.

Were you fazed by that, given that you had no real background in the sector?

Not really, because it held a lot of interest for me and I was looking forward to the fact that it was going to stretch me intellectually.

What was the hardest part of making the transition from being a lawyer to being a fund manager?

There were probably two things; one was having to make pretty major decisions on the basis of incomplete information. Given my background and training as a lawyer, you expect to be able to cross all the i's and dot all the t's before you make a decision. So, one of the biggest things that I've had to learn was to accept that even though you've tried to cover all your bases, there is still always that unknown element in making an investment decision. You could spend another week or two researching that final part and getting your comfort level higher, but I think in this business you have to accept that in most of the decisions you make, unless you are very fortunate, your confidence level isn't going to be 90%, it's probably going to be nearer 60% or 70%. You are always living with an element of uncertainty. A legal training can encourage the avoidance of risk, with an emphasis on cast-iron contracts and water-tight guarantees — just look at the small print in any insurance cover.

Do you think that the average investor fully appreciates that risk?

No, I don't. Analysts, strategists, and investment managers tend to present their views in the media or in their publicized research in very confident and definite terms. Partly that's because on the sell-side you are selling ideas, so you really have to sell them very firmly and give the impression that your conclusion is the obvious conclusion. Most often, it's only one of a range of possible outcomes. Confidence is a highly priced commodity in the industry, rightly or wrongly. Another issue in this business that we have to deal with is accepting the fact that you don't pick up all the information or data that is out there. For example, as we speak, there are stocks that are performing that I haven't spotted; there are moneymaking ideas that I haven't grabbed. There are opportunities out there that we miss because nobody can monitor the markets twenty-four hours a day. Learning to live with that, and managing your time to focus on the best available investment opportunities in your market or sector, is a critical discipline.

Are you suggesting that markets aren't perfect?

I don't think that markets are perfect in the *short term*, but they are very efficient in the *long term*. Markets can overshoot widely in times of excess optimism or excess pessimism. An important part of our investment philosophy is that it's very difficult to outperform the market if you are investing over the shorter term.

Why is that?

In the short term, it's momentum that drives stock prices, rather than valuation. Short-term price movements are inherently difficult to predict, but a focus on long-term value enables you to buy stocks when markets are too pessimistic and valuations are too low. Also, the bulk of our competitors are focused on short-term considerations, and that's where some of the best brains in the business are trying to make their money. We try to take a longer-term perspective on things and are more interested in knowing where a company will be in three to five years, not three to five months.

And where does the sell-side add value?

I like the way you put the question. I think as responsible adults, we have to recognize the way the sell-side makes their money and make sure that as fund managers we fully understand that. Everybody has a motivation when they are making a recommendation, and I think that part of my job is to understand why someone is recommending a particular stock or a particular course of action. I think we are quite relaxed about that and understand that it's rare to come across research that combines our type of value discipline with a long-term investment perspective as well. So, we are very used to reading brokers' research or speaking to brokers and putting our own filter on what's being said.

Now, how does the sell-side add value? I think we get value from speaking to individuals who, through their knowledge of a particular industry or company, can really increase our understanding of the prospects for that business. We don't get value from the stock recommendations as such, and we don't even necessarily get value from the numbers that brokers produce. However, what we *do* get value from is a clear and deep understanding of long-term industry and company trends, the profitability outlook for individual companies, and their positioning within their industry. So, we're not looking for brokers to have a 300-strong analytical team full of MBAs who are all very bright but who have limited experience and therefore follow market trends. Sell-side analysts add value when they can offer something more than just the consensus view.

That seems quite different to the traditional perspective.

It comes back to what is difficult about the business. Sir John Templeton always said that you will never achieve a superior investment record by doing what everyone else is doing. Intuitively, that's very clear, but to make those decisions and go against the market when most people are saying that's the wrong thing to do — for example, saying "sell" when everyone else is saying "buy" — is an incredibly difficult discipline; it's very difficult to shut out the white noise.

So, courage is important?

I'm not sure if courage is the right word. I'm cautious about saying that we are more courageous than our competition. I would rather say that we have a disciplined framework, which means that we rarely follow the crowd. And, in fact, one of the great benefits of working within a disciplined framework is that you have a *very* clear understanding of what you are trying to achieve. But whether that is being courageous or not, I'm not sure.

What are the benefits of having a global approach?

We believe that there are three or four major benefits from adopting a global approach to investing, and we would argue that the main one is that industries, or sectors in general, are becoming increasingly global. Therefore, the logic of comparing across borders is becoming more compelling, whereas twenty years ago, an awful lot of industries were either very country-specific or regional in their orientation. So, that's, I suppose, a fairly obvious issue.

The second issue is that businesses or industries are becoming more commoditized and there is greater substitution. For example, no matter where you invest, an auto manufacturer is an auto manufacturer, a pharmaceutical company is a pharmaceutical company, and a bank is a bank, and while there might be local or regional nuances, there is still a fundamental profit model that is generalizable in all of those businesses. So the basic economic models are starting to converge, no matter where you look. And so for us, one of the most important things is to try and understand the structure of company balance sheets and income statements and how that could change over time and through a cycle. That's important because, in particular countries, while investment cycles will differ in their amplitude and duration and there will be legislative issues, or social issues, or competition issues that will be potential points of departure, nevertheless, the fundamental industry trends in most instances will be very similar. So, we find it very useful to be able to screen companies by using that sort of framework and analysis.

Could you give an example of that?

A good example would be Pechiney[5] in France. If you were a French specialist, how would you value Pechiney, because you have no other benchmarks within France to value it against? You could try stepping out regionally and valuing the company against other steel and metal producers or other cyclical companies in Europe, but the best way to look at Pechiney would be in a global context and that would also be the best way to look at BP or Shell, for that matter.

Do "commodity"- or "service"-based companies tend to lend themselves more to this type of approach — for example, banks, natural resource companies, and airlines?

Well, yes and no. For example, if you look at companies like Canal Plus[6] in France, which is a specific French company operating within a specific media environment, the company's share price is performing quite dramatically today based on media consolidation issues that are driven by factors in the global entertainment and media industries. So, even something like the media sector, while there are issues that are specific to the local media industry, is as a whole, becoming more global. Whether an industry is global or regional, I think that having a basic understanding of the way an *industry*, or a company within that industry, works, and putting it into a framework really helps you to think more critically about price and value.

What about industries that operate in protected environments or markets?

Where a company is operating within a protected market or protected industry, with very little international competition and consequently generating above-normal returns, the immediate question is, how sustainable is that? And if you are only a *local* analyst looking at that company, you are unlikely to be making the right comparisons and saying, "Wait a minute. This company is earning X% more than a company 200 miles away, or 1000 miles away, doing the same thing — how sustainable is that?" The global approach, however, gives you the perspective to do that.

As more people become more global in their perspective, does that mean the returns are going to be harder to generate?

Yes, that's true, because the flip side for us at Templeton is that we have been looking globally for decades. As others follow this pattern, it's becoming more and more difficult to spot valuation anomalies. That's mainly due to the fact that the investment industry on both the buy-side and the sell-side is moving more toward global methods of analysis.

What do you think has been driving that?

It's been driven partly by the sell-side, as you see global investment banking teams offering their services to their large clients on a global basis and, moreover, their clients demanding it. Subsequently, that feeds through to secondary research. Moreover, there is also increasing convergence, because the buy-side, of its own accord, is also moving toward the global approach. Europe is perhaps a good example of that trend. Five years ago, Europe was very country-specific, whereas today most people are moving toward Pan-European industry teams. How do we at Templeton respond to that? It comes back to something we were talking about earlier, where I believe that we have to be very careful that we're not static. Looking at industries on a global basis has been for us a very profitable way of investing for a number of years. Will it be so profitable over the next decade or thereafter? Not necessarily, because, by definition, the more people that are engaged in that activity, the smaller the number of valuation anomalies that will appear. Are we *absolutely* wedded to looking at industries on a global basis? No, I don't think we are. We are, however, wedded to the idea of looking for *value*, whichever way that arises and however that is defined. It may well be that at some point in the future, we'll have to look at another way of dividing up the investment pie. That's not the case today.

How do you define value, and how do you approach the issue of valuation?

We have a very strong value discipline, but at the same time I think it would be a mistake to say that we have a very narrow view of what value is. We would define value as a situation where a company is trading at a significant discount to its long-term worth. Now, what is the long-term worth of a company? We spend a lot of time normalizing[7] earnings through a cycle, and that provides us with a very important benchmark. The next question I would ask myself is, "Given the cyclical trends and structural trends in this industry, what sort of return on capital would this type of company in this type of industry generate in four to five years' time?" We could ask the question a different way and say, "What sort of cash flow on its invested capital, or what sort of earnings, or what sort of net asset value, will it have in five years' time?" We could also ask in certain circumstances. "What would that company be worth to a third party in the industry?" The point is that there is no *absolute* way to determine these things, because you have to be very flexible in asking these sorts of questions.

Could you give an example?

If the market falls in love with a particular valuation approach or methodology, like EVA,[8] or discounted cash flow, or a particular investment statistic or ratio, then it becomes much more difficult to identify valuation anomalies using that method. You're not going to find value by looking at things the way everybody else looks at things. I think it's important to have an awareness of the various methods of valuation that are in vogue *at present*, and to ask yourself whether those methods are going to continue, and if so, for how much longer and what could potentially replace them.

But by the sounds of it, you accept that cash returns and cash generation are the fundamental building block?

True. At the end of the day, long-term value comes down to cash earned or cash created. But markets and share prices are, from time to time, driven by other mechanisms — for example, in certain types of markets, people will put very high values on assets that aren't necessarily generating cash at that point in time, so you need to be able to have an anchor from which to gauge whether you believe that the market is overpaying or discounting too heavily.

Why do you think these pricing anomalies occur?

I think that the market can only focus on two or three things at one time and that, broadly speaking, markets tend to be obsessed with particular issues at particular points in time and to ignore other issues, for better or for worse. Consequently, that drives excessive optimism or excessive pessimism. My job is to use those periods of excessive optimism or excessive pessimism to generate buy or sell decisions.

Could you give an example?

Take the Asian banks, for example. At present, the big question is whether the market is excessively pessimistic about the outlook for nonperforming loans, and whether that is creating long-term opportunities where you might want to buy into some very attractive and dominant franchises. At today's pricing levels, you are seeing people trying to estimate the franchise value of banks based on deposits bases and the size of customer bases. But you *weren't* seeing that sort of thinking nine months ago. There may have been very good reasons why that wasn't the case, but when you think about it, nine months ago *was* the time to be doing those sorts of calculations and making those types of estimates.

Are you implying that markets are inefficient?

In the short term, yes; in the long term, much less so. Market participants tend to take short-term trends, one or two years, and extrapolate them indefinitely. This creates pricing anomalies. Emotions — fear and greed — are also very influential in relatively short time frames — say, under one year. In hindsight, they can look relatively inefficient, because they can be largely driven by emotion in the short term.

Even though there are a variety of perceptions out there, do investors still seem to make similar mistakes?

One of the biggest is the "straight line" mistake of assuming that current conditions, whether they be good or bad, will remain in place in perpetuity or certainly for as long as any reasonable person could expect. Recognizing that an economy or a company is dynamic, that individuals are dynamic and things are constantly changing, is a major issue that investors have to think about, rather than engaging in "straight line" thinking.

Or assuming that things won't change?

Exactly. That's another common mistake. For example, I was reading a piece of research today that said an investment in a particular company was "dead money for six months" despite the very low valuation of the stock on the basis of this analyst's longer-term numbers. Now, I don't see how the analyst is in a position to draw that conclusion. There are any number of catalysts that could alter that analysis or scenario.

Apart from simple extrapolation, are there any other common errors that the average investor makes?

I think that another common error is the idea that you'll have time in three months' time to make the investment decision that you think you ought to make today. In many cases, people think, "Yes, the stock is cheap today, but the numbers are still being downgraded or sentiment is against it." Consequently, they too often delay a particular decision because they tend to believe that the recent performance will be perpetuated, and because of a fear of being too early or too far ahead of the market. A fundamental part of taking large positions in stocks is to recognize that you should always leave something on the table for the next person. It's better to buy too early and wait for some months than to miss the opportunity altogether. Sometimes you are lucky, but more often than not you are too late, and it's exactly the same case when you come to sell. So, sometimes you've got to be prepared to leave 20% or 30% on the table, because when the markets are in that last euphoric phase of a liquidity-induced boom, that magnitude of price movement can be quite common. Now, that can be very painful to watch, and you have to be prepared to accept a lot of criticism from your client base for making some of those decisions. However, no-one can consistently call the top or the bottom.

Does portfolio management come into this? Someone said that portfolio management is designed to protect investors from their own stupidity.

How you manage portfolios is a fascinating topic, and yes, protecting yourself against your own stupidity or mistakes is one way of viewing diversification. However, diversifying a portfolio and spreading your risk doesn't relieve you of the responsibility of knowing exactly what you are buying. I think a lot of people forget this. You are buying a claim on the *underlying assets* and the *dividend stream* of a company. You are buying a legal claim, and your legal claim may be weaker or stronger in particular countries — that's what you are fundamentally buying. You're not buying a currency. You're not buying a market. You're not buying an interest rate option, or whatever — you're buying a company, a business. So you have to try and understand what it is you've got at the company level and then construct a portfolio from a fundamental or bottom-up basis.

Whereas a lot of investors tend to construct their portfolios from a top-down basis.

Yes. In many ways, I think that's a more difficult job. We emphasize to our clients that they're not employing us to make big market or macroeconomic decisions. They're asking us to make eighty or ninety small decisions, because that's what a typical portfolio will contain. Whether that's too many or too few stocks can be debated, but notwithstanding that, you have a diversified set of *individual* decisions being made on the back of a substantial amount of fundamental analysis; that's the service that we offer to our clients based on the argument that that strategy will deliver superior long-term returns. Investment managers have to be very clear in their own minds as to what it is they are offering their clients. Other managers may be offering a currency expertise or some sort of asset allocation expertise, but it's very dangerous to try to be all things to all people and to pretend that you've found the holy grail or a complete solution, because there are all sorts of tensions between your top-down asset allocation process and your bottom-up stock selection. And I think that the buy-side tends to mask over a lot of these issues and pretend that they don't exist, especially when you read some of the marketing material that's produced.

So, you primarily buy based on company fundamentals, rather than on some sort of macroeconomic or industry-related call as part of an asset allocation argument?

Yes, we always have a very clear idea of why we are putting a stock into a particular portfolio and that gives rise to a very *focused* way of managing portfolios.

Could you be more specific?

I was discussing Thai banks with a broker earlier today. The broker was making an investment case for one of the larger Thai banks. Now, in my view, that particular bank is only alive today because of government intervention. Our valuation on that stock is some 40–50% below the current market price. But the argument that was advanced was that you can't afford to ignore that particular stock because it's such a large part of the Thai market index and a 5% price movement in that stock will translate into a significant part of the overall price movement in the Thai market index. I think that's a remarkable sort of rationale for owning a stock. It's bizarre, because if you are going to manage clients' assets on that basis, then I think your clients have to ask what value you are adding to the investment process and, more importantly, what risks you are taking with their money. So, consequently, we are very cautious about investing clients' money by reference to an index.

But as a manager you can't afford to ignore the indices because, rightly or wrongly, that's ultimately what your performance is judged by.

Well, that's true to some extent. There is a huge move within the industry globally toward indexing, so you can't ignore that. But at the same time, I can't understand why you should be so hypnotized by an index, because while a portfolio of stocks may be worth $X yesterday as measured by a composite index, you have no certainty that they will be worth $X tomorrow. So, investing solely on the basis of using indices is, in my opinion, investing blind. Unfortunately, I think there are a lot of managers who claim to be active managers but in reality are closet index investors, and they would be serving their clients far more honestly if they just declared themselves as index managers, cut their fees, and removed all of the hype from their marketing material.

Another issue is that indices always include companies that you would *never* want to own.

Exactly. Or, put another way, are you prepared to invest money in stocks which you have a pretty good idea are going to lose your clients' money? This was the issue that struck me in the case of the Thai bank that we were discussing earlier. If you went ahead and invested your clients' money in a stock that was a significant part of the Thai stock index, knowing full well that the company had negative shareholders' funds and was significantly overvalued, that seems to me to be totally irresponsible and even unethical.

Nevertheless, why has there been this big swing toward indexation of portfolios?

I think indexing has been very much a product of the bull market in the United States, because it has become apparent as the party has gone on, that the important thing is to be "on board" and it doesn't actually matter how you do it, because in a rising market everybody makes money. Underperformance by a large number of "active" managers over this period has also been influential.

A rising tide floats all boats?

Exactly, but if you look at the history of Corporate America over the past seventy years, many of the bellwether stocks of the 1930s, the 1950s, and the 1960s are nowhere to be seen today. You're not going to gain exposure to the value-creating companies by investing in the titans or the dinosaurs of today. So, I don't understand why you would index. It just doesn't make sense to me.

Another mitigant to creating wealth is probably high stock or portfolio turnover.

Yes, I would agree with that, too. In fact, I was reading this morning an article in *Fortune*[9] on Warren Buffett. He estimated that the U.S. market pays something around US$36 billion to provide investment advice and execution of one sort or another. If you deduct that from the net profit of the Fortune 500 companies, you start to get a perspective on the fundamental *economic inefficiency* of the U.S. stock market. So, I think that indexing is an issue and that high portfolio turnover associated with momentum investing also begs some questions. For example, I think the average portfolio turnover in the U.S. is over 100% per annum, whereas our turnover is typically about 20%, reflecting a five-year investment horizon.

In view of that, what's the hardest part of taking a longer-term investment horizon?

I think one of the toughest challenges is resisting the temptation to tinker with your portfolio. Sometimes, taking action seems better than taking no action. It's tempting to believe that you can improve the quality of your portfolio and get that incremental bit of performance by engaging in some trading — but, to be honest, it doesn't work. All you end up doing is incurring more transaction costs and enriching brokers.

Like falling prey to the switching call, for example?

Correct. For example, I received a call today from a broker trying to push a switch on me. He was bullish on both HSBC[10] and Standard Chartered,[11] but he said that they were putting out a switch recommendation from HSBC into Standard Chartered. So I asked him why, and he gave me various reasons and none of them seemed particularly compelling. These were two stocks that he was positive on and that offered a very similar sort of economic and business exposure. The valuation differentials weren't huge, but he was recommending a switch out of one into the other. Now, if he was a seller of HSBC, fair enough, but he wasn't. So, to make that kind of recommendation seemed very tenuous to me. It looked like a turnover-generating idea that they were putting out to all their clients, rather than making any real fundamental business or investment case.

Are the better sell-side analysts those that don't change their recommendations very often?

We don't follow recommendations, so it's not really a fundamental issue for us, but notwithstanding that, at the same time I'm looking for a degree of integrity on the part of the people making those recommendations. I get very frustrated when I see analysts changing their recommendations with no change in news or no real change in the outlook for the company. Quite often, you see analysts changing recommendations or promoting switches between stocks for no compelling reason, or you see them initiating coverage of stocks with a forty-page note saying "Buy, etc., etc." The stock then falls 20% for reasons such as changes in the macro environment, which have nothing to do with specific issues relating to the company or its management. But the analyst then changes their recommendation to a hold! We have never followed that sort of advice, so I can't get too wound up about it, but the real point I'm making is that the stock call as such isn't important to us; what *is* important is the integrity of the analyst. We're not looking for saints, but credibility and consistency are very important qualities to us.

In terms of stocks calls, what was your worst call and what did you learn from it?

Probably my first big lesson was Dawson International,[12] which is a U.K. company. If my memory serves me correctly, the share price fell from around £4 to about £1.20 on the back of some very bad management and difficult trading conditions. The company was basically a clothing manufacturer who had the Pringle knitwear and various other clothing brands. Management was replaced, and I looked at the underlying business and thought there was a good core business in there that hadn't been appreciated by the market and so it was worth buying. We made an investment at somewhere around £1 to £1.20, and the price is now, four or five years later, around 30 pence. The lesson? Just because a stock has gone down a very long way, it doesn't mean that you can't lose all your money.

In other words, don't fall into the trap of always thinking that you know better than the market?

Correct. The market was right, and I was wrong. That was a simple but very important lesson, especially when you adopt a value discipline that can lead you to stocks that have disappointed and significantly underperformed. I think the second valuable lesson that I was handed was a much better understanding of cash flow and stock management issues.

Inventory?

Yes, inventory and working capital management, because the worst thing that you can do to a franchise is overproduce. The company had warehouses full of sweaters with the Pringle brand on them that people didn't want to wear because they were the wrong color and the wrong shape, and it's very difficult to resurrect brands from that kind of mismanagement. The company tried to sell the stock off in Eastern Europe, but it all came flooding back into the U.K. and was then sold at a discount. So, I think working capital, inventory management, and the damage that can be done to brands if they are mismanaged was a very good lesson for me with that company. Once you have cheapened or damaged a brand, it can be *very* hard to restore it to its previous status. The world is littered with brand names that have been permanently damaged or destroyed by poor management.

Were there any accounting irregularities with regard to inventory?

No. Over the past five years, I think that the new management team has done its utmost to turn that situation around. I don't think you could have asked more from them in that they are very honest and very hard-working, but it just hasn't happened.

By contrast, did you overestimate the capabilities of the management team?

Yes. I overestimated management and underestimated the difficulties of that particular industry, where the barriers to entry were very low and the opportunities for cheap import substitution were quite high, as well as the general fickleness of the fashion industry. At the other end of the scale, another valuation lesson that is closer to home was the South Korean bank, Cho Hung.[13] I recommended the stock shortly after a large capital issue, believing the prospectus when the company declared that they had decent credit management. The prospectus was great — in fact, I've kept it as a permanent reminder of the danger of believing everything that management tells you. It had four or five pages on their credit disciplines and exposures, etc., but it was a complete piece of fiction as to how the management structure and credit process worked in that bank. The other lesson from that was that sometimes stocks are cheap for a very good reason. That stock was trading at a 30% or 40% discount to most of the comparative valuation ratios in the sector. But the discount was entirely appropriate in retrospect.

How would you summarize the lessons from making bad stock picks?

Sir John Templeton always said that if you get two out of every three decisions right, then you'll have a superior investment record for your clients. And again, coming back to the earlier issue about what is difficult about this business, it's recognizing that you'll make mistakes and they'll be there for everyone to see. As a lawyer, if you make a mistake in drafting a document, that mistake may not surface for ten years when the document is being litigated and it's more than likely that you are long gone. There are all sorts of industries and businesses where, if you make a mistake, it isn't immediately obvious. But in the investment management world, your "mistakes" can be seen almost instantaneously. When you make mistakes, you have to be humble, accept responsibility, and learn from your experience. The decisions that lost money can often teach you a lot more than the successes.

Do you use charts?

Not really. I occasionally look at them if only to get a good understanding of the sort of ratings companies have been on historically at previous points in previous cycles. So, I only look at them to gauge a stock's performance relative to comparable investment opportunities. I don't think charts have any predictive value, and it's very dangerous to look at one line or one performance chart of one stock in isolation.

Could you give an example?

Take a mining stock, say an aluminum producer. To argue that, based on past points in the investment cycle when the aluminum price was 75 cents a pound this company commanded an enterprise value[14] of X and a price/earnings ratio of Y, or a cash flow multiple of Z, and therefore it should command that sort of multiple today at the same price, is a superficial conclusion. Unfortunately, that's the sort of logic that a lot of people use on both the buy-side and the sell-side. But there are so many other variables that may have prevailed when the aluminum price was 75 cents. So, we can't draw hard-and-fast conclusions like that. You have to put everything in context. Charts are of limited value; they are only another part of the information flow and need to be interpreted *very carefully*.

But it would be to your peril to ignore them?

Definitely. But the point I'm making is that I don't want to be confused with being a chartist!

If someone said they were thinking of entering this industry, what advice would you give them?

Tricky. Most firms will start with qualifications as a sifting process, but one of the problems in the industry is that we too often look for the wrong sorts of qualifications in a person. Today, the industry is obsessed with MBAs, who can be very narrow in their focus. Now, to earn a top-quality MBA is a very demanding task. You have to respect anyone who comes out with an MBA from one of the top colleges or universities. It's not easy, but does it qualify you to run a portfolio of your clients' money? No, it doesn't. One of the dangers in the industry is that there are a lot of people coming into it who think that, because they have had a particular type of background or training, they are ready to get their hands on the money and to make those big decisions. Unfortunately, the industry does allow people with very limited experience, in their tender years, to inflict a lot of damage. The best portfolio managers are often those with wisdom, possibly an unusual CV, and an inquiring mind. Big egos, by contrast, aren't an asset.

What qualities are required to be successful?

Humility rates very highly, because arrogant individuals can find it difficult to listen to alternative ideas and are a pain to work with. I think discipline is also important, because, compared to many jobs, you have a very unstructured working day and no-one is there making you come up with ideas. It's a creative job, and I don't think people outside the industry entirely appreciate that. I'm not asking for people to recognize us as artists, or anything like that, but it's fundamentally a creative, self-motivated sort of job. You have to be very disciplined. It's very easy to spend all day talking on the telephone or reading and then think that you've done a day's work, when in fact you haven't. All you've done is amuse yourself intellectually, but you haven't actually made any decisions. You haven't done anything that impacts, or potentially impacts, your clients' portfolios. All you've done perhaps is keep yourself up to speed so that you can "gossip knowledgeably" in the wine bar that evening, or so that you can see a less-knowledgeable client and impress them with your knowledge of whatever particular stock is hot that day.

Someone said to me in another interview for this book that a lot of people equate being busy with being successful.

Yes, I think that's the case. What does it take to be successful in this industry? It depends on what your barometers of success are, because in this industry it's possible to have a very successful career without ever actually being a good fund manager or adding value to your clients. But I think that in order to be successful in this business you have to be disciplined; you have to be intellectually disciplined. A questioning mind is also important, because you'll get huge amounts of information thrown at you, some of which will be relevant and a lot that will be irrelevant; some of which will be accurate, and a lot that will be misleading. So, I think you have to have a questioning mind and not be afraid to ask the obvious questions. It's very easy to come into the industry and listen to people talking and think, "Well, I could ask a question about that, but I won't because everyone else probably knows the answer." You may actually find that a lot of people *don't* know the answer.

There's no such thing as a dumb question, just dumb answers?

That's right. Moreover, don't feel that you have nothing to learn from other people. This is something that touches on the broker-fund manager relationship; the buy-side/sell-side relationship, if you like. I think that on the buy-side, whilst we recognize the limitations and motivations behind a lot of sell-side research, there are an awful lot of very bright people on the sell-side who have value to add. They may not be looking at things the same way as you are, but that may be just the reason to ask them what approach they are using, because it's very easy, particularly in a house with a strong record of investment discipline, to get into a bunker mentality or to develop a degree of arrogance. So, I think that it's important to recognize that you can learn from other people and that there are an awful lot of brains out there you can use to your benefit. There is a lot of knowledge and experience out there that you can tap, especially in the early years of your career, but perhaps even more so in your later years when you realize how little you know.

So, it's a knowledge- or information-based industry, and you need to know how to extract that knowledge and use it profitably?

Correct. You have to question a variety of people, assimilate different ideas, and use the knowledge to your clients' advantage. The best way to do that is to ask questions, and not be afraid to ask and to listen to others. So often, you go into company meetings with perhaps other buy-side people and you get buy-side analysts telling the management how to run their company. Some company managements may be strong, some may be corrupt, and some may be incompetent, but most of the people running these businesses have worked hard for twenty or thirty years and know their industries pretty well and know very well the difficulties that they face. Now, they may not necessarily know what the market is looking for at that particular point in time, so communication is important. And they may not be well-versed in all of the latest shareholder value concepts, but to sit there and tell people how to run their business I think borders on arrogance.

A three-foot putt always looks easy from the commentary box?

Exactly. In fact, taking that sporting analogy a little further, someone once said to me that investment management was one of the best spectator sports in history.

Do spreadsheets and the profusion of financial modeling also contribute to this arrogance or presumption of management ignorance or ineptitude?

Yes. I think that this overconfidence in spreadsheets and computer models is in many cases unwarranted. For example, the belief that if you have a twenty- or thirty-page spreadsheet model, then you've got "the answer" and therefore the stock is expensive or cheap, is a bizarre notion to me. I remember one guy that we employed who was an MBA, a great guy. We were training him and I gave him a chemical company to look at. I was genuinely interested in the company, because I thought it might be cheap. The company's share price had gone from £3 to £1, and so it looked interesting. The company had spent a lot of money building a couple of plants that weren't working out. The analyst put together a huge spreadsheet on the company and concluded that it was cheap because all management needed to do was double their operating margins in line with the rest of the industry; therefore, the stock was worth buying. So, I asked him, "Why don't you think they haven't done this? Why are their operating margins half the rest of the industry? Why do *you* think they can do it? What is it that they can do to their plant to change the ways they do things?" In other words, how is it going to happen? And he said that he didn't have an answer to the first, second, and third parts of my question, but his answer to the last part of the question was, "Well, I'm sure they can get Boston Consulting in." So, people who are trained to believe that there is no problem in life that cannot be sorted out by a management consultant or a spreadsheet, or who are intellectually arrogant, aren't going to do very well in this business. Needless to say, we didn't invest in the company!

Looking over the other side of the fence, what about arrogance at the corporate level?

It's also a warning sign for investors. Arrogance can often be the result of past successes rather than current reality, and that's particularly the case where you get industry leaders who have dominated for a long time and maybe aren't cutting the mustard today. BHP[15] in the early 1990s was probably a good example of that. I think it's a very strong warning sign when you meet arrogant management.

Apart from BHP, are there any other examples that spring to mind?

There was a European coal mining company that we avoided. I wasn't at all sure about it at the time, but its share price had climbed and brokers kept coming back to me saying that I really should take a look at this company and that they would line up a meeting for me.

So, this was a European coal miner — deep mines, high costs, and with all sorts of operational issues and risks. And the guy I met was incredibly arrogant. One of the things he said was that they were thinking of buying coal mines in Australia, because they believed they could operate those mines a lot better than the Aussies could. And I said, "Well, there are all sorts of unique and critical operational issues in Australia; why do you believe that you can go over there and deal with a very different type of mining operation that has a highly unionized workforce, etc., and be successful?" But this guy was unequivocal about it. I felt he was insulted that I'd even asked the question, and he gave me no reason as to why they could run things better than the Aussies. So, for me that was enough, because I just thought, "Well, this guy is very arrogant and isn't prepared to consider whether my questions are valid." Now, maybe they weren't valid, and maybe the company was potentially the best manager of Australian coal assets the world would ever see, but asking if he could demonstrate that was, I thought, a fair question — even an obvious one — from someone considering an investment in his company. So, we never invested in that company. And I'm very grateful that that guy demonstrated his arrogance to me at that meeting, because the stock looked attractive on a variety of measures, but has subsequently collapsed.

Can we extend this issue and talk about minority shareholders' rights? To what extent does the sell-side have a role to play in protecting them?

I think there are a couple of issues there. Is that part of a broker's role? If anything affects the economic value of the entity, and particularly the value of the minority shareholders' interest, then it's very clearly a part of their job to point that out. Now, it obviously causes complications on the sell-side of the business in terms of maintaining access and communications with the company, but, again, if companies aren't prepared to accept criticism from a broker and aren't prepared to accept that a broker won't always be a buyer of their stock, then that's a concern. And it really concerns me when you hear of companies putting pressure on brokers not to issue negative reports, or cutting brokers off completely because they have a sell on their stock. That seems immature. I'm sure that the correct approach is to argue the fundamental merits of that piece of research, and if the research is wrong or inaccurate, then the company should try to convince the broker of that. If a piece of work is poor and inaccurate, then it should be in the analyst's own interest to try to check their facts beforehand, because they have their career to think of.

With regard to shareholder activism, there are two things to bear in mind. First, if you buy a stock where there is either a controlling family interest, a dominant corporate shareholder, a controlling government interest, or a very clear potential issue with regard to minority shareholders' rights, and you are buying that stock at a valuation that reflects that — that is, it's in the price — then I don't think you really have any comeback. That isn't to say, however, that you can't use all the available remedies, legal or otherwise, to protect your position. If you're a global investor, it's a part of your fundamental analysis of any company to understand the ownership structure, the legal framework, and the regulatory political environment, and to incorporate that into your analysis. Eyes wide open. So, there is that angle. The second issue is that despite that, having made an investment, it's open to you to try and improve the value of your investment through shareholder activism. Shareholder activism can take many shapes or forms. It could involve working with other shareholders if it is in your interest to do so and the legal environment allows it.

Are there any examples that come to mind?

Eramet[16] in France was a case in point. The company was a nickel producer, and the bulk of its assets at that point were in New

Caledonia. The company was being partially privatized, with the French government retaining a controlling interest. In response to separatist demands, they proposed an asset swap, and a portion of its reserves that were less viable were transferred to another party with no competing bids involved. So, it was very clear prejudice of the rights of the minority shareholders of that stock. The remedies available within the French legal system to the minority were very limited. Notwithstanding this, a number of shareholders, partially together and partially independently, put a fair amount of pressure on the French government to provide appropriate compensation. Due to that shareholder pressure, and various political considerations, reasonable compensation was eventually paid. Sometimes it's necessary as an investor to fight these sorts of battles, but if you're going to go down that route you have to be pretty clear as to what your aims and intentions are and what you expect to achieve. Some of the shareholder activism one sees is unprofessional, and can be positively dangerous, because it gets a very high profile in the media and can end up being contrary to the longer-term interests not just of yourself, but of other constituents as well.

Finally, what skills in this business do you think can be taught and what can't be taught?

The technical skills can be taught, and doing something like the CFA[17] program is valuable. It will help you with the nuts and bolts, the mechanics, of the business, like the accounting, the use of ratios, and basic economic principles. All of those can be taught, but that won't make you a successful investment manager. What *can't* be taught? That's a good question and there's no simple answer. There is no hard-and-fast model. It's a bit like asking what the difference is between an ordinary football player and Ronaldo. There are very few Ronaldos in the industry. There is no recipe for success in this business; there's no mold into which you can pour people and create successful fund managers. In fact, that's what I think makes the industry so interesting. There are a multiplicity of models out there that can work for you, but the glue, perhaps, is discipline. Discipline and the willingness to ask questions, and a willingness not always to accept the consensus viewpoint or conventional wisdom. I would also say the ability to work with people is important. Maybe that's humility. I don't think the single-minded, loner-genius will succeed either, as there's no correlation between intelligence and success. I think there are very few successful models like that, because if you are relying on your own wisdom all the time to produce results, you'll be up against it. You are much better being able to rely on people both internally and externally, and to be able to communicate with them and get ideas. Although I think humility is essential, you also have to have the self-confidence to make tough decisions and to see them through and bear the consequences, good or bad.

❋ ❋ ❋

Murdoch Murchison believes that as businesses and industries become more commoditized and their basic economic models continue to converge, the case for investing on a global basis becomes more compelling. However, apart from adopting a global approach toward investing, many aspects of Murchison's investment philosophy are fundamental to all markets. The key ones are:

- You will always be dealing with incomplete information. Don't assume that the market has complete or perfect information either, because in most cases it doesn't. Learn to accept that, in making an investment decision, your confidence level will be less than 90%, and in most cases is going to be nearer 60% to 70%.
- Be wary of brokers or investment advisors who argue a case (either buy or sell) with absolute certainty about an issue and who can't entertain alternative scenarios. A good test is to see if the advisor or broker can identify three key issues or events that could change or alter their argument.

- Beware of companies with arrogant management. Despite its attractive valuation and market popularity, Murchison's against-the-market call and subsequently correct decision not to invest in a European coal mining company was largely based on the arrogance of its management.
- Don't get distracted. The world is full of interesting investment opportunities; however, part of the cost of remaining focused is that you will have to ignore a lot of alternative and interesting investment opportunities.
- Focus on the longer term. Try to understand where a company will be in the next three to five years, not the next three to five months.
- Liquidity can drive stock prices higher (or lower) than a stock's intrinsic value.[18] Therefore, it's important to have an anchor valuation for a stock against which you can judge whether the market is becoming overly optimistic or overly pessimistic.
- Understand the difference between price and value, and take advantage of periods of excessive pessimism or optimism. Roger F. Murray, who helped write the fifth edition of the value investor's bible, *Security Analysis*,[19] likened the stock market to a broken clock. "Price will tend to fluctuate around value. The price of a security is like a stopped clock — it will be right twice a day, and will be wrong all the rest of the time. The main principle in what we are saying is that securities are chronically mispriced in relation to their intrinsic value."[20]
- You will never achieve a superior investment record by doing what everyone else is doing. A value-orientation approach to investing often requires going against the market and buying securities that are out of favor. Value investors take courage in the aphorism by the poet Horace that is cited by Benjamin Graham in the first edition of *Security Analysis* (1934); "Many shall be restored that are now fallen and many shall fall that now are in honor." As Murchison also attests, "You're not going to find value by looking at things the way everyone else looks at things."

- Don't engage in simplistic linear extrapolation or believe that the circumstances or prospects of a company can never change for the better or worse. Moreover, don't be enamored of market indices, because that is all they are, just indices, and they contain companies that you would never want to own. As Murchison argues, "You aren't going to gain exposure to the value-creating companies by investing in the titans or the dinosaurs of today."

Sir John Templeton, who founded the Templeton organization and is widely regarded as one of the pioneers of global investing, formulated sixteen principles for successful investing. And although the Sir John Templeton has retired and is no longer associated with the Templeton Group, his principles continue to underscore the investment process at Templeton Funds.

Sir John Templeton's Sixteen Rules for Investment Success

1. If you begin with a prayer, you can think more clearly and make fewer mistakes.
2. Outperforming the market is a difficult task.
   The challenge is not simply making better investment decisions than the average investor. The real challenge is making investment decisions that are better than those of the professionals who managed the big institutions.
3. Invest — don't trade or speculate.
   The stock market is not a casino, but if you move in and out of stocks every time they move a point or two, the market will be your casino. And you may lose eventually — or frequently.
4. Buy value, not market trends or the economic outlook.
   Ultimately, it is the individual stocks that determine the market, not vice versa. Individual stocks can rise in a bear market and fall

in a bull market. So buy individual stocks, not the market trend or the economic outlook.

5. When buying stocks, search for bargains among quality stocks. Determining quality in a stock is like reviewing a restaurant. You don't expect it to be 100% perfect, but before it gets three or four stars you want it to be superior.

6. Buy low. So simple in concept. So difficult in execution.
   When prices are high, a lot of investors are buying a lot of stocks. Prices are low when demand is low. Investors have pulled back, people are discouraged and pessimistic. But, if you buy the same securities everyone else is buying, you'll have the same results as everyone else. By definition, you can't outperform the market.

7. There's no free lunch. Never invest on sentiment. Never invest solely on a tip.
   You would be surprised how many investors do exactly this. Unfortunately there is something compelling about a tip. Its very nature suggests inside information, a way to turn a fast profit.

8. Do your homework or hire wise experts to help you.
   People will tell you: investigate before you invest. Listen to them. Study companies to learn what makes them successful.

9. Diversify — by company, by industry.
   In stocks and bonds, there is safety in numbers. No matter how careful you are, you can neither predict nor control the future. So you must diversify.

10. Invest for maximum total real return.
    This means the return after taxes and inflation. This is the only rational objective for most long-term investors.

11. Learn from your mistakes.
    The only way to avoid mistakes is not to invest — which is the biggest mistake of all. So forgive yourself for your errors and

certainly don't try to recoup your losses by taking bigger risks. Instead, turn each mistake into a learning experience.

12. Aggressively monitor your investments. Remember, no investment is forever.

   Expect and react to change. And there are no stocks that you can buy and forget. Being relaxed doesn't mean being complacent.

13. An investor who has all the answers doesn't even understand all the questions.

   A cocksure approach to investing will lead, probably sooner than later, to disappointment if not outright disaster. The wise investor recognizes that success is a process of continually seeking answers to new questions.

14. Remain flexible and open-minded about types of investment.

   There are times to buy blue-chip stocks, cyclical stocks, convertible bonds, and there are times to sit on cash. The fact is there is no one kind of investment that is always best.

15. Don't panic.

   Sometimes you won't have sold when everyone is selling, and you will be caught in a market crash. Don't rush to sell the next day. Instead, study your portfolio. If you can't find more attractive stocks, hold on to what you have.

16. Do not be fearful or negative too often.

   There will, of course, be corrections, perhaps even crashes. But over time our studies indicate, stocks do go up ... and up ... and up. In this century or the next, it's still "Buy low, sell high."

1   The term "value based" is generally accepted as being developed by Benjamin
    Graham and is based on focusing on a company's fundamentals and future
    earning potential. Moreover, value investors tend to ignore the price cycle of
    individual stocks or broad stock market shifts and to welcome major downward
    price movements, as this provides the opportunity to purchase good businesses
    at a discount to their intrinsic value.

2   Sir John Templeton, who founded the Templeton organization, is widely regarded
    as one of the pioneers of global investing.

3   BP Amoco Plc is an oil and petrochemicals company. At the time of writing, the
    company had a stock-market capitalization of £125.6 billion.

4   Royal Dutch Petroleum Company owns 60% of the Royal Dutch/Shell Group of
    companies. The company explores, produces, refines, and markets petroleum
    products, manufactures chemicals, and mines coal and other non-ferrous metals.
    At the time of writing, the company had a stock-market capitalization of Eur
    138.9 billion.

5   Pechiney S.A produces aluminum and ferroalloys, beverage cans, plastic
    packaging, and tube packaging. At the time of writing, the company had a stock-
    market capitalization of Eur 3.9 billion.

6   Canal Plus broadcasts motion pictures, sporting events, documentaries, children's
    programs, and news services. The company operates in Belgium, Spain, Poland,
    Switzerland, Germany, and Africa. At the time of writing, the company had a stock-
    market capitalization of Eur 26.6 billion.

7   Normalizing earnings is the practice of gauging what sustainable or "normal"
    earnings or return on equity would be under "normal" business or economic
    conditions. It is also the practice of adjusting reported earnings for nonrecurring
    or abnormal items of income or expense.

8   Economic value added, or EVA as it is often referred to, differs from most other
    measures of corporate performance by charging profit for the cost of all the
    capital a company employs, debt as well as equity. Capital is also adjusted to
    reflect economic reality by taking into account off balance sheet debt and adding
    back unwarranted write-offs against equity. The result is better information and
    insight about a company for its managers, which enables them to make better
    decisions. EVA is not particularly new, as the concept, a registered trademark of
    Stern Stewart & Co., was first written about by Alfred Marshall, the English
    economist, in 1890.

9   Carol Loomis, "The Market – Mr. Buffett on the Stock Market", *Fortune*, November
    22, 1999.

10 HSBC Holdings plc is the holding company for the HSBC Group, one of the
    largest financial services and banking groups in the world. At the time of writing,
    the company had a stock-market capitalization of US$99.7 billion.

11 Standard Chartered plc is an international banking group operating primarily in
    Asia, Africa, Latin America, and the Middle East. At the time of writing, the
    company had a stock-market capitalization of Eur 9.1 billion.

12 Dawson International PLC is an international textile company which produces
    apparel products, cashmere, thermalwear, shower curtains, and home furnishings.

Key brands include "Pringle of Scotland," "Duofold," "Morgan," and "Ballantyne Cashmere." At the time of writing, the company had a stock-market capitalization of £ 36.2 million.

[13] Cho Hung Bank Co., Limited is a South Korean bank that provides commercial, retail, and international banking services. At the time of writing, the company had a stock-market capitalization of KRW 1.3 trillion.

[14] Enterprise value is defined as a company's market capitalization plus the market value of its debt less cash plus long-term liabilities plus deterred tax plus minority interests.

[15] Broken Hill Proprietary Company Limited is an Australian-based international resources company whose principal business lines are steel production, minerals exploration and production (coal, iron ore, gold, copper concentrate), and petroleum exploration, production, and refining. At the time of writing, the company had a stock-market capitalization of A$32.4 billion.

[16] Eramet SLN mines, refines, and produces nickel, ferro-nickel, and special steels. The company operates plants in New Caledonia, Doniambo, and Sandouville. At the time of writing, the company had a stock-market capitalization of Eur 1.3 billion.

[17] Chartered Financial Analysts program offered by The Institute of Chartered Financial Analysts, Charlottesville, Va.

[18] Intrinsic value was a term originally used by Benjamin Graham. His basic formula to gauge intrinsic value was the company's current EPS multiplied by two times the expected earnings growth rate plus the PER multiple of a company with no growth, divided by the yield on AA corporate bonds. Arithmetically, the formula is: EPS(2R+8.5)/Y. Graham believed that 8.5 was the appropriate PER multiple for a company with static growth, but in view of the fact that PERs and growth rates have risen, the appropriate PER multiple is open to debate.

[19] Benjamin Graham and David L. Dodd, *Security Analysis* (New York: McGraw-Hill, 5th ed. 1987).

[20] Catharine Davidson, "Graham and Dodd's *Security Analysis*: The Fifth Edition," *Hermes*, Fall 1987.

9

Michael Mauboussin: Shift Happens

*"When I'm wrong, I change my mind. What do **you** do?"*

Michael Mauboussin is a managing director at Credit Suisse First Boston Corporation in New York City and chief U.S. investment strategist and co-chair of the firm's Investment Policy Committee. He is also an adjunct professor of finance at Columbia Graduate School of Business and continues to teach the course that was first introduced by the father of modern security analysis, Benjamin Graham,[1] whose greatest disciple was Warren Buffett.[2] Michael Mauboussin has been repeatedly included in *Institutional Investor's* All-America research team, as well as *The Wall Street Journal* All-Star survey in the food industry.

Mauboussin is an acknowledged leader in the application of value-based tools in security analysis, and has lectured, consulted, and published widely on the subject. His series of eclectic articles, published under the series name "Frontiers of Finance,"[3] are some of the most stimulating and thought-provoking that investors are likely to come across, and challenge many of the conventional theories about stock-market behavior and stock valuation. In "Frontiers of Finance" there are three themes that underscore Mauboussin's thinking about markets and stock valuation. The first is what

Mauboussin calls "The New Corporate Finance," which is about developing frameworks for determining whether companies are creating or destroying shareholder value. This expands on the seminal work in this area by Alfred Rappaport.[4] The second theme is about the transition from the Old Economy (i.e., capital-intensive) to the New Economy (knowledge- and technology-intensive), and how investors can apply shareholder value frameworks to determine the value of New Economy stocks such as Internet stocks. The final theme of Mauboussin's work is on the New Theory of Capital Markets and the *behavioral* aspects of finance. This looks at the reflexive nature of markets and how investors' perceptions of how the stock market works significantly influence their investing style. Moreover, while Mauboussin argues that classical capital markets theory isn't dead, he suggests that the metaphors we currently use to describe and understand markets will change. Thinking about markets as biological or natural world phenomena — specifically as a complex adaptive system[5] (CAS) — appears to be a better *descriptive* theory of how markets work, and could represent the next major paradigm shift in finance and economic theory.

How did you get started in the equity markets?

I came out as an undergraduate from Georgetown University as a liberal arts major and went to work at Drexel Burnham in 1986. My first sell-side job was at Nomura Research Institute America, a Japanese firm, in the late 1980s. I've been with Credit Suisse First Boston since 1992.

What have been the major influences on the way you think about stock markets and stock valuation?

In the late 1980s, I read Alfred Rappaport's book *Creating Shareholder Value* which had two important messages. One was the link between corporate strategy and valuation. And the other was what he called "market signals analysis" — that is, the ability to take stock prices and actually read what the market believed, or implied, about a company's financial prospects. I integrated that work into my research in the late 1980s and early 1990s well before it became mainstream. The other major influence has been the last seven years teaching as an adjunct professor at Columbia Business School. I teach security analysis, which is the same course that Ben Graham taught sixty years ago; consequently, I spend a lot of time every year thinking about the right approach to take when you start in this business.

For example?

The reality of our business is that a lot of people throw facts around, but very few people have a framework upon which to hang those facts. So often when analysts receive data points, it's almost as if they are reinventing the wheel in how they analyze those data. It's my belief that if we have frameworks, or mental models, for hanging these facts on, rather than trying to start from zero when some data or news comes out, it can fit into a mosaic offering some understanding of what's going on. For example, sometimes when a company misses its earnings, it's a disaster. But sometimes, it's an opportunity. And distinguishing between the two is important in fundamental analysis.

The structure of the results or data is more important than the bottom line or outcome?

Correct. However, while process is very important, outcomes are also important. But when you have the correct process or framework, statistically you are going to have a better chance of succeeding over long periods of time. That's really the idea behind it all.

And coming back to process, part of the process of becoming a good investor or analyst is being able to learn from your mistakes. What was your worst call, and what did you learn from it?

The biggest and the most challenging call I had was Kellogg's,[6] a global cereal producer. It was a spectacular stock through the 1980s and the first part of the 1990s. And even today, by any objective measure, it's a very good value-creating business. But valuation compressed as the company ran into global unit volume problems. One thing about the investing process is that it can be explained to some degree with statistics. So, statistically speaking, when you recommend a stock as an analyst, you've got some probability of being *really* right and some of being *really* wrong. I think that a lot of young analysts confuse the luck of being correct with brilliance. And some money managers do the same thing.

You can be right for the wrong reasons?

Absolutely.

And wrong for the right reasons?

Correct. Often, if analysts get poor results, they consider themselves to be inept. Provided they followed an appropriate process, I would argue that's not the right conclusion. Now back to Kellogg's. I had been following the industry for some time when I made this call. Ultimately, I overestimated management's ability to straighten out the company's problems. My biggest analytical error was overestimating management and its ability to change the business. Even though I understood the economics of the business, I misjudged what management could do in terms of improving the company's financial performance.

That's interesting, because assessment of management's ability to deliver always seems to be the area where people make the most mistakes.

Absolutely. And I think that what's going on in Silicon Valley today is very interesting. If you talk to the venture capitalists, they always say that they want people first and ideas second. Their attitude is that they would rather have a brilliant manager than a brilliant idea, because a brilliant manager will make them money in some way, shape, or form. And when you study this issue, what you find is that most successful managers, those driven to create value, have a lot of what I would call good hard-wiring. Their behavior and style are intuitive and innate. So, finding people that have integrity and who can make money for you is very often as important, or more important, than finding great businesses. And let me be clear about the Kellogg's example — I'm not placing the blame on management. It was my error in assessing their capabilities incorrectly. And the longer I'm in this business, the more I believe that the character of the people that are running the companies is very important. There's no question about that.

Should we regard mistakes as great learning opportunities?

Absolutely. It's a fascinating area. I have spent a lot of time in recent years looking at human cognitive skills and capabilities — the *behavioral* aspects of finance and markets. I wrote a piece about this called "What Have *You* Learned in the Past 2 Seconds?" [7] The formal study of behavioral finance really started with Kahneman and Tversky about twenty years ago. They outlined Prospect Theory, [8] which dealt with human attitudes about risk. And what they came up with were a number of areas where humans tend to be very bad in their decision-making. One example that really caught my attention is called the confirmation trap. What tends to happen is that once an analyst has made a decision, they fall into the confirmation trap in an attempt to remain *consistent* with that decision. So every piece of information that confirms the thesis is talked about, and every piece of information that disconfirms or challenges the thesis is either ignored or discounted. So you get into this confirmation trap. And it's a totally human reaction. Managers do it, investors do it, and analysts do it. And it's so pervasive that I have pinned a card on my bulletin board that spells out the five cognitive errors people tend to make. One of them is the confirmation trap. The reality is that even with a high level of self-awareness, it's still hard to avoid these traps. We are all just human.

Then you would agree that one of the big risks in investing is being stubborn and not being flexible or open-minded enough in your thinking?

Yes. As humans, we all strive for consistency — in the way we brush our teeth or shave, for example. Now there's something to be said for that, of course, but change is obviously the only way you evolve. You have to have a balance between the two. It was Keynes[9] who said, "When I'm wrong, I change my mind. What do *you* do?" That's a great line and a great motto for life.

It's also not dissimilar to the philosopher Karl Popper's[10] view that knowledge can only grow by making mistakes, and that most theories or assumptions about the world should be treated as temporary or conditional hypotheses or conjectures waiting to be corroborated or refuted. Likewise, I suppose, when it comes to investing, we would be better off if we viewed most things as a conjecture or hypothesis and held on to it only until something came along to refute or disprove it.

Correct. But there's only a relatively small percentage of the population that thinks like that. One of the things that follows from this is how to ask questions of management teams. I've found that when investors are favorably inclined toward a security or a management team, they ask them leading, and often favorable, questions. For example, "Isn't it true that if Japan did this, then your business would be up 20%? Isn't that true?" and they say, "Oh yes, that's a brilliant observation." So, what I have learned to do is ask everything in a *negative* way, even if I have a favorable outlook on the stock. For example, "It strikes me that your business in Japan has no chance of getting back to historical profitability because of these factors. Isn't that so?" And then I see if management comes back and actually presents the positive view or facts that would support the positive view. So there's a lot of that needs to be thought about when approaching the issue of how to question management.

We don't need the right answers, just the right questions?

Yes. It's very much like what an attorney learns to do. You have to be able to understand both sides of every story clearly. And when you are trying to confirm something, it's best to work at it from the *negative* side or the side that is counter to your own view, rather than trying just to confirm your own view of the world. For example, it is now routine to have conference calls with companies after they release their earnings. If the earnings are good, the bulls will get on the conference call and say, "Hey, Sally, great quarter! Congratulations! Isn't it true that if …" So it's very interesting, and that's why I think a lot of the errors we make are due to the kinds of questions we ask. It's a suboptimal process.

You are also suggesting that courage is an important part of the process — the courage to ask the right questions, the courage of your convictions, the courage to change your mind.

Yes. For an investor or analyst, it's probably one of *the* vital success elements. In fact, if you are *truly* independent in your views, you are a contrarian. And being a contrarian is very difficult, because a lot of the time the consensus is correct. So as Warren Buffett says, courage means that, given the facts, you have to have the confidence of mind to actually believe something, even if it's counter to what everyone else perceives. And some of the great investment ideas are when you buy something when you're going against the tide of what everybody else believes. In fact, most of the great investors seem to have that philosophy. But the problem is, of course, that the market is very often correct. So, just being contrarian for the sake of being contrarian isn't going to make you a lot of money. You really have to be objective in understanding the facts and that's really courageous. That's really hard to do.

What about the objectivity and quality of research today? Arguably it's hard to be courageous as a sell-side analyst because of the conflicts that analysts face. Do you think the objectivity of equity research is under threat?

I would say that the quality of research certainly hasn't improved, or at least doesn't appear to have improved, in recent years. But there are a number of strands to that. The first strand is that the master of the sell-side analyst, to a large degree, is the investment bank and the fees that are created there. In fact, this business is similar to the newspaper business, insofar as newspapers make money due to advertising, not circulation. But you need circulation to have the advertising. And a lot of investment banks seem to embrace a similar philosophy. They need analysts to do investment banking as investment banking is driving the profitability of the firm. The second issue is that I'm not so sure that the torrent of information we have today actually helps us to make decisions. In fact, it probably confuses us more than helps us. Furthermore, there is this illusion of precision that computers bring. People can now crunch a lot of numbers, but it doesn't necessarily mean that they will come up with any greater insights.

Is it better, then, to be vaguely right than precisely wrong?

Absolutely, and that's a Keynes quote that I also use all the time. Recently, Bill Miller[11] of Legg Mason made a comment to me which I thought was right on the mark. He said that because of the cornucopia of information, many analysts rely on what he called "stock" factors versus "economic" factors. Stock factors are all the traditional metrics — pricing/earnings ratios, cash flow multiples, dividend yields, etc. — the statistical measures that are widely available on companies. These are cheap, ubiquitous, and quite accessible, and so people throw them around a lot, but there's not necessarily a lot of value in them. But when you think about it, it's the *economic* factors that are really going to tell you what's going on. And that goes back to the true craft of security analysis. Miller believes that's where the real money is made. But given that the number of stock factors has blossomed, sell-side analysts can operate very nicely within that domain. What's more, it keeps them busy.

This suggests that the "science" of security analysis isn't in such a good state.

That's an interesting point. Economics is really a *social* science rather than a hard science, and finance is a subset of economics and securities analysis is a subsector of finance. So, what we are really dealing with is much more of an *art* than a science. But the foundations of the *science* part aren't particularly good either. Modern portfolio theory, for example, makes securities analysis look like a science, which in reality it's not. So, a lot of people are winging it.

Are value and risk ultimately in the eye of the beholder, then, and not necessarily in an Excel spreadsheet?

I think that speaks to the fundamental indeterminacy of economics, which is a major issue in all of this. When it comes to valuing securities, it's about gradations. Here's what I mean. Valuing fixed income securities, for example, is a relatively straightforward process. We have a steady stream of cash flows, which are contractually obligated, and if a government backs those cash flows, there's usually a perception of low risk. And we also have an explicit forecast period, so we can value the security quite well. But with equities, valuation is to a large degree a product of *expectational drivers*. So, it's not quite as clear an issue as it is for a fixed income security. But the foundations essentially remain the same.

So, it's possible to achieve a certain level of objectivity in valuing stocks, because value is ultimately defined as the present value of the future stream of cash flows. But, given the fact that valuation is forward looking, there is a high degree of subjectivity and forecasting risk. That said — and maybe this is more of a judgment call than an empirical statement — I believe that stock values do follow, even if it's loosely, some sort of intrinsic value over some extended period of time. Put another way, if you had two companies starting out and they go twenty-five years and one is remarkably successful and the other is a remarkable failure, it's unlikely that the values will be completely inverted. That's because perception will be a moderating variable and there are enough people out there that are self-interested, motivated, and bright to assure that those gaps don't get substantially out of whack for extended periods of time.

In a broader sense, price is what you pay but value is what you get?

Yes, that's correct. And on that issue, I'm currently collaborating on a project with Alfred Rappaport. One of the central things that we address is the price versus value issue. And if, indeed, a gap exists, how does one identify and exploit it?

Which brings to mind the subject of Internet stocks. Warren Buffett said that if he set a question in a final-year security valuation course on how to value an Internet stock, he would fail anyone who could answer it. Are Internet stocks Bubble.com rather than Cashflow.com?[12]

That's a good question and time will tell. Warren Buffett is probably the most famous graduate of Columbia Graduate School of Business. As an adjunct professor teaching security analysis, his comment was something that really struck me. But in fairness, I think there are a couple of dimensions to this issue of Internet valuation that Buffett may be underweighting. There are two or three observations that I would like to make. The first is that the *cash flow economics* of certain Internet stocks are actually much more attractive than the *income statement economics* would suggest. The fundamental observation is that in *traditional* businesses, physical capital or physical resources are the source of competitive advantage. Furthermore, in traditional businesses, all the investments made are *capitalized* — they go right to the balance sheet and don't run directly through the income statement. Now, that's important because the income statement, or net income, *overstates* the cash that an investor can put in his or her pocket. In contrast, for the so-called New Economy companies — these knowledge-based companies — investments include items like R&D and marketing costs. These investments are expensed and what's more, their physical capital needs are very modest. So, it's an important point of distinction. With Internet stocks, cash flow and earnings are much more synonymous than they are with traditional businesses. Further, in some instances, Internet companies are able to generate cash inflows from their balance sheets because of the nature of their business models. So, the whole thing seems to be the reverse of what we are used to seeing. When you look at Internet stocks on a straight cash flow basis, the scenario is much more constructive.

Could you give a specific example?

In 1997, Amazon.com[13] had revenues of about US$150 million. I thought, "Why don't we compare this to what we know is a great retailing concept, Wal-Mart."[14] So, we went back in time to the year that Wal-Mart had the same revenues as Amazon.com did in 1997 — and that was 1973. We dusted off the financials and stacked them up, and what we found was that cash earnings for Wal-Mart were US$6 million. In contrast, Amazon.com lost US$29 million. So we have a US$35 million difference. Not good. But then we saw that Wal-Mart spent US$18 million on their new stores and inventory, and

Amazon.com actually had an *inflow* from their balance sheet because of how they managed their cash conversion cycle. So, *free cash flow* was negative US$12 million at Wal-Mart and a lesser negative US$7 million at Amazon.com. So, superficially, the income statement wasn't telling you the cash flow story. That would be one major dimension. And that analysis was contained in the document we published, called "Cashflow.com."[15]

And the second dimension?

The second major dimension to the Internet stocks story, and this is also about investing for the twenty-first century, is the transformation from capital to knowledge as the real source of competitive advantage. One of the interesting dimensions of this story is that knowledge travels in a very different way than capital. More formally, capital is a rival economic good, or a good that one person at one entity uses at a time. Things like factories, stores, or your pen, for that matter, are rival goods. Knowledge, however, is a non-rival good. That means you can create ideas, put them into place, pass them on, distribute and replicate them very cheaply. So, knowledge-based companies scale very differently and can grow much faster than capital-based companies.

How can investors get to grips with valuing those sorts of companies, as it would appear that we are using Victorian science to tackle a twenty-first-century issue?

Well, that's the final dimension, which is the counterweight in all of this. Ultimately, everything comes back to first principles: value is the present value of all future cash flows. But we may have to look beyond the standard discounted cash flow models to capture all the dynamics of the New Economy. For example, option-pricing theory can be very useful for understanding some of these issues. We have done a lot of work on real options[16] and their applicability to

Internet companies. So, that's the good news — there is a lot of utility in using real options as a valuation tool. On the other hand, the benefit of real option value is offset by the very true economic liability of employee stock options. And our accounting system is doing a poor job of reflecting the issue of employee stock options. So, that's the bad news.

The comment I'd make about the Internet in general is that I think a lot of the Internet stocks are benefiting from the so-called proxy effect. This is a term that came from Geoff Moore, one of the authors of *The Gorilla Game*.[17] His argument is that everyone knew that the Internet was going to be a monster phenomenon. But the question is, how do you play it as an investor? And the answer is that there aren't that many ways. There aren't that many companies to invest in and their public floats aren't that big. So, as a result, every IPO that has come out with dot.com in its name has benefited from the proxy effect — that is, it is a proxy for how big this phenomenon is and, as a result, people have been piling money in. The issuers and the investment banks are still creating supply as fast as they can, so the market is working on trying to match demand with supply. At some point, we may be close to where the supply and demand for paper will balance out. Then there will be a sorting-out period. My suspicion is that you'll see a lot of the recently floated companies drop significantly in price at some stage in the future.

An interesting point to this effect was one made by Jeff Bezos, the CEO of Amazon.com. I think he actually got this idea from Warren Buffett. He said that what's going on with the Internet will be something like the Cambrian explosion 550 million years ago, when the number of species exploded. That's the good news. The bad news is that the proliferation of species was followed by a record number of extinctions in the subsequent years. Survival of the fittest, if you like. So, realize that while there's this explosion in the number of businesses today, very few of them will actually exist in the future because the survival challenge will be beyond them.

In view of that piece of fatalism, what is the best strategy that the average person can adopt when it comes to investing in Internet stocks?

Jeffrey Moore's basic thesis in *The Gorilla Game* was that typically, in New Economy environments, it's a winner takes all, or a winner takes most, outcome. So, unlike traditional businesses where it tends to be reversion to the mean, in the case of the Internet it's a repulsion from the mean. One company can run away with the spoils while everybody else slogs it out. And so his approach, which makes a lot of sense to me, is to buy a portfolio of businesses in a given Internet space. Then, when one of them starts to emerge as the leader, you pare back on the ones that seem to be the losers and put the money back into the ones that look like the winners.

So, buy-and-hold strategies are out? You have to actively manage your portfolio?

Correct, but only for a period of time. Then it becomes a one-stock decision: you buy the leader in any Internet segment. Then it's smooth sailing until a disruptive technology comes along.

Another twist to all this, which you raised earlier, is that the accounting system — historical cost or accrual accounting — is totally inadequate to deal with Internet companies, especially if expenses can be viewed as assets.

There has always been a chasm between accrual accounting and economic reality; it's just widening. What investors have to appreciate is that our dual-entry accounting system was formalized by Luca Pacioli, a Venetian monk, about 500 years ago. So, to expect that a system that was literally developed 500 years ago will serve our purposes today is unfair. Add to this that we are evolving from a tangible to an intangible world. Our system is relatively okay about reflecting tangible assets on balance sheets. However, where we are deficient, or at best very inelegant, is in dealing with intangible assets, because it's really difficult to value them. How do you capitalize or value that?

I have met fund managers who have said they will never buy a company with a high proportion of intangible assets, which means you are ruling out certain companies, especially service-based companies.

Yes, and it's ridiculous. Take Microsoft[18] for example. It has a US$480 billion market capitalization, and the way we calculate it, has invested capital of about US$1 billion. So, the most valuable company in the world trades at 480 times book! And as a portfolio manager in the States, where you are measured against the S&P 500, if you don't have a market weight in Microsoft, it could be a meaningful demerit to your performance.

Another dimension to this, which we talk about in an article called "A Piece of the Action,"[19] is that the world is going from a reliance on physical capital to people as the source of competitive advantage. And as these talented people come to work, they will want something that the plants or hard assets never asked for, a piece of the action. They say, "I'm bright, I'm coming to work for you, give me upside." And upside means equity ownership — partnerships. So, a greater percentage of compensation is going to be in the form of equity. Now we are seeing that phenomenon clearly in both Silicon Valley and biotechnology companies, which are almost pure intellectual capital businesses. And what's more, the whole world is probably going to evolve in that direction. So, there is this huge employee stock option issue that's not being recognized by conventional accounting.

For example?

Take Microsoft. By *their* numbers, the value of their outstanding employee stock options was about *US$81 billion*. So, their invested capital is US$1 billion, but the value of the outstanding employee stock option liability is US$81 billion! Now, that's an important step toward understanding valuation of intangible assets. But the overriding consideration is that the value of any business is ultimately the present value of the stream of future cash flows. And so whether you are using archaic or modern accounting systems, whether you're domiciled in Australia or in the U.S., it doesn't make any difference. Ultimately, it's *cash-in* versus *cash-out* for the life of the business. That's what will ultimately dictate value.

And how are you defining cash flow?

It's the cash earnings that businesses would have assuming no financial leverage whatsoever, minus the investments made in the balance sheet. So, it's really the income statement minus what happens on the balance sheet.

So, it can be determined using the standard financial statements?

That's right. What we do is we take sales and multiply it by the EBITDA[20] margin, which gives you operating income before goodwill, times one minus the tax rate. If you want to be more precise, it's a cash tax rate. And that calculation delivers what is called NOPAT — net operating profit after tax. So, that's an unlevered number. And then there's the balance sheet. The required investment includes changes in working capital, fixed expenditure capital (net of depreciation), and then any business acquisition requirements. And that gives us an investment requirement for future growth. NOPAT minus investment equals free cash flow.

That analysis would also highlight credit weaknesses as well. It should work for both debt and equity stakeholders.

Correct. But, regarding the veracity of the accounting which you raised, sure, it's not too hard to doll up an income statement or a balance sheet for a period of time. In fact, we are doing a major study on how Corporate America is managing its capital. We look at the cash conversion cycles, or how corporates manage their working capital; how they manage their fixed capital; and what's happening with goodwill and other intangibles.

And what have you found?

The long and short of it, as far as we can tell, is that working capital is being managed better today than ever in the U.S. Moreover, fixed capital is being managed better than ever before. But goodwill and intangibles are ballooning.

And what about margins and cash flow?

One of the ways to improve your margins is to buy goods at a lower price but at worse terms. So, you say to the supplier, "I'll buy and I'll pay you faster than I would have otherwise." So, you get a 2% discount and that helps your *margins*, but consequently you're also paying your bills faster, so that doesn't necessarily help your *cash flow*. In other words, you have to be very careful about saying that the fact that margins are up or down is categorically good or bad, because you have to look at the *cash flow* impact.

Are there any examples that come to mind?

One example we've seen is McDonald's, where the margins are improving but their payables are shrinking. We suspect that part of the margin impact is due to the fact that they are focusing on managing for margins and, consequently, they're giving their suppliers better terms. So, they're getting better prices in return for better payment terms. But that may not be good for cash flow or valuation.

I suppose that raises the issue of the debtor/creditor cycle in Internet stocks as well, where they go cash positive relatively

quickly due to the lag between their debtors and their creditors. Does that mean that Internet stock valuations will be more sensitive to interest rates?

Yes. I think we saw that dynamic clearly in action in the summer of 1999, when rates spiked in the U.S. and the Internet stocks really took it on the chin. But I think there were other factors behind that as well. For example, the second-quarter earnings numbers weren't particularly inspirational. But I think a big part of it was the spike in interest rates. When you think about it, it's just bond mathematics. Internet stocks, when you think about it, are long-duration assets. It's like a zero coupon bond; you're not getting your payments until way out in the future. So, valuations are going to be highly sensitive to changes in interest rates. Traditional companies or stocks are more like high coupon bonds.

But let's be crystal clear on one point: Internet companies have to make money for the current valuations to make economic sense. They can't perpetuate losing money forever and be a good business. They have to make money.

What I think is intriguing are the competing business models out there. Amazon.com's prime business today is still books. But their business model is vastly different to their competitors'. And I would argue that Amazon.com's is a more attractive business model than Barnes & Noble's,[21] for example. So, it really has to do with where the consumers ultimately go. And the answer is, where the value proposition is best.

How difficult is it to devote time to thinking about these sorts of strategic issues, because so much of sell-side research is about what I would call maintenance — the routine stuff?

I agree. The dullest and most difficult part of the job as an analyst is the maintenance element. The question is, how much time do you spend reporting versus analyzing? And the answer, especially for sell-side analysts, is that there's a lot of time spent reporting. What you want to do, ideally, is adopt what I call the barbell approach to analysis. This is where you make sure you are on top of the short-term events that are obviously important in order to understand possible future developments. But you also need to understand structurally what's going on in the big picture. Then you leave all the issues in the middle for someone else to do. Unfortunately, I think most analysts get sucked into doing the material in the middle — it's very difficult to avoid.

The other thing that I have always found very challenging is that there exists an extraordinarily diverse group of investors or clients. As a sell-side analyst, you're always taking your basic framework, your own approach, and mapping it or matching it up with the many very different ideas, objectives, and thought processes that exist on the buy-side.

How do you communicate what are some fairly non-traditional ways of looking at valuation and analysis to the client base, who by your own admission, look at things from a variety of perspectives?

It's always been my belief that basic solid economics cuts through it all. Most successful investors have shorthands that get them to the right place. Nevertheless, I always spend a lot of time with our salespeople asking, what is this account about? What do they think about? How do they approach it? And I make sure that we present the story in a way that's consistent with how the clients look at the world so that they may be as accepting as possible.

How important is the binary call — the buy or sell recommendation?

I have never believed that the recommendation was very important, but it's an interesting question. The average sell-side analyst probably follows fifteen or twenty stocks. Typically, they'll be hot on, say, three or four at any given time. So, what a fund manager can be almost assured of is that the analyst is going to be most current and up to date on the three or four stocks they're recommending. Whether that fund manager is interested in buying or selling, or doesn't really care, they still know that the analyst is current on those stocks, if nothing else. So there's that side to it.

But fundamentally, what fund managers get paid to do is buy and sell stocks and make money from that, and to be honest, I think they are much more interested in *information* and *perspectives* than they are in actual recommendations. I also think that it's fair to generalize and say that the majority of fund managers view it that way too.

But there are some fund managers that want to be told what to do. In fact, a fund manager said to me about six months ago, "All this valuation work you do, I actually believe in all this stuff. So, I'm going to give you a free pass on this. Just tell me what I should do, what I should buy, what I should sell." And I thought to myself, "That's fine, but intellectually it's extraordinarily lazy because a lot of it is about the process. What value do you add as a fund manager if all you do is just follow broker recommendations?"

But could that reaction be due in part to the fact that the buy-side are in many cases covering hundreds of stocks, as well as being subject to quarterly performance and benchmarking?

Yes, that's right. And I think that money managers in the U.S. are, by and large, operating in an extraordinarily suboptimal way.

In what sense?

If you study how to construct, maintain, and manage a portfolio, certain points come out that are relatively self-evident. Turnover shouldn't be high, taxes and transactions costs should be minimized, and portfolio sizes should be within a certain range. For example, having over 100 names in a portfolio probably doesn't make much sense. Unfortunately, it's a very rare portfolio that's run on that basis. Robert Hagstrom,[22] who wrote a book on Warren Buffett and focus investing, used one of my favorite quotes: "A lot of people equate being busy with being successful. But it's not really about that, it's really about being right." Likewise, Warren Buffett's also got this story that illustrates the point. He says, imagine coming out of business school and being given a piece of paper and being told you're allowed to make only twenty investment decisions in your life, and that every time you make a decision you punch a hole in that piece of paper. Well, with only twenty decisions in your life, you would want to make sure every one of those decisions made sense. It's obviously an exaggeration of reality, but that's a bit of the mindset that investors should try to develop.

Now, the other issue you raise about quarterly performance is also interesting. I was talking to Bill Miller — who I mentioned earlier — about this very subject. He is probably one of the best fund managers in the United States, and his portfolio turnover is about 10–15% a year, versus his competition who are turning over 100%. He said to me, "You know, the average portfolio in the U.S. turns over 100% once a year. If you think about it, these guys are competing in the most efficient part of the market, as the market's really good at discounting (pricing) the next six to twelve months. But the market's just not as good at understanding structurally what's going to happen over longer periods of time. So, consequently, you've got high transaction costs, bad tax consequences, and you're competing in the most efficient part of the market." Now, Bill Miller has outperformed the S&P 500 nine years in a row and, statistically, he's on the far right-hand side of the distribution — the top 1%. But what he said to me is, "On average, when you look at our quarterly performance, it's only a 50/50 proposition." So, what he's saying is that using quarter-by-quarter benchmarks isn't a particularly good measuring device. But obviously, over time, you have to have more ups than downs.

The reality is that 75% of fund managers underperform the market year in, year out — after transaction costs and fees. What that tells me is that you've got these bright people, motivated people, ambitious people, trying to beat one another, but by and large, they are doing a poor job. And the irony is that 75% of people can buy an index fund and outperform the highly paid professionals. Now, do you know any industry where 75% of people who walk in off the street can do better than the professional? Can they do a better job than, say, the car mechanic, or do better than the doctor in the hospital? It just doesn't happen. But it happens in our business every day. You buy an index fund and you will outperform the majority of the professionals. Statistically, it's been true for forty years, and will probably be true forever. It's amazing.

In view of that paradox, do you think that stock markets are efficient?

My definition of efficiency isn't really the traditional one. My definition is, "Is there a *systematic* way to outperform the market?" And by that measure I think the markets are largely efficient. Now, why do some people systematically outperform? I think there are two fundamental reasons. The first one is going to be due to pure statistics, or chance if you like. For example, if you've got a certain number of investors and you create a thousand portfolios by throwing darts at a dart board, you're going to have some of them outperform, some underperform, and the distribution of those returns is going to approximate the normal distribution.

The second issue, however, is that some investors are *truly* much better investors, and that, to me, has a lot to do with their hard-wiring, cognition, and innate abilities. And I think guys like Warren Buffett and Bill Miller fall into that camp. So, there's nothing, statistically or fundamentally, that says that there can't be people who outperform the market. The word I emphasize is *systematic*. The interesting question is, are their skills transferable? The answer, in my judgment, is no. So, in other words, when we read those Berkshire Hathaway annual reports, which include Warren Buffett's famous essays, they may give you a warm, fuzzy feeling. They are clever, homespun, and funny. But the critical question is, can you apply it? And I like to compare it to a diet — call it the Warren Buffett diet — and diets are very easy to understand but very hard to do. It's not understanding the diet that's hard, it's implementing the diet that's hard.

It requires discipline and patience.

Yes, discipline and patience. But in Warren Buffett's case and Bill Miller's case, and in fact in a lot of the great investors' cases, they have the hard-wiring and extraordinary minds, and so they've got an advantage. I like to use a sports analogy. It's like Michael Jordan and basketball. Back when he was a great basketball player, there's no question that his physique, his size, his agility, etc., was a prerequisite to being successful, but it was that size and physique combined with great coaching and a drive that made him *great*. One without the other didn't work. And I think guys like Warren Buffett have the equivalent mental makeup.

What's the ratio between talent and sheer hard work then?

That really becomes a sell-side versus buy-side thing. On the sell-side, "successful" seems to be about getting notoriety. You don't necessarily have to be all that talented. The sell-side is, by a large degree, a marketing game. There have been a lot of sell-side analysts who have been very successful simply by calling their clients a lot and getting quoted a lot in the media. So, there is a relatively straightforward way to achieve some measure of "success." But on the buy-side, all that matters is performance, so in order to be truly successful, you don't have to work hard physically, but you have to be mentally engaged. You have to be passionate about what you do — you have to love it. What's more, you have to have an eye for detail and do your homework. Successful investors aren't making lots of decisions, but they're looking at a lot of situations. And that, to me, is the key thing. They are busy in the sense that they are always reading, thinking, and looking at the world, but they're not acting every five minutes. And I think that's where a lot of fund managers make a mistake, because they feel that they *have to* do things. It's great for brokers, but not necessarily good for them.

Is there a natural conflict between brokers and fund managers?

I think there is, but I think most people on the sell-side are truly good people and truly want to do the best for everyone. We would all like to see wonderful outcomes for everybody. But at the end of the day, we get paid based on commissions from stock turnover, and fund managers get paid based on performance.

And talking about efficiency, coming back to Internet stocks, how do you measure the operational efficiency of an Internet company?

You should look at the cash-generating ability, but that's got more of a link to valuation. At the operational level, you can start by looking at the gross margins. For example, the gross margins of Amazon.com are the same as the gross margins at Wal-Mart.

Pre-marketing expenses?

Yes. In other words, Amazon.com sells goods at the same gross margin as Wal-Mart does. And obviously the losses are due to marketing and R&D expenditure. So, the question is, what's the potential scale of this? Will these costs grow in lockstep with revenues, or will they grow at a slower rate? And that's where the income statements scale up. The second thing is balance sheet efficiency. How do these companies use capital? Do they need more or a lot less? And as you have invested capital, turnover, and margins, you can create a trade-off curve [*draws a utility curve*].

Let's say you have 15% returns. Obviously, returns are a function of capital turnover and not margins. So, here's a business with a 15% margin turning its capital over once a year, and here's a business with a 1% margin turning over its capital fifteen times. From an economic standpoint, these are identical businesses — but they get there very differently. This is a jewelry store (high margins, low turns), this is a grocery store (low margins, high turns). So, the question is really, when the balance sheet matures, where is it on the curve? And what you find is Barnes & Noble is well down the curve and Amazon.com is well up the curve. Compaq[23] is here, Dell[24] is here, All State Insurance[25] is here, GEICO Insurance[26] is here. And so they're very different business models. And what happens is that if you're only looking at one facet of the equation, in this case the income statement, you're missing the other part of the equation.

It looks very similar to DuPont[27] analysis.

It's the same thing. Exactly the same idea. And it's interesting that DuPont[28] itself has mostly abandoned the DuPont approach. But nevertheless, it's a very, very important way to understand how returns are generated.

Where do banks fit in this framework, or do you approach them differently?

They're similar, but not quite identical.

In terms of looking at banks, do you regard price-to-book ratios as an outcome or a starting point?

They are definitely an outcome.

So, a bank can be cheap at three times book and expensive at one times book?

Yes. And what we do a lot of is we create these curves and we've done this all over the world. What we do is calculate the return on capital less the cost of capital spread. Then firm value is enterprise value[29] divided by invested capital, which is priced at book essentially, and it's an economic theory that says if that is zero, then the company should trade at one times book. Anything above that should trade at a premium to book, and anything below that should trade at a discount to book based on your economic returns.

Is it an accounting-based definition of shareholders' funds?

One is accounting-based, and the other is obviously market-based. We make about a half-dozen adjustments to the accounting numbers to try and make it more economic-based, so we add back reserves, etc., so there's a fair amount of adjusting between the book number and the cash number. For banks, it's the same relationship, but instead of return on invested capital (ROIC) we use a modified return on equity (ROE). So, instead of enterprise value to invested capital, it's price to book.

The point is, buying a higher return business at a high multiple is no different than buying a low return business at a low multiple. Except for the fact that, as Buffett says, when you buy a business with good returns, time is your friend, and when you buy a business with low returns, time is your foe.

Coming back to valuation, despite all the textbooks and theory, is it still more of an art than a science?

It's a combination. But it's more of an art than a science. When doing the DCF[30] valuations, our argument is that the forecast horizon should be intimately linked to the period of sustainable competitive advantage. We've developed a concept called Competitive Advantage Period, or CAP. CAP is the period of time where a company can generate excess returns. So, we're saying that the value of the business is its cash flow streams, discounted at the appropriate rate for the CAP, or period of excess returns.

How do you determine the terminal value?

We use a perpetuity value. Mathematically, it's the NOPAT earned in the last year of the CAP, divided by the cost of capital. For example, say we look at a three-year period. First, we calculate a present value of the free cash flows in each year. Then we calculate the cumulative present value of the free cash flow. Now, to get the terminal value, we take the third year's NOPAT and capitalize it at the cost of capital. Let's say that year 3 NOPAT is $10. If we assume a 10% cost of capital, we have a $100 terminal value. We then present value that. So, it's a very conservative terminal value.

What happens when you use CAP is that approximately 60% of the value is accounted for by the cash flow values in the explicit forecast period and less than 40% by the terminal value. If you look at most of the DCF valuation approaches, about 20% of the value is due to the forecast period and 80% is due to the terminal value.

What about the valuation arguments contained in the book *Dow 36,000*?[31]

The authors argue that, over time, the equity risk premium for stocks may trend to zero. So, stocks should earn the same rate of return as bonds, spurring a massive revaluation of stocks. That argument doesn't make a lot of economic or common sense. In all of their calculations, the authors forecast dividends out for five years and then employ a turbocharged terminal value. Say the last year's dividend is $1. They take the $1 and divide it by the risk-free rate (5.5% for their examples), minus the long-term growth rate (say, 4.5%). The end result is $1 divided by 1%. This effectively capizalizes the last year's dividends at 100 times. So, what happens in their model is that 90% of their value is terminal value, which in my opinion is flawed analysis. When people ask me about the appropriate CAP for a business, I invoke the Keynes quote that you mentioned earlier: "I would rather be vaguely right than precisely wrong." In other words, I'd rather have an explicit forecast period that gives me a rough sense of the economics, which is fundamentally the thing that you're trying to value.

That's interesting, because with banks, we have used zero as the terminal value.

If you go out far enough, you can do that.

What's interesting is the number of debates you get into when you say to people the terminal value isn't that critical in the valuation; the underlying economic profile is more important.

Exactly. If you ask most investors whether the value of a financial asset is the present value of its cash flow stream, they usually agree. But they often add, "Yes, but the terminal value is an issue." And they use the terminal value as an excuse to dismiss the model completely. I find it amazing that a fund manager will willingly pay twenty-four times earnings or fifteen times earnings — this arbitrary P/E multiple number — and feel completely comfortable and yet say, "Oh, by the way, your terminal value assumptions are bogus." So what they're really saying is that they don't understand a particular dimension in the correct economic model, so they dismiss it. Yet they're perfectly willing to use a *shorthand method* — a P/E multiple that is removed from the actual valuation process — with complete facility. If you think about that, it's ridiculous. So, I hit people hard on this issue. P/E multiples and cash flow multiples are *not* valuations. They are shorthands for the valuation process. Shorthands and the process are two different things. So, when people say, "Oh, forget the DCF because of the problem with the terminal value, but hey, you should pay eighteen times earnings for the stock," I just shake my head.

Do you look at charts?

No. But I'm going to be slow to dismiss technical analysis, because some of the best finance professors today are finding that there is persistence in price trends. So, random walks don't work in the real world. That said, for the *average* investor who is bringing up charts and trying to divine what's going on from those charts, what's going on is they are just wasting their time. There are probably some sophisticated ways to use the data, but the *average* person is wasting their time.

I look at them because, as human beings, we love to look at patterns, and we try to find patterns in most things, including stock prices. So I bring them up for the same reasons everyone else does: (1) to know literally what happened; and (2) to try and get a pleasing pattern recognition image for my brain. But in terms of actually helping you to make money, I've come across very few people that it has really helped.

Could you talk about what you mean by the "expectations approach"?

One of the cheapest, but at the same time most valuable, pieces of information about a company is the stock price. You should be able to read the stock price and understand the expectations inferred by the marketplace by using economically sound value drivers. That's one of the most logical and best ways to understand expectation mismatches. So, the expectations approach suggests going *backward* from a stock price to find expectations mismatches.

There will be forecasting risk associated with that approach, though, and that touches on another area concerning risk. One of the fundamental premises of modern finance theory and CAPM[32] is that risk is normally distributed. Is that the case?

The answer is that *returns* aren't normally distributed. It's not a Gaussian distribution,[33] and yet all the statistics we use to value markets are based on normal or Gaussian distributions. And here's what it looks like in the real world [*draws a distribution with a taller mean and fatter tails*]. That's obviously an exaggeration, but basically what we find is that the mean (average) is higher than it's supposed to be and the tails are fatter than they are supposed to be. What is also interesting is that the guys who found this out forty or fifty years ago just explained away the fat tails. Now, as an aside, but related to this issue, is that I'm hosting a conference forum in Santa Fe, New Mexico, called the New Economy Forum. And we're speaking about these sorts of issues. We picked Sante Fe because that's the home of the Santa Fe Institute, which is a multidisciplinary think tank. And a lot of the work they've been doing is on statistical distributions, and one of the key things they study is the so-called Complexity Theory and complex adaptive systems. Now, complex adaptive systems are ubiquitous — e.g., ant colonies, cities, immune systems are all complex adaptive systems and the basic idea is very simple. You have a number of agents with decision roles. The agents interact with one another. Then there's what they call an emergent phenomenon. The result is a meta-system[34] — that is, a system that has properties and characteristics that are separate and distinct from the sum-of-the-parts, yet they come from some of these parts. When you think about it, it's an appropriate analogy for the capital markets, because there's no additivity — you can't just take the sum of all these individual investors and create a market.

Similar to a musical canon[35] or fugue created by the interaction of different and independent voices?

Yes. It's really what Adam Smith meant when he talked about the invisible hand. In other words, there's an almost miraculous, magical creation of interaction that we can't explain very well as a result of these individual participants. And so, what happens is that decision rules are individually dispersed, while errors are independent and evolutionary. But what is fundamental is that the characteristics of all complex adaptive systems are that they are *nonlinear* and have critical points.[36] I recently had an opportunity to hear a talk by Myron Scholes from Long Term Capital. He won the Nobel Prize for his contribution to options pricing theory. He said, "You know, we were playing off statistical probability distributions based on Gaussian distributions," and Long Term Capital would take a spread between bond X and bond Y and the theoretical spread was supposed to be five basis points but was in fact eight basis points. So they leveraged 1000 to one on the assumption that it was going to narrow back to a normal distribution. Then they went through August 8, 1998, which saw a seven- or eight-sigma event. So we had an event that wasn't supposed to happen in multiple lifetimes. And when you're leveraged 100 to one or 1000 to one, it doesn't take long before you're dead.

Doesn't that blow CAPM and beta[37] away, including the way we calculate the cost of capital?

Yes. Absolutely. And eventually it's all going to be blown away. Now, my argument for that is analogous to the hard sciences where Newtonian physics is extremely valuable for getting around from day to day or for explaining planetary motions or the fall of an apple from a tree. But in terms of *really* understanding what's going on in the world, you have to bring in things like quantum physics and Einstein's theory of relativity. So, I think that CAPM is a stopgap solution. It's very elegant in theory and reasonably practical. It just doesn't work all the time in reality.

So, it's intuitively appealing but, practically speaking, flawed?

Yes.

What about Fama and French's[38] views? Does that lend further weight to their argument?

The problem with their work is that they are following the same framework. What Fama and French said was, "We've tested beta and CAPM and guess what, it doesn't work. And what's more, here are two things that actually *are* associated with high rewards: low price-to-book ratios and firm size." However, Fama and French still assumed a linear risk to reward relationship. So, they were still saying that if, indeed, there were returns, they *must* be related to risk. I wrote an article on this.[39] And you can't get to the next level without having the modern portfolio theory that we have today. Going from what we knew seventy years ago to what we know today in terms of modern portfolio theory, it's been a quantum leap in understanding. But the question now is, how do we go to the next step? There are people who have made phenomenal contributions — Merton Miller, Franco Modigliani, William Sharpe, Myron Scholes, and Robert Merton, all Nobel laureates. But it's not going to end with their contributions. Other chapters will be written. Take the Copernican revolution as an analogy. I'm sure some philosophy professors will take me to task on this, but the framework for understanding shifts in theories, specifically scientific revolutions, was developed by Thomas Khun. The Khunian framework is: develop an idea, test it, put to one side facts that are counter to it, patch up the theory with band-aids, and then have new theories supersede old ones. And where are we right now? Well, we had a problem: capital markets theory came along to explain it, test it — it doesn't really work, it's a little fuzzy on the sides, and the finance professors are still patching it up. But eventually, I think, complex adaptive solutions will take over. That's my prediction. It's going to be complexity science.

The sad part about it is that the mathematics aren't as precise, and one of the reasons that all hard scientists are drawn to Newtonian physics is because it consists of equilibrium equations that can be solved with fancy mathematics. It's a fabulous use of probability calculus. However, the bad news about Complexity Theory is that the mathematics are much messier, meaning that sometimes you have either no solution or multiple equilibria. So, the question becomes, will you trade off this beautiful equilibrium-based theory for the messy, opaque one? Inevitability it's going to happen, as the mathematics are getting better. But you're right about the flaws in the current theory and CAPM. Eventually the whole system will be overturned, just as Copernicus changed astronomy and Einstein changed physics.

So, should undergraduate finance courses include a semester on philosophy of science?

Yes, they should. I don't get into philosophy of science at Columbia, but we still cover the sort of things that we are talking about. My whole argument is that when it comes to understanding markets and building models of them, you have to understand how ideas develop. There's a great book written by a Tufts professor, Philip Mirowski.[40] He traces a lot of these economics-as-physics issues back to Alfred Marshall.[41] There are some great Marshall quotes. For example, he suggested that markets are metaphors that we should be drawing up biologically. However, there are no good mathematics around for biological metaphors, hence we use physical metaphors or mathematics. So Marshall understood that it's a biological world. There's eventually going to be an evolution in the theory of capital markets. While economics is currently modeled on physics — Newtonian physics — it's only because that's where the mathematics works.

Taking the biological metaphor a step further, do Fibonacci numbers[42] therefore have a place in the investment world?

No, they don't.

Getting back to one of the earlier points about evolution and data, the developments in technology mean that there is now a huge data overload that people can't digest. We probably consume more data and think less. Is that also affecting the fundamental nature of markets?

Absolutely. I think that is why Buffett is such a successful investor — because of his ability to be rational. Buffett's ability to think about probabilities in everything that he does would account for a lot. And it's probably a function of his hard-wiring — most people aren't disciplined or structured enough to do it like he does. He thinks about everything in terms of probabilities. Everything.

And because emotions and perceptions drive markets, a rational and disciplined investor can consistently outperform?

Yes. Bubbles, crashes, and manias are subjects that hold a lot of interest for me. And this is where thinking about complex adaptive systems can be very useful. For example, take a group of people betting on a particular outcome. Provided their errors are independent — in other words, the way they make their mistakes is distinct from one another, separate — you will tend to get an answer very close to the correct answer. However, when errors become non-independent — when everyone starts to think the same way — that's when you get bubbles and manias. So, manias and bubbles tend to happen when errors become non-independent and everyone starts to think the same way.

Is the Internet an example of that at the moment?

It's not clear to me that the Internet is a bubble. There seem to be many people who are extremely bullish, as well as a whole group of people who are extremely bearish. So, it seems to me that there's a full ecology of investors interacting here. That's one point. But there is also another point about volatility. Treat this as a mental exercise. Use Amazon.com as an example. Imagine that Amazon.com, after the close of business one day, made two announcements. The first is that they would never get into a new business in the future. So, what you see in terms of the Amazon portfolio is what you get. They will do the best they can at managing the portfolio, but they'll never do anything new. The first question: What happens to the stock the next day? The second question: What happens to the subsequent volatility of

Amazon's stock? Typically, people believe the stock will go down. The finance point is that their real option value is getting marked to nil. So, what Amazon.com *could* have done to create value goes away. As for the second question, the volatility of the stock will decline. I think that this intuition can be supported. It is best explained by real options theory. A lot of the value in some Internet companies is based on their real options value. And the *observed* volatility of those stocks is as much a function of the real option value moving around as it is of the core business. Said differently, if we had no option value, the volatility would intuitively dampen, because options are a derivative of the underlying core business. Now, an Internet business is riskier than the average business, so risk is moving around and so is the option value. So I'm not sure if the volatility in Internet stock prices is either incorrect or inappropriate. But I do think that as Internet core businesses become better defined, the volatility is going to dampen. So I'm not sure that what we're seeing isn't about right.

Sir John Templeton[43] said that the four most dangerous words when it comes to investing are "this time it's different." In relation to Internet stocks, is he wrong?

I think that it *is* different every time, although some of the fundamentals are the same. But the point I always stress is that the curve that explains the diffusion of technology hasn't really changed. For example, when telephones were launched it was a diffusion curve. A few people started with them and then the take-up grew exponentially. Television, rail, steel, electricity were all the same too. But it was *fundamentally* different when we migrated from agrarian to industrial economics — clearly, things *were* different. You had specialization of tasks, you had much more efficient production, so you went from handcraft to line production and it was a very real, fundamental change. And then the second thing is that we have gone from the industrial age to the information age. And it goes back to the point I was making earlier: physical capital doesn't travel very well because it's a rival economic good. Knowledge, in contrast, is a non-rival economic good. So the way value is dispersed is very different. In every case, I think the underlying *diffusion* of technology is similar, but in every case there is something different underlying it.

Let's come back to complex adaptive systems. Is the criterion to get predictability or understanding? If you have predictability but no real understanding or theory behind it, have we really achieved anything?

I agree. We need to improve our *understanding* of the phenomenon, because just having a black box that is good at predicting price behavior isn't totally satisfying. What I have argued in particular is that complex adaptive systems are a better *descriptive* framework of the world today, but still not a predictive model. And maybe the mathematics will come along to allow it to be predictive. But in terms of the stock market, I don't know of any long-lasting predictive theories. But what you need to start with is a better descriptive theory, because once you have a better descriptive theory then you can work on it being predictive.

So, despite the existence of CAPM and other asset pricing models, we really only have a fairly crude *understanding* of the underlying phenomena?

True. And, unfortunately, that's the way it's likely to continue. Richard Thaler, who is regarded as the father of behavioral finance, has a simple exercise that underscores the fundamental indeterminacy that underlies economics. I do it in my class as well. You get a group of people together, and say, "Write a whole number, from zero to 100, on a piece of paper, and I'll pay $20 to the individual whose guess is closest to two-thirds of the average guess." The heuristic that tends to be used is zero to 100 averages fifty, two-thirds of fifty is thirty-three. Most people are smart enough to figure that out. So, two-thirds of thirty-three is twenty-two. Now what happens, and I've done this in my class at Columbia for five years, is the number one guess is always twenty-two, or two-thirds of thirty-three. The number two guess is typically thirty-three, and then you get all the random stuff. But the winning guess is always between thirteen and fifteen. If you're ever in this contest, always put thirteen. Thirteen is a good number to put down. And this is a good example of Keynes' quote about the stock market and beauty contests. The point isn't what *you* think the right answer is, it's about what you think the *other* participants think the right answer will be. Because the heuristic should be that you say to yourself, "How clever are my peers and how many iterations are they going to go through? If they're not very clever, they'll do one iteration. If they're clever they'll do two, and so on and so forth." And this goes back to the fundamental issue about markets and the behavior of crowds. It's also about the issue of the indeterminacy of economics insofar as you will never really know the answer.

At the other end of the spectrum, the coin tossing experiment[44] is an interesting one, as it can illustrate how perceptions of expertise can be incorrectly shaped because, as you mentioned earlier, success can be due to random or statistical outcomes rather than any great skill.

Correct. I do the coin tossing exercise in my class every year as well. I have sixty-five people on average, so statistically I'm going to get one over two to the power of six. So I'm going to get one student who calls five or six tosses correctly in a row. And I make it into a fun event. Every student is allowed to call the first four tosses. Then I ask, "Who got zero out of four?" I then suggest their future is driving a taxi cab. But the person who calls four out of four right is identified as a star. I typically suggest that the person is a "coin guru." But jokes aside, you want to be very slow to dismiss probability distributions when you think about successful investors. I think super-successful investors will fall into two camps. One will be the statistically lucky;

the other will be truly the "hard-wired to do well" group. Now, there's bad news on both fronts. Obviously, with the statistically lucky ones, there's nothing that they are doing that's exceptional; they just happen to be in the right place at the right time. However, the other guys have typically wonderful skill sets and hard-wiring, but their skill sets are largely nontransferable. So, it's not a very sanguine conclusion about money management.

What advice would you give to a novice analyst coming into this business?

I would say that successful security analysis requires an understanding of four basic dimensions. The first dimension is an understanding of capital markets: how prices are formed, market efficiency issues, what the market cares about, what it doesn't care about. For example, does the market care about earnings or cash? Why? So, that's all about fundamental risk and reward. The second dimension is the strategic issues: corporate strategy, value chains, and understanding how value is added and about increasing shareholder returns. So, having a really well-structured strategic framework is the second key thing. The third dimension is valuation. Understanding should cover the gamut of issues ranging from earnings multiples to very sophisticated DCF valuations. I would want to understand all the pros and cons of those methodologies. And the last dimension is the behavioral finance — basically, the issue of cognition and psychology. What are your biases going to be? What are the biases of the market going to be? If you have those four things down, then I think you'll be equipped to wade into the world of equities and be successful.

How important is humility?

Huge. Having been in this business for quite a while, I don't see how anybody can't be humble in this business. I believe that markets are very smart. My assumption has always been that the market understands, and I don't. Not the other way round — which is the usual way of thinking. So, if you're not wrong, and in some cases wrong big time, a number of times, then you're not in the game. Because everyone's proven to be wrong on things, big time. Moreover, a big ego is potentially a huge liability in this business, especially on the sell-side. And the investors that I've gotten to know and that I respect the most are the most humble because they've been around for so long. And for these types of people, it isn't about the money anymore. It's all about the whole game. The challenge. I think these people are very measured, controlled, and humble. I think this has a lot to do with a person's personality rather than anything else. And the other thing you have to be careful about, as I mentioned previously, is equating money with success. You can be successful in this business out of pure luck. It can make you very wealthy only because you were in the right place at the right time. So, you have to be careful about that, and I think a lot of the ego in the industry might come from people equating their money with being smart, and that's not necessarily accurate.

How do you judge success? What are the criteria?

Success is all about having an environment where you can continue to learn and where your mind can keep working. Success is also about demonstrating balance with personal matters — that is, family. The never-ending journey of security analysis is one of the things that intrigues me about it. I tell the young analysts, "Understand one thing — you'll never master this trade, because you have to be a great finance person, you have to understand markets, you have to understand psychology, you have to be able to write, you have to be able to talk. So you're always rolling that boulder up the hill, as the skill set required is huge." To be competent isn't that tough. But to be really exceptional in the required areas — well, there's always something to work on. And what's intriguing is that the markets are always dynamic and fluid, so you're always learning. You're always going to be taught lessons by the marketplace. So that's why you get these people who have been around forever — like Warren Buffett — who are continually energized because there's so much going on out there.

While the financial rewards in this business are a benchmark by which a lot of people judge success, to me it's all about having an environment where you can continue to learn. And that's what I get paid to do. I get paid to identify issues, learn about them, and teach others about them. The goal is to create wealth along the way, and in the business world where there are billions of dollars moving around, that's a very important activity.

❋ ❋ ❋

Michael Mauboussin's views on investing, valuation, and markets are as refreshing as they are challenging. Moreover, his emphasis on trying to overcome our innate biases — or hard-wiring, as he calls it — is perhaps one of the most important keys to successful investing. In a piece titled "What Have *You* Learned in the Past 2 Seconds?"[45] Mauboussin lists five key things that we should try to avoid when it comes to investing:

- **Don't irrationally escalate commitment to an initial course of action.** As sunk costs are irrelevant, your reference point should be the present. Consider only future costs and benefits.
- **Don't anchor judgments on irrelevant information, including historical prices or multiples.** The past is only a guide; change on the margin is critical.
- **Don't be overconfident.** Try not to overestimate your abilities. Weigh all potential outcomes with probabilities. Carefully consider both sides of any investment case.
- **Don't be overly influenced by how information is presented.** How a situation is framed can alter the choice. Be objective in weighing risk and reward.

- **Don't fall into the confirmation trap**. Try not to seek confirming information at the expense of non-confirming evidence. Be honest and objective.

Mauboussin argues that in order to overcome our behavioral and psychological limitations, we must first be aware of them. In essence, we should avoid simple traps such as extrapolating past trends or being overconfident, and not be overly influenced or swayed by how information is presented. However, like diets, these principles are simple in theory but very difficult in practice.

---

[1]   Many investors regard Ben Graham as the father of modern security analysis and value investing and Warren Buffett as his greatest pupil. Value investors take courage in the aphorism from the poet Horace that is cited by Ben Graham in the first edition of *Security Analysis* (1934): "Many shall be restored that are now fallen and many shall fall that now are in honor."

[2]   Warren Buffett is chairman and CEO of Berkshire Hathaway and is widely regarded as one of the globe's most astute investors. He is the third-wealthiest person in the United States, with an estimated net worth of US$31 billion.

[3]   "Frontiers of Finance: Mental Models for Market Outperformance," Michael J. Mauboussin, Credit Suisse First Boston, 1999.

[4]   Alfred Rappaport is professor emeritus at Northwestern University's Kellogg School of Business and author of the seminal work, *Creating Shareholder Value*.

[5]   Complex adaptive systems are used to explain phenomena that occur in the natural world, such as ant colonies, cell cultures, and the flocking behavior of birds. See "Shift Happens: On a New Paradigm of the Markets as a Complex Adaptive System," Michael J. Mauboussin, Credit Suisse First Boston, October 24, 1997, and "The Invisible Lead Steer: New Answers to Old Questions About the Stock Market," Michael J. Mauboussin, Credit Suisse First Boston, December 11, 1998.

[6]   Kellogg Company manufactures and markets breakfast cereal and other convenience food products. The company's products are marketed under brand names such as Kellogg's, Rice Krispies, Pop-Tarts, Eggo, and Nutra-Grain. At the time of writing, the company had a stock-market capitalization of US$14.2 billion.

[7]   "What Have *You* Learned in the Past 2 Seconds?" Michael J. Mauboussin, Credit Suisse First Boston, March 1997.

[8]   D. Kahneman and A. Tversky, "Prospect Theory: An Analysis of Decision Under Risk," *Econometrica*, 1979.

[9]   John Maynard Keynes (1883–1946) was one of the twentieth century's most influential thinkers and economists. His principal legacy was his book *The*

General Theory of Employment, Interest, and Money, as well as the international banking institutions, the International Monetary Fund and the World Bank, which were established as a result of the post-second World War Bretton Woods conference in the United States, which was dominated by the presence and works of Keynes.

10 Karl Popper was one of the twentieth century's great philosophers. George Soros, who met Popper in his final year at the London School of Economics, cites Popper's thinking and writings as among his earliest influences, especially his views on Scientific Method. Philosophy [according to Popper] "is a necessary activity because we take a great number of things for granted, and many of these assumptions are of a philosophical character; we act on them in private life, in politics, in our work, and in every other sphere of our lives — but while some of these assumptions are no doubt true, it is likely that more are false and some are harmful. So the critical examination of our presuppositions — which is a philosophical activity — is morally as well as intellectually important." In the preface to the 2nd edition of *Conjectures and Refutations* (Routledge, 1969), Popper wrote: "It is part of my thesis that all our knowledge grows only through the correcting of our mistakes."

11 Bill Miller runs the Legg Mason Value Trust, and in an era when most fund managers have had trouble performing in line with the S&P 500, Miller has beaten that benchmark every year since 1990. No other fund manager comes close. Through the 1990s the Legg Mason Value Trust has returned an annual growth rate of nearly 21%.

12 "Cash flow.com: Cash Economics in the New Economy," Michael J. Mauboussin, Credit Suisse First Boston, March 2, 1999.

13 Amazon.com, Inc., an online retailer, sell books, music, videotapes, audiotapes, and other products. The company offers a catalog of approximately three million titles, search and browse features, email services, personalized shopping services, Web-based credit card payment, and direct shipping to customers. At the time of writing, the company had a stock-market capitalization of US$23.3 billion.

14 Wal-Mart Stores, Inc. operates discount stores which offer merchandise such as apparel, housewares, small appliances, electronics, and hardware. At the time of writing, the company had a stock-market capitalization of US$256.6 billion.

15 "Cashflow.com: Cash Economics in the New Economy," Michael J. Mauboussin, Credit Suisse First Boston, March 2, 1999.

16 Real options apply traditional financial option theory to real investments such as plant, equipment, R&D expenditure, and technology newtworks. See "Get Real: Using Real Options in Security Analysis," Michael J. Mauboussin, Credit Suisse First Boston, June 23, 1999.

17 Geoffrey A. Moore, Paul Johnson, and Tom Kippola, *The Gorilla Game: An Investor's Guide to Picking Winners in High Technology* (HarperCollins, 1998).

18 Microsoft Corporation develops, manufactures, licenses, sells, and supports software products. At the time of writing, the company had a stock-market capitalization of US$474.9 billion.

19 "A Piece of the Action: Employee Stock Options in the New Economy," Michael J. Mauboussin, Credit Suisse First Boston, November 2, 1999.

[20] Earnings before interest, taxes, depreciation, and amortization.

[21] Barnes & Noble, Inc. operates superstores and mall-based bookstores throughout the U.S. At the time of writing, the company had a stock-market capitalization of US$1.1 billion.

[22] Robert G. Hagstrom Jr., *The Warren Buffett Portfolio: Mastering the Power of the Focus Investment Strategy* (John Wiley & Sons, 1999).

[23] Compaq Computer Corporation develops, manufactures, and distributes networking and communication products, commercial desktop and portable products, and consumer personal computers. At the time of writing, the company's stock-market capitalization was US$32 billion.

[24] Dell Computer Corporation designs, develops, manufactures, and directly sells standard and custom-specified computer systems that include desktop computer systems, notebook computers, workstations, and network server and storage products. At the time of writing, the company had a stock-market capitalization of US$105.5 billion.

[25] All State Insurance Group is a major U.S. casualty insurer.

[26] GEICO Corporation (acquired by Berkshire Hathaway in January 1996) is a multiple property and casualty insurer.

[27] DuPont analysis is a financial ratio system that decomposes the drivers of return on assets and the return on equity.

[28] E.I. du Pont de Nemours and Company is a global chemical and life sciences company. At the time of writing, the company had a stock-market capitalization of US$50.6 billion.

[29] Enterprise value is defined as a company's market capitalization plus the market value of its debt less cash plus long-term liabilities plus deferred tax plus minority interests.

[30] Discounted cash flow, which is the net present value of the future cash flows discounted at an appropriate hurdle rate.

[31] James K. Glassman and Kevin A. Hassett, *Dow 36,000: The New Strategy for Profiting from the Coming Rise in the Stock Market* (Times Books, 1999).

[32] The capital asset pricing model is one of the cornerstones of modern finance and portfolio theory. It is a linear equation based on the premise that investors are risk averse, returns are normally distributed, and if two portfolios have the same risk (as measured by the expected variance in returns), investors will prefer the portfolio with the higher returns.

[33] The Gaussian distribution, also referred to as a normal distribution or bell-shaped curve, was named after the German mathematician Carl Freidrich Gauss (1777–1855). The Gaussian distribution has some special mathematical properties that form the basis of many statistical tests. Although no data ever follows the mathematical ideal, many types of data follow a distribution that is approximately Gaussian. Of note is the fact that Gauss made a systematic study of the financial news of the day, and he was able to gain a considerable fortune through his dealings on the stock exchange. He died a very wealthy man.

[34] Meta, derived from the Greek, means outside or beyond. The market as a "Meta System" is discussed in "The Invisible Lead Steer: New Answers to Old Questions about the Stock Market," Michael J. Mauboussin, Credit Suisse First Boston, December 11, 1998.

[35] The idea behind a canon is that a musical theme is played against itself. In a canon for three voices, for example, each note of the theme must act in two distinct harmonic ways as well as melodically. Nursery rhymes like "Three Blind Mice," when sung in rounds are examples of simple musical canons. Thus, each note in the canon has more than one musical meaning, and the listener ultimately works out the meaning of the voice according to its context. J.S. Bach perfected the art of the canon and fugue. D.R. Hofstadter's Pulitzer Prize-winning book, *Godel, Escher, Bach: An Eternal Gold Braid* (Penguin, 1979), explores the nature of human thought processes, and links the music of J.S. Bach, the art of Escher, and the mathematical theorems of Godel together with ideas from logic, biology, psychology, physics, and linguistics. For an interesting discussion on musical allegory and analogies and financial markets, see Chapter 14 of Victor Niederhoffer, *The Education of a Speculator* (John Wiley, 1997). For example, Neiderhoffer likens the mathematics underscoring Bach's six-part fugue in the Musical Offering to "be on a par with that of the greatest options and spread traders I have had the privilege of knowing."

[36] Commonly known as "the straw that broke the camel's back." Avalanches, for example, are often caused by the accumulation of small amounts of snow. See "Shift Happens: On a New Paradigm of Markets as a Complex Adaptive System," Michael J. Mauboussin, Credit Suisse First Boston, October 24, 1997.

[37] The beta of a stock is a measure of its relative risk. It is the covariance of a stock's price with the market index, and is standardized by dividing by the market variance. A stock with a beta of 1.0 would be expected to move in line with the market, whereas a stock with a beta higher than 1.0 would be expected to rise or fall at a greater rate than the market.

[38] E.F. Fama and K.R. French, "The Cross-Section of Expected Returns," *Journal of Finance*, Vol. 47, pp. 427–66.

[39] "Shift Happens: On a New Paradigm of Markets as a Complex Adaptive System," Michael J. Mauboussin, Credit Suisse First Boston, October 24, 1997.

[40] *More Heat than Light: Economics as Social Physics: Physics as Nature's Economics* (Cambridge University Press, 1992).

[41] Alfred Marshall (1842–1924) was one of the twentieth century's most influential economists. His chief work is *Principles of Economics*, published in 1890, and is still today a standard textbook. Marshall employed his mathematics background and training to develop and refine microeconomic theory. He clarified the concepts of value, utility, and consumer surplus, and was responsible for introducing the now widely accepted concept of elasticity. A leading figure in the development of modern economic theory in his own right, Marshall also encouraged and influenced Keynes.

[42] Fibonacci numbers are named after the Italian mathematician Leonardo Pisano Fibonacci. A Fibonacci sequence consists of the numbers 1, 1, 2, 3, 5, 8, 13, 21, …, each of which is the sum of the two previous numbers. Fibonacci numbers are of great interest to mathematicians, biologists, scientists, and even stock-market technicians, and have been found to occur in nature and in stock price data. For example, the spirals on seashells follow a Fibonacci sequence, as do petals on flowers and the arrangement of seeds on flowerheads. Moreover, if two

successive numbers in Fibonacci's series (1, 1, 2, 3, 5, 8, 13, ...) are divided by the number before it, the following series of numbers results: $1/1 = 1$, $2/1 = 2$, $3/2 = 1·5$, $5/3 = 1·666$ ..., $8/5 = 1·6$, $13/8 = 1·625$, $21/13 = 1·61538$. The golden ratio $1·618034$ is also called the golden section, or the golden mean, or just the golden number. It is often represented by a Greek letter, phi, and has been used to design many buildings, from the Parthenon in Athens (400 BC) to the United Nations building in New York. It was known to artists such as Leonardo da Vinci and to composers like Bartok, Bach, and Beethoven, and to the violin maker Stradivari.

[43] Sir John Templeton, who founded the Templeton organization, is widely regarded as one of the pioneers of global investing.

[44] Take a group of people, and ask them all to stand up and toss a coin. Those who toss heads have to sit down. In a group of 100 people, for example, it would take anywhere from six to eight tosses before only one person is left standing.

[45] "What Have *You* Learned in the Past 2 Seconds?: Why Hunting and Gathering Comes Naturally — and Successful Investing Does Not," Michael J. Mauboussin, Credit Suisse First Boston, March 14, 1997.

10

Joe Petch:
Asian Values

"In Asia, being technically good isn't adequate. You have to understand the political issues, you have to understand the relationship between companies, and you have to understand how people do business here."

With over fourteen years' experience covering Asian markets, Joe Petch, currently head of Hong Kong research at ING Barings, is one of Asia's most experienced and respected analysts. Few analysts have Petch's depth and range of experience, having headed research teams in most of Asia's key markets — Hong Kong, Singapore, Malaysia, Indonesia, and South Korea. Formerly a number-one-rated analyst for Indonesia and a top five All Asian analyst, Petch established the highly rated South Korean research team at Dongbang Peregrine. During his time in Asia, Petch has seen many changes in equity research and investment philosophies, and, despite the nuances and subtleties involved in emerging market equities research, he still tries to combine the best of developed market analytical techniques and thinking with local knowledge of the emerging markets. While Petch acknowledges the role of proper analysis and valuation techniques in investing, he is acutely aware that understanding the unique political and cultural issues that influence Asia's stock markets is an important part of successful investing. In Petch's view, technical excellence isn't sufficient; it's also necessary to understand how companies do business in Asia.

What attracted you to the equities business?

I think it goes back to my university days. I've always had an interest in economics and companies and, having an inquiring mind, I like to know how companies work, and how that relates to broader industry structures and economies. Moreover, I've always wanted to challenge different perspectives on things and to understand the link between the macro and the micro, so the stock market naturally held a lot of appeal.

And making money from those efforts?

Money wasn't one of the great motivators.

I meant more from the perspective of creating wealth for people as a result of your efforts.

Yes. I think that with this business, if you do make a good recommendation, you can see the tangible results of what your efforts are and that's very important. A lot of people's jobs are so detached from the end result that it's actually quite alienating and consequently there isn't a great deal of job satisfaction. But in this business, you can see results. That wasn't something I was aware of before I went into the industry.

Why are you on the sell-side, as opposed to the buy-side?

I think the buy-side is easier in the sense that you are fed with a considerable amount of information and analysis. I think you deal with things at a much higher level than you do if you're on the sell-side, and I think that goes back to what I was saying earlier — that the initial motivation was really to understand things, and not have to accept the conventional wisdom. Getting to the heart of an issue is what interests me. However, when you are on the buy-side, you just don't have the time. You've got a wide variety of markets or sectors to look at, and therefore you can only deal with things at a relatively high level.

What is the hardest part of the job?

I think, over time, it's just keeping the motivation up, but I think that is a function of being in any job over a long period of time. I've been lucky in the sense that I have worked in a number of different markets, which has helped to sustain my interest. However, I think it's also important to stick with a sector or a specific industry over the longer term. The hardest part of the job is disciplining yourself, because there is no end to the job. At the end of the working day, you can't just leave and say, "Okay, it's over." There are always projects that have to be managed. So, it really comes down to managing your time and ensuring that you meet the deadlines, because this industry is so time-sensitive that if you don't complete things within a certain period of time, they become stale and lose their significance.

The job isn't glamorous?

Despite the popular perception that broking is a glamorous occupation, research isn't, as it involves a considerable amount of grunt work. But while you can see the product of your work, in the sense that you get orders from clients, it's quite rare that you get a tremendous sense of satisfaction out of making a very good call, because a lot of the job is just maintenance — keeping salespeople aware of what's going on, visiting companies with or without clients, calling clients to keep them up to date. It's only very occasionally that you are way ahead of the market in terms of making a call and everything goes right. There is a lot of mundane work, and keeping the excitement and motivation there is the hard part.

What are the challenging things about analyzing companies in emerging markets compared to developed markets?

I think it comes down to disclosure of information and whether or not you believe the information you are given. I'm reminded of a story that I was told when I was in Indonesia, about a cigarette company that was having a regular review with its main banker. The accounts appeared to show that the company was in a sound financial state, and the meeting went smoothly until the banker asked where the loan from his bank was reflected in the company accounts. It turned out that he had been given the wrong set of accounts! I understand that the bank later withdrew its loan, but it was replaced by another loan from a syndicate led by a leading U.S. bank. The cigarette company later ran into financial difficulties and certain irregular practices were revealed. It turned out to be one of Indonesia's major financial scandals of the early 1990s.

If you look across Asia, the level of disclosure varies considerably. I would say it's probably best in places like Korea and Malaysia, where you can get quite a lot of information — particularly in Korea, where you can get industry information. However, it is appalling in Hong Kong, as industry associations and individual companies here are very reluctant to give you information. When you've got poor disclosure, your relationships with the companies then become more important. People value that much more, whereas in developed markets, because the disclosure is better, you can apply your analytical skills in a better way. For example, research in Asia is very descriptive — traditionally, it has been very descriptive — and the difference between analysts has been whether you can provide a bit more of an inside track on something and get ahead of the game in terms of getting information. So, relationships here are much more important. It was only when the U.S. houses set up here, leveraging off their sector knowledge from the more developed markets, and when the technical industries started to grow, telecommunications being a classic, infrastructure being another, that analysts had to have a much keener understanding of how their industries worked.

There is only so much you can write about a prawn farmer in Indonesia?

Absolutely.

Do you think that if you are a good analyst in, say, a developed market, you'll be a good analyst in an emerging market?

I think it's easier to come into Asia as a good analyst and fit in quite well. But what you've got to be aware of is that, in Asia, being technically good isn't adequate. You have to understand the political issues, you have to understand the relationships between companies and politicians, and you have to understand how people do business here, which is very different from how management is in developed markets, where there is largely independence of management. By contrast, in Asia, there are many examples where major shareholders are actively involved in the day-to-day management of their businesses. I remember when I first came to Hong Kong and worked for an up-and-coming broker, Crosby Securities. We were involved in the listing of Sime Darby Hong Kong, which was engaged in the distribution of cars and heavy equipment, as well as trading in Hong Kong. It was a well-managed company with a good business, but the perception of its parent in Malaysia was very negative — it was seen as being controlled by the government and lacking independence. We, or rather our sub-underwriters, ended up with a substantial portion of the issue. Ironically, Sime Darby became the darling of the market when Malaysia enjoyed a boom in the late 1980s and 1990s.

So, the fundamental issues and goals are different?

Yes, shareholder/managers have different motivations. I think they are willing to accept lower rates of return, for example, because they are actually the owners of the business, so that there isn't the kind of pressure on companies here to generate the types of returns that you would get in more developed markets. There have been some very good analysts, for example, who have gone into countries and failed to understand the politics. Politics is so much about which stock is going to get promoted, how it's going to be restructured, and who is going to benefit from the restructuring and the subsequent asset injections. New analysts to these markets haven't always understood that, and have made some very bad calls as a result. But if you are an analyst going from Asia into the developed markets, I don't think you have the kind of skill set that is going to make you differentiate or compete, because that hasn't been the tradition of analysis here in Asia. Innovations have been introduced from the West, in particular the United States, with the increased presence of the major U.S. brokerages and their emphasis on sectoral research.

With over fourteen years in Asian equity research, how would you describe the progress in sell-side analysis then?

It has come a long way, but previously it was very superficial. You were basically providing information, you weren't providing analysis. I remember going for an interview with a regional head of research who bragged that they would send a team into somewhere like Indonesia, who would spend a week going around visiting companies. They would then spend a week writing up the research and completing their models. They would have a book on the whole country published within another week. That shows you how superficial the analysis was in the early stages when these markets were first developing. Salespeople used to get calls from clients saying, "Well, if you can spell the company's name correctly, I'll give you the order." That's how poor it was. But I think, again, it goes back to the fact that the U.S. houses have really come in here and raised the standard, particularly with respect to understanding highly technical sectors, such as telecommunications, and the introduction of more sophisticated valuation techniques.

Are there any areas that still require further development?

Where we have got light years to go, is that we are still just focusing on investment analysis. In the developed markets it is moving, shifting more toward strategic analysis and understanding the dynamics of how industry works and how that interrelates with the strategy of the management, and how that affects the P&L, balance sheets, cash flows, and everything else. That isn't really happening here in a coherent way. The other thing is that you've got some techniques that are being brought over, like EVA,[1] but no-one in Asia is really applying them properly because there are very few people who are actually forecasting over an entire price or investment cycle. They are still stuck with their arbitrary three- to five-year forecasts and are then saying, "In that period it is showing positive EVA. That sort of supports a PER[2] of X and that makes the stock a strong buy." Now, that sort of interrelationship doesn't make sense. The cost of capital is another area, with conglomerate analysts still valuing divisions using the group cost of equity. And while analysts in Asia are getting excited by EVA, U.S. research firms are already using real options, a technique that the corporate finance departments of corporates have been using for twenty, thirty years now, which illustrates generally how far the industry is behind the curve.

That's the future — could we can talk a bit about the past? Where were you during the crash of 1987?

I was in Singapore.

What were your thoughts back then?

We all thought it was a great buying opportunity. But that was a big mistake, because we were sitting there looking at companies and saying, "Well, nothing has fundamentally changed." But we completely misunderstood the kinds of pressure our clients were under. They were getting redemptions. They wanted to be told what they should sell and get out of, what was going to fall further or underperform. That's all they wanted to know. It was more, "How do we realize cash?" than being told, "This is a great buying opportunity." They didn't want to be told that Asia was fine and therefore they should be using this time to get in. They couldn't do that.

What about Tiananmen Square in June 1989? Where were you when that happened, and what was your reaction?

I was in Hong Kong. I think people got very emotional about it. The problem with Tiananmen was that the international press were there, and CNN and everybody played it up very much. I think people in Hong Kong could see that the students really weren't achieving very much.

So, another great buying opportunity?

Another great buying opportunity. Because, fundamentally, nothing had really changed. But the international press really blew it up out of proportion and everyone got very emotional. I later worked for Peregrine who, under the leadership of Philip Tose, capitalized on the state of depression that enveloped Hong Kong at the time — even amongst the tycoons. Philip showed greater vision by opportunistically buying a stake in Kwang Song Hong, a listed property company, from Li Ka-shing. The profit that was subsequently made from trading property through that vehicle was instrumental in building up the capital base of Peregrine, which became the largest Asian investment bank outside Japan. Peregrine later collapsed, a victim of the Asian crisis, but that's another story.

In contrast, would it be fair to say that Indonesia is arguably not a great buying opportunity at the moment?

I think Indonesia is something different again. Indonesia has a structurally unsound economy, in the sense that you have an ethnic minority that, in collusion with the ruling elite, has pillaged that country of its wealth for a long time. Everyone looks at cronyism and associates it just with the First Family. They got rid of the First Family, but they forget about the rest of it. So, I think there is a deeper issue there in Indonesia. The thing with Suharto is that he concentrated power so much on himself that there weren't the institutions to support his legacy. People were very fearful that if he went, there would be a complete collapse because there was no democratic means of transferring power. There were no institutions that could ensure stability once he was removed. All they did was replace him with Habibie, who carried on in the same sort of vein. The election of Wahid is an interesting turning point. We will have to see if he can radically overhaul the existing institutions to achieve true democracy and encourage the development of an indigenous, Muslim entrepreneurial class, which is necessary for self-sustaining growth to be achieved.

A lot of people talk about value investing, but given that the focus in Asia is so short-term, is it still possible to take a value investment approach to a country like Indonesia, for example?

I think it's very difficult, because you've got to be able to realize that value over the longer term. Prices may be cheap at the moment and Indonesia may rally, but it will be a liquidity-driven rally as people take a view on the market, a view on Asia, and some of it may fit in. But for me, value investing is that you are actually going to see structural changes that make something intrinsically worth much more over the longer term. The problem with Indonesia is that the same people that have run the country or stripped the country of its wealth are still in control. However, if you said to me that there is a new entrepreneurial class developing in Indonesia from the middle class, and that it is taking over control and running businesses, independent of ownership, and applying some of the more modern management techniques, that would say to me that there is a fundamental change going on and so it's probably worth buying into

as you will probably see that value being realized. Examples would
be if we saw investment going into education, or into raising the
productivity of people. But if you said to me that future policy is to
try and stabilize the situation with the same companies run by the
same people that have extracted so much wealth, and who are
notorious and ruthless accumulators of capital rather than re-
investors in what should be long-term sustainable growth, then I
think you're not a value investor.

**What was behind your decision to leave Indonesia? Did you
make an unpopular call on a stock?**

My departure was more about what we, rather naively, at the time
thought was integrity. It all stemmed from an issue concerning
minority shareholders' rights.

What was the stock?

The popular view was that it was Plaza Indonesia,[3] but it wasn't; it
was actually an automotive component manufacturer. What it was
really about was, the stock exchange in Indonesia was run by what I
would say were some very enlightened people. They were trying to
gauge foreign opinion about how they could develop and move the
stock market forward and make it more attractive to foreign
investors. One of the issues was protection of minority interests. We
highlighted in our research a number of situations where a particular
group was abusing minority interests. For example, a listed company
acquired a loss-making company from its parent company at an
inflated price, justified by a projected turnaround in the business.
The turnaround didn't materialize and no action was ever taken. This
obviously upset the majority shareholder, and pressure was therefore
put on the company I was working for at that time to have me
removed, and then I was advised to leave. By way of contrast, there
were no repercussions as a result of the "do not subscribe" we put on
the first privatization in Indonesia, which was Semen Gresik.[4] The

stock price collapsed subsequent to listing, as it became apparent the company wouldn't achieve the numbers projected at the time of listing.

Why were you so negative?

Basically, because we didn't think the profits were likely to be achieved. The Ministry of Finance was possibly upset about that, but no pressure was exerted in that situation. But when you start to get involved with powerful, private shareholders, it's a different issue.

What was your best call, and what did you learn from it?

I think my best call was in fact the "do not subscribe" recommendation on Semen Gresik. What did I learn from it? From my skeptical point of view, I learned that in those situations, in those types of markets, investors don't care, as there is too much of a vested interest in making the issue succeed. We got lambasted for that call. And with an IPO, where there is so much vested interest in making things go well and succeed, in those situations, people just weren't prepared to pay attention to the fundamentals. The lesson from that is that, from an analytical perspective, you must always do your homework. For example, the company was embarking upon a major expansion and we visited the site and talked to middle management and learned that the new capacity was unlikely to be commissioned on time. We had learned from prior problems with the listing of a cigarette manufacturer, where we placed our faith in what senior management was telling us, rather than in what we heard from independent sources. The company had raised prices dramatically just before the listing but insisted there would be no impact on sales because they hadn't gone through the consumers' price sensitivity thresholds. Current sales data were also withheld from the market, and subsequent to the listing it became apparent that sales volumes had collapsed and profits were going to fall well short of projections. The company also used part of the proceeds from listing to buy land for property development rather than invest in plant, which didn't help sentiment either. I received an anonymous letter pertaining to this from employees, complaining about funds being siphoned from the company, jeopardizing its future, and asking for us to investigate the matter and reveal what was going on. However, the company hired an expatriate investor relations manager and subsequently became the darling of the market, helped also by a recovery in earnings.

In light of your experiences, and the traps out there, what are the qualities that you look for in an analyst?

Well, let's set aside the qualifications. Let's talk about the actual interview process. I want someone who is going to come in and present to me. I don't want someone who is going to come in and wait to be asked a whole series of questions. I ask questions basically to clarify points, to really try and understand whether the person knows what they are talking about or are just winging it. You want someone to come in and say, "Right, I'm here to sell myself," but at the same time I don't want a hard sell. I want someone who says, "I want to tell you about me and what my skill sets are, how I think about the world, and explain my processes to you. This is my analytical framework. This is how I start to project things. This is how I run my models. This is how I think about the world." And you want someone who has some originality of thought and has some new ideas about ways of looking at things.

But a lot of people have new ideas that can't be implemented, or are so difficult, or the timing is so tricky that you can't make money from them.

Yes, that's true, but you want someone who is commercial. They've got to be commercial. The other thing is that you want someone — and this is why I think it is important that people go in and present themselves — you are looking for somebody who is relatively hungry about getting on with the job, and who is going to persevere, because getting information out of companies is really hard. So, you want someone who has drive and initiative, and who isn't just going to sit back and wait for things to fall in their lap.

How would you balance the criteria? If there are three or four things that you need — say, first, good models; second, an ability to pick stocks; third, be able to market; and fourth, be able to write decent reports — how would you rank those, in terms of importance?

I think they are all related, but as there is a growing tendency amongst the bigger institutions to have their analysts make their own stock calls, the stock calls aren't number one. But as institutions probably cover such a large number of markets, they want an analyst to be able to give an insight into the dynamics of the industry, the regulatory environment, the structural changes that are going on, so that they can have a framework. So you refine their screening process for them, but ultimately it's the funds that actually make the stock picks. Those people who are more portfolio managers, be they global or regional, will value analysts for their stock ideas and company contacts. In Asia, I still feel that they value more the inside track than they do whether or not you can explain to them the underlying technology.

Is it more important to be right, or to be logical?

Both, but I suspect, at the end of the day, I would say it's better to be logical. I don't think it's necessary to be right. I think you've got to be *consistent* and it's a matter of people trusting your opinions and views on things. Credibility. For example, fund managers ultimately take responsibility for their own decisions, but if all they did was rely on analysts for their stock picking ability, then it's hard to see how fund managers are adding value for their clients. I think that if you've been logical and consistent and they accept your argument, then you have served them as best you can. If they go and make the investment and something goes wrong and they come back and say, "The stock price has gone down 20%, and it's your fault," well, yes, you presented them with the information, but ultimately they made the decision to invest.

What do you think are the most popular misconceptions about the job of a sell-side analyst?

I think that basically people see it as a very glamorous job, particularly in Asia. It's a job people like to aspire to, because the financial markets have status. However, I think people don't appreciate that the work is very hard and it's actually not as glamorous as it's perceived to be. There's a lot of grind. Going back to the points we discussed earlier, you have to collate, analyze, produce, and market. And that's why a lot of people cut corners, because they're not prepared to put in the effort to go and get all that information. What they will do is visit a company and then say, "All right, this company is prepared to give me this amount of information. That's how I'm going to build my model." Instead, they should be asking, "How do I build the *best* model?" and then try and get all the right information, which may take a year or so. So, there is that side of it. People tend to think it's a glamorous job and it's easy.

The other misconception is that I don't think people understand how the job is changing. It's not just about analyzing companies; marketing is very much more important these days. The salesperson is no longer the principal person conveying information. They are more involved in relationship management and various other things. So, the skill set is much broader than I think people really appreciate. Plus there is the other side of it, which is getting involved in the corporate finance business. But in summary, people come into this industry saying, "I've got my financial accounting skills, I'm now qualified to be an analyst." What they really should be saying is, "Do I really understand any industry in depth?" And that's why I encourage people to spend some time working in industry as a marketer, or in operations or operational planning, or whatever. First get involved in the industry you plan to cover.

How important is stability?

Very important. People like to switch around sectors because something gets bigger, they get bored with it because their attention span is too short, the industry goes into decline, or various other things. What you tend to have here are people with very limited periods of time covering a sector. In the U.S. by contrast, they may be doing it for ten or twenty years, but people just don't stick at it here. Plus, as research is hard work and people tend to underestimate that, their objective is to migrate over to the buy-side because they see that as being easier. And it's viewed as being just as glamorous, because they are still in the financial markets. If you are going to get into this industry and be taken seriously by the major global institutions in the future, first go and work in the industry that you want to cover and then come in and work in the financial markets covering that sector for the longer term.

There are some major trends happening that are also worth considering. For example, there is globalization. I think if you come in and say you want to be a country analyst sitting in Thailand or Indonesia, that's limited. You have to think much more about being in a sector, or being part of a sector or regional team. We're going to see far more integration in research in the future, and it's more likely that analysts will be part of a sector team on a regional or global basis. If you have ambition, you won't want to be working in one sector in one country. You have to think about that in the broader sense.

You spoke about the increase in corporate finance work that analysts have to contend with. Is it a threat to research objectivity?

The big U.S. houses have consciously made a decision to become more corporate finance-driven, and I think most of the big global houses are saying that they can't make money in secondary broking, which I don't believe to be true in all cases. We may see a rise in boutique research houses as a result of this trend, but I think we will also see that the better and more objective analysts will go over to the buy-side. I think objectivity has been such a problem because there haven't been any analysts of sufficient stature in the past actually driving the corporate finance deals. It's always corporate financiers coming to analysts and saying, "Right, come up with a positive slant on this." I think where you might start to see some change is, as analysts become more authoritative, they'll be the ones that start to identify the deals and drive the corporate finance departments, so you're not necessarily going to get that conflict that has arisen in the past.

Are analytical skills starting to improve at an increasing rate?

Not really, because you've still got huge funds flowing in, and more money is going international and consequently, more money is coming into Asia. And the flow of funds ultimately determines things — that has been a much more important factor. Therefore, people haven't had to bother about the skills behind those investments, but it's now starting to happen. I think that the entry of the U.S. houses has made quite a considerable difference to the level of professionalism, but the quality of the work that analysts have to do still has a long, long way to go. I don't think it will be an internal dynamic within Asia that will change that. I think the transfer of expertise is still happening. If you look at some of the U.S. houses, they have their valuation models that they developed in the U.S., they've transferred them here and refined them, but you don't see much indigenous R&D going on in Asia itself and people coming out and saying, "This is how we value XYZ in the emerging markets context." Furthermore, I think we need to address the issue of cost of capital in Asia, because in emerging markets the whole issue of cost of capital is a much more difficult concept. But you don't see cost of capital being researched and analyzed, or people thinking about it. They just use the techniques that have been developed in the West. As I said before, the buy-side could do more to exert pressure to raise standards, but they would have to upgrade themselves first. Even some of the institutions with their own research capabilities are deficient in their analytical techniques. This has been graphically illustrated by the Asian crisis, and the fact that their past performance has been flattered by the huge liquidity inflows into Asia.

How do you classify Hong Kong as a market?

Hong Kong is property and banks, but what it has in common with emerging markets is that disclosure of information is pretty poor.

Do emerging markets lend themselves to a bottom-up or top-down approach, or a combination?

I think top-down is important if you are talking about a situation where you have huge liquidity flows playing around the region. Where it becomes more interesting is when those factors are less significant — then, you have to start really searching for good companies. I think what is going to happen in Asia as a result of the crisis is that, as there are a lot of dynamics, foreign investors are probably benchmarking themselves more and it's therefore becoming more of a top-down call than it was previously. Moreover, they are farming out a smaller proportion of their portfolios to specific stock picks. But I think from an analyst's perspective, the credibility of management has been undermined by this crisis. They were given cheap money, so they basically went in and invested it, in low-return/high-risk assets. So, people are going to be much more careful about management, how companies are managed, and what strategies they are adopting. So, if you are in Asia, analyzing Asia, you have to be able to justify the argument for an investment from a much more bottom-up approach. Whether people invest on that basis, however, is irrelevant, as I suspect it is increasingly going to be from the top down.

What are your views on analyst polls and quarterly performance measurement for funds? Five years is probably a good time frame for assessing a company's management, and likewise probably a fund manager.

Yes. I rated number one in Indonesia a year after I left the country! So what does that tell you! I think polls are subject to too much manipulation. They are not very sophisticated in the way they are compiled. They are arbitrary, subjective, and not very scientific in the way they are put together. They are marketing tools and hype. Quarterly performance for funds? I think this preoccupation is a big danger for the industry, because it's having an impact on the quality of analysis behind the investment decisions and is bringing in other factors that are seen as being more important than whether something is a good fundamental buy. So, it's an influence that has potentially negative implications for the longer-term performance of the business. Moreover, it puts enormous pressure on people which is largely to the detriment of good decision-making.

The media has also changed the nature of investing, arguably because they contribute to volatility and this makes intelligent investing even harder.

Yes. There is so much information about that you get inundated with it and don't have enough time to properly interpret it. There are classic examples where retail investors will react to the news or white noise. It will drive stock prices, but be completely meaningless. So, yes, we are in the information age and everyone has all this information, but how do you sift through it and make sense of it on a timely basis so that you can advise your clients appropriately?

We consume more information but think less?

Absolutely. What tends to happen is there is a gut reaction to a piece of news, a stock price moves, and it becomes completely inappropriate. Analysts need to recognize this and the fact that their job, as it has traditionally been defined, only contributes to this information overload. Consequently, there is a need to focus on providing investors with the tools to screen information, diagnose forecasts, and assimilate the most important information so that they can make an informed decision quickly.

I suppose the flip side is that for value investors, that's really a great opportunity, because it means that the gap between price and value will continue to widen as prices will be driven more by sentiment than by long-term, considered analysis.

Yes. When you put a combination of those factors together — quarterly performance and benchmarking — yes, that will happen. But I also think that the great danger you are faced with is that there are now other factors that are driving stock prices but which bear no relationship to fundamentals. So what you end up doing is asking yourself how do you actually assess that. And you then get caught out when trying to make your call. You can say something's worth this, but people may see a bit of news and the market then gets excited. For example, recently market speculation was that the company Hutchison[5] was going to make a big-hit acquisition. They were raising money, and that got into the press and the stock price traded up to a significant premium. And yet nothing has happened! You can really get caught out following short-term sentiment.

Do you think that risk is greater in emerging markets than in developed markets, or is the gap narrowing?

Well, you've got Internet stocks in the U.S., but the distinction between emerging markets and developing markets is going to be eroded because there are new industries out there — technology, in particular, where the dynamism, the rate of change that is going on, is phenomenal. If you define emerging markets not only by their immaturity in terms of structure, but also in terms of their rates of growth, then you are getting those types of features in developed markets in certain industry sectors as well. So, the distinction is becoming much more blurred because the impact of technology is so dramatic.

What are still the great emerging markets? China, India?

Yes, those two have got to be. They have to go through major structural change for that potential to be realized, though.

In the case of China, is it a continuation of the thesis that communism doesn't work; therefore, as democracy grows and communism falls away, income levels will rise, adding to stock-market capitalization and GDP, and that education, infrastructure, television, telecommunications, etc. — all those things will become more in demand? Is that still a valid macro theme?

Well, I don't know whether it is democratization, because I don't know that a democracy really exists anywhere. I think it's just a matter of unleashing the full productive potential of people. However you want to achieve that.

Maybe "capitalism" is a better term.

Yes, capitalism rather than democracy. But I think there are different constraints on that happening in places like India and China.

But as imperfect a model as capitalism is, people realize it's probably one of the better models to emulate.

I agree. What communism has achieved in China, however, is to ensure that everyone has had a reasonable basic standard of living. To improve upon that standard of living, there have to be significant changes in the model that they have adopted which will unleash, not so much the entrepreneurialism but the dynamism of what people actually have, the work ethic, and everything else. You are going to have to have change.

What do you think is the most common mistake made by the average person when it comes to investing?

Unless they have inside information, a common pitfall is to think that they know more than the market. If you believe a stock is fundamentally undervalued or overvalued, understand why the market hasn't already discounted what you believe are the reasons for this mispricing. If the market is either missing or misinterpreting something of significance, then invest.

What advice would you give the average investor when it comes to investing in emerging markets?

If you can, meet the shareholders (or at least talk to someone who has) and try to understand their rationale for being a listed company and gauge the extent to which management is independent. Most companies in emerging markets are still family-controlled, and there is little understanding of the obligations of being a listed company or of minority shareholders' rights or interests. Most shareholders and managers still believe that capital raised from the stock market is free and, therefore, they are insufficiently concerned with returns.

What do you think of charts?

I had the privilege of working with a very competent chartist early in my career and was impressed by the power of technical analysis. However, I don't use them except for identifying trading opportunities and fine-tuning the timing of a recommendation.

Finally, what advice would you give to someone considering a career in this industry?

People come into this business for different reasons and with different things they want to get out of it. I probably fell into it by accident, more than by design. My advice goes back to the sorts of things that I expect from an analyst. I think that if you really want to come into this business, you should spend some time in commerce or the real world, get that experience, because I think that it's a very good foundation to come in on. It's a matter of getting all the prerequisite skills. It's not adequate to do an MBA or a CFA. You've got to really have some proper accounting and financial analytical skills or industry expertise. I think that the industry is going to shift more toward understanding the concepts of strategic analysis. It's a matter of arming yourself with the right types of skill sets, because it's all about differentiation. We're going to see further consolidation in the industry, so it's going to be increasingly difficult to get a job with the right types of companies. The threshold is being raised. In the past, expatriates have turned up in Hong Kong and have just walked into jobs. That's not going to happen anymore, because Asians are far better educated and far harder working. The idea that you can just walk into a job, whether you are local or foreign, is evaporating. So, in order to be successful, it's a matter of arming yourself with the right skills set.

Joe Petch's experiences and views complement those of Mark Mobius — that is, they provide the sell-side view of the risks and issues that should be considered when investing in emerging markets. Moreover, Petch's approach to analysis and investing is likely to be of most interest to people just starting out in their careers. The key elements of Petch's philosophy are:

- Don't always accept conventional wisdom, and be prepared to challenge the consensus view.
- Know your strengths and play to them, and take a disciplined approach toward developing a deep understanding of your sector. Don't get distracted by other sectors, as longevity and experience in a particular sector is rare and highly valued by the market.
- Being technically good isn't sufficient; no matter how numerous or good your qualifications are, there is no substitute for industry experience or knowledge. Moreover, understand how companies do business in Asia in the context of the local political environment.
- Develop strategic analysis skills and an understanding of the dynamics of how industry works, and of how that affects financial performance and, ultimately, valuation.
- Value investing is difficult as Asian stock markets have traditionally been driven by a combination of leverage and growth, with little value-added from management. However, try to identify structural changes that are occurring in either economies or companies which may result in a stock being intrinsically much more valuable over the longer term.
- Some analysts are rated because they are feared, and others because they are right. It is impossible always to be right, but you can always be logical and credible. What's more, credibility is a more enduring and sustainable quality.
- Equity research is a grind and isn't a glamorous profession.
- While company and stock analysis is important, be aware of the fact that foreign investors are allocating money on more of a top-down basis. It is therefore important to understand the macro themes and sector issues that will influence asset allocation and stock prices.
- As a consequence of the Asian crisis, investors are much more focused on the quality of company management. Understand how management runs the company and for whose ultimate benefit.

---

[1] Economic value added, or EVA (a registered trademark of Stern Stewart & Co.) as it is often referred to, differs from most other measures of corporate performance by charging profit for the cost of all the capital a company employs, debt as well as equity. The result is better information and insight about a company for its managers, which enables them to make better decisions. EVA isn't particularly new. The concept was first written about by Alfred Marshall, the English economist, in 1890.

[2] Price/earnings ratio.

[3] PT Plaza Indonesia Realty manages hotels and leases shopping centers, office space, and apartments. The company owns Grand Hyatt Jakarta and Plaza Indonesia Shopping Center. At the time of writing, the company had a stock-market capitalization of IDR 724.5 billion.

[4] PT Semen Gresik (Persero) Tbk manufactures cement and is involved in the development and operation of industrial real estate, manufacturing of packaging materials, and packaging and distribution of cement. At the time of writing, the company had a stock-market capitalization of IDR 724.5 billion.

[5] Hutchison Whampoa Limited operates in real estate, ports and related services, retail, manufacturing, telecommunications, media, energy, and infrastructure, finance. At the time of writing, the company had a stock-market capitalization of HK$423.4 billion.

11

Gordon Hall:
The First Virtue

"This is a very humbling business. If you aren't humble, it will eventually make you humble."

Gordon Hall is an analyst with few peers. As a managing director in the equity research group at Credit Suisse First Boston Corporation (CSFB), based in Houston, Texas, Hall is responsible for coverage of the oil service and equipment sector and is head of the equity group in Houston. Hall has been recognized as an "All Star" by the *Institutional Investor* poll for the past ten years and as a "First Team All-American" for the past six years with a "commanding lead." In the most recent Reuters survey covering US mid to smaller capitalization companies, Hall was ranked as the number one sell-side analyst across all industries, and number one in the oil and gas drilling equipment sector. He has also been recognized in *Institutional Investor* by European investors for coverage within the European energy sector. Hall has received several citations for his stock-picking prowess in *The Wall Street Journal*'s annual "All-Star Analyst" review. In addition to his institutional rankings, Gordon Hall has significant transactional experience, with involvement in more than sixty deals, having assisted numerous companies in raising more than US$10 billion in capital, and advising on mergers and acquisitions exceeding US$20 billion.

How did you get into the equities business?

It was very much unplanned. I originally trained and worked as an engineer at Raytheon. I continued to work for Raytheon[1] while attending business school at MIT. One of my classmates at Sloan was Dr. Burt Richards who ended up going to work for Credit Suisse First Boston. For whatever reason, maybe because I was an engineering type and he had a doctorate in chemistry, Burt told the people at First Boston that they should come after me. At that time I had no interest whatsoever in investment banking and intended to go into marketing with a technology company. However, Dan Meade from CSFB convinced me to come work for them as a technology analyst. When I showed up for work, though, Dan made it pretty clear that of the nine new analysts he had hired in 1987, I was not near the top of his "most likely to succeed" list.

And what were the stocks you covered?

Companies like Hewlett-Packard,[2] Perkin Elmer,[3] Millipore,[4] Teradyne,[5] — mainly instrumentation companies in the semiconductor area.

How did you move across from technology and high-tech into the less glamorous area of oil services and equipment?

The market crashed in October 1987. I had been with the firm for less than a year, and, while *today* we are the leading firm in the technology sector, back then it was a weak spot for the firm. So the firm planned cutbacks on the technology side following the crash and my job was in jeopardy. Natural resources has always been a power alley for CSFB and there was an open slot in that research group. Rather than sending me packing, they gave me a shot at the job which I took, thinking I might as well be employed while looking for something else to do. Energy turned out to be more interesting than I would have thought.

When you came out of business school and came into the industry, what were your expectations of the business and how did it subsequently compare?

That is a very difficult question to answer. I had so little knowledge of the industry coming in. I remember in my first interview with the firm, they said, "Why would you prefer the sell-side to the buy-side?", and I said, "What is the sell-side and the buy-side? *You* called *me*. I don't know the difference." Fortunately, they were forgiving of my ignorance.

And how long does it take to become a good sell-side analyst?

My guess is probably fifteen years [*laughs*], but I really don't know the answer to that. I think you can probably get pretty strong in five years — *if you are fortunate*. But in terms of really scoping it out and understanding all the different aspects of what is expected of you and what you need to deliver, I think it's probably a different path for everybody. It really depends on what sector you cover and your background. Moreover, in order to be good, or at least competent, you really need to go through some cycles. If, for example, all you ever did was cover companies that were just rocket ships the whole time, you would probably never quite get the full breadth of experience. You really need to have gone through some of the different types of economic environments, cycles, and stock-market conditions.

And is industry experience in the sector that you cover important?

I don't know if it would be a plus or not. I'm a technology guy who's covering oil services and it hasn't been a problem for me so far. In some ways, not having come out of the industry, I found it was an advantage, because I could take a fresh look at the sector without all the historical baggage. I found that a lot of the analysts that followed the sector were so embroiled in the good old days that they couldn't see the paradigm shift and the long-term implications of what had transpired in 1986. Many had simply slipped into being cheerleaders for the industry, hoping things would return to the way they were. Now that being said, having a technical background has been very helpful to me in covering the oil service business, as the application of technology has played a major role in the reshaping of the industry post the 1986 oil price collapse. However, being new to the energy sector, the first thing I did was to get out into the field and spend time with the people that were working in the business day-to-day. I went to the West Texas oilfields, the Gulf of Mexico, offshore California, Alaska, and the North Sea. I still make it a point to get out in the field every year. I made friends and contacts with the people in the business. I spent as much time with company executives as I could get. I learned a lot from operating people like Ed Spatz, who was a visionary on the direction of technology in the business.

Is technology ever going to change the long-term structure of the oil price?

That process is already in place. In fact, technology is a major reason behind continuing real-price deterioration in the commodity. Following the oil price collapse of 1986, the industry responded to extreme pressure on its very survival with technical ingenuity. Also, bear in mind that there is a high degree of politics in the oil business, and that is something that can create major deviations from long-term trends. The tremendous influence of politics was evident in the 1970s and 1980s. So, I guess you have to not only take into consideration the logical *influence of* technology, but you also have to understand the grander schemes of what is going on in the world and how that can affect the oil price. Fortunately, my long-time partner, James Clark (Integrated Oil analyst for CSFB), is very insightful in the area of factors driving oil price trends.

And are the recent mergers that we have seen in the oil industry a part of that?

Yes, but I wouldn't put them nearly in the league of what can happen as a result of Middle East politics. You would have to have a lot more mergers than we have had to have a major alteration in the structure of the energy sector. Nevertheless, the recent round of mergers was unusual activity for the big oil companies by historical standards. Importantly, this was something that we were able to anticipate through teamwork. My partner, Jim Clark, put out a piece called "No More Mister Nice Guys," long before the mergers started happening or the theme became popular on Wall Street. Jim envisioned the companies deviating from their historical bent toward independence and following the merger trends that had occurred in many other industries. This was a big enough trend that a number of the Integrated Oil analysts tried hard to steal the credit from Jim by claiming to be first to recognize it was coming. But again, we wouldn't see it as something that will really alter the *macro* oil cycle in a dramatic way, because it will have little impact on the marginal portion of the cost curve for oil development. It will impact the capital and exploration spending levels for two or three years as some of the big spenders focus internally. This could serve to bolster oil prices above normal levels until development programs are restarted.

So what is the critical variable that investors need to focus on when investing in the sector?

The cycle and valuation. What is going on cyclically is number one. If you look at the performance of this sector versus the overall equity market, it's a picture of secular decline. The oil service sector underperforms long term because the companies are serving an industry that is developing a commodity that is declining in real price terms over time. Furthermore, the underlying demand growth rate for the commodity is only 2–3% per annum. Compared to the broader stock market, many industries have significantly faster underlying growth rates. That being the case, what is interesting within the energy envelope, and the oil services sector in particular, is that it is *so cyclical* and the stocks so volatile that the stock market essentially creates multi-year outperformance opportunities. So, within long-term underperformance trends are windows that can be exploited for profits.

So, timing is critical?

Yes. Timing is almost everything in this sector. Where is the industry in its cycle, and what are the stocks discounting? You develop a risk-reward profile for investing in the group. You want to play the group in a *big way* when the risk-reward profile is highly attractive. However, this takes an iron gut. The risk-reward profiles are most attractive when consensus thinking is very negative and naysayers are proclaiming that the world is awash in oil.

Given that it is so cyclical, what about the manpower skills and the delivery and infrastructure risk in the sector?

Manpower issues come up time and again.

Is that a big risk factor in the business?

Yes, it is. The oil service industry has cut more than 20% of its work-force over the past eighteen months. And they are going to need them back someday; employment levels will probably be 25% higher by 2002. While training and manpower is a big pain for managers of these companies, the cycles and valuations are still the key investment issues. You can't let yourself get distracted from what really drives investment performance — "Where am I within the cycle in terms of industry fundamentals, and what is the market discounting? How much of a recovery is being factored in?" Say, for example, you are at the bottom of a cycle, which is close to where we are today. In fact, our numbers would say May 1999 was the bottom from an economic or industry fundamental perspective. Of course, the stocks have had a significant bounce off of the bottom as well. We would argue that the change in industry conditions that is coming in 2000 should be much more significant than the move in the stocks has been so far. To come to that conclusion, one has to have a perspective on the group's equity valuations.

And what is your preferred valuation approach?

We look at a number of different things: cash flow multiples, asset values, and earnings multiples. Cash flow multiples are one of the screens we are most comfortable with, particularly in conjunction with an analysis of returns. We like to look at not only individual companies, but also the group and its historical ranges. We put a lot of weight on historical trading ranges within the group, and especially the post-1986 time period. We do this because we look at the world as having made a paradigm shift post-1986.

Which was?

From the early 1970s through 1985, Saudi Arabia assumed the role of swing producer, reducing production to support oil prices. Saudi production (market share) fell sharply over time and they abdicated that role in 1986. The lesson was that artificially holding prices above the marginal economics of alternative oil results in severe market share losses. Today, we have OPEC functioning as a price stabilizer; a bit more difficult to coordinate, but the goals are less ambitious. An underlying assumption in our investment framework is that a unilateral swing producer will not exist again in a timeframe that we care about. So, given the market structure we expect, what kind of multiples is the market affording the stocks, and are they cheap versus their own historical trading in absolute terms and/or relative to broader market valuations? In bad times, the oil service stocks tend to go to the low end of historical multiples in absolute terms on cash flows and assets. In good times, the stocks tend to trade up to the high end of historical multiples relative to the market on cash flow and earnings. It's the opposite of what you would expect from a cyclical — cheap on depressed numbers and expensive on peak numbers. This historical pattern is part of what creates the enormous volatility in the shares.

And to what extent is capital expenditure, over-or-under spending, a big factor in stock price and earnings performance?

Capital spending patterns of customers are what create the cycles. Capital expenditures by the service companies aren't the driving issue, at least over the past fifteen years. It started to become an issue in 1997 as the industry began building some large rigs (long-life assets), but the cycle cut the building programs off fairly quickly and most of what was built was for new frontiers such as deepwater. The oil service companies live off whatever the oil company is after, and thus most of their capital is for short-term needs, responding to day-to-day demand trends.

So the depreciation policies tend to be very long term in this business?

Actually, it varies significantly. The oil service business is made up of dozens of different niches with unique business characteristics. There are all different kinds of equipment; some assets have a very short life and some have a long life.

How do you get around those problems? For example, in banking I've got banks that have different bad debt provisioning policies, and that makes comparative analysis difficult at times.

We try to break the industry into different sub-groups. One of the distorting factors in this sector is that the companies have had *massive* write-offs at various times, and some of those assets written off are still being employed. This is in part why earnings are such a *bad* indicator of the economic reality, especially when comparing companies against each other. And that is why we would rather take the cash flow multiples which help cut through the issue of inconsistent carrying cost on assets. However, I think within the context of working with cash flow multiples there are two things you need to understand. First, you have to understand the cash returns of the company; and second, you have to understand the capital intensity of the company. Obviously, if a business is extremely capital-intensive and has short-life assets, it should be afforded a lower cash flow multiple than a company that has longer-life assets and is not so capital-intensive. We try to cut through all of those issues using a proprietary value-added framework. Without getting into the details, we (Jim Clark, Phil Pacc, and I) looked at what made the stocks work over time and designed a framework to analyze the factors that were driving stock performance. When we do return analysis, we employ gross invested capital or the actual cost of the operating assets at original cost. That way the figures we are producing are real returns, not accounting ratios. We try not to get caught in the EVA[6] trap because there are several real distortions that result from that methodology, particularly when you get into capital-intensive industries. Furthermore, we have never seen anyone demonstrate in a straightforward and scientific manner that EVA works for picking stocks.

Because of the cost of capital issues?

That's a big issue from two perspectives. First, you cannot compare an accounting ratio to a real required return on investment. You must have a sound methodology for calculating returns that is not distorted by bookkeeping. Second, the rote calculation of cost of capital has problems as well. I believe that stock performance is much more about the *direction* of returns. It's not so much about whether a company is exceeding its cost of capital at a given point in time; it's about how returns are going to change going forward.

So, it's about knowing where the underperforming businesses are and whether you can improve them, and if not, you exit them?

Yes. And I'm going to be bold and be willing to break from the academic norms on this. In fact, I can cite cases in point in the real world that cause you to break from the academic norms. I'm convinced by real experience that the beta[7] of a stock is not a good measure for deriving cost of capital. For example, in one of the companies that I cover, things were going great in the *industry* in 1995, 1996, and 1997, but this company kept stumbling. The overall equity market was doing great, and all of the oil service companies were doing great, but this particular company was having blow-up, after blow-up, after blow-up. Management kept making mistakes and meeting with misfortune on a range of issues. Consequently, their beta dropped and so their cost of capital went to about 5%. So, on a mathematical basis, they were getting rewarded for being bad! Pragmatically, I can tell you what kind of returns *I need* from a company. Furthermore, good CEOs know what kinds of returns are needed as well. As much as I like math, I'll take strong intuition over a weighted average cost of capital calculation based on beta any day.

So you have to be very commercial?

Right, you can't get distracted by the wrong ideas or get too obsessed with quantitative methods. When I started, my engineering background had the better of me — I wanted to make everything into a model — mathematical and straight-up. I figured if I did that, I wouldn't even have to report to work after a few months. But the reality is, the system dynamics overwhelm the models. There is no substitute for experience and intuition, supported by appropriate frameworks.

But do you think that this is a common mistake that a lot of inexperienced analysts make; they forget that companies are run by people who occasionally screw up, and you can't model that?

I think you are probably right on that. Although the greater problem on the sell-side today is gun-slinging — you know, when they just jump out of the box and try to make a name for themselves by making a lot of noise and being controversial or colorful. The background work, the real research, and the modeling are passed over completely. It might work for a while, but then the sophisticated investors figure it out, they realize it's all hot air.

Speaking of mistakes, what was your worst call and what did you learn from it?

That's a very good question, because engineering is generally a precise science — you get the answers right almost all of the time. You test and prove that you got it right, and at Raytheon, you *had* to get it right. So, the transition from that exacting and precise environment into this business was probably the hardest challenge for me. The call that was perhaps the best learning experience for me and frustrated me the most was Smith International.[8] In 1995, Smith International, a well-run company that I was very familiar with, was poised to see its business take off and I *knew* it would do extremely well in the environment that was coming. Meanwhile, the street was skeptical and the stock was trading at US$12. At that point in time, I thought there were some very interesting reasons why this company was going to do well in the up-cycle with some major changes within the drilling fluids business, a business that they had recently bought into and had bought at an extremely attractive price. There were some big changes in store, and I went and studied those and wrote them up. The valuation was there, the internal trends were there, the industry trends were there, everything was there that you needed. I wrote a thirty-page report that highlighted these details on the company's prospects, but then the stock started moving before I got the report out. I just couldn't bear it. It was $12 when I wrote the report, and then it went to $14 and I thought "I'm just going to wait a little bit" and then it hit $16, then $20, and this continued almost non-stop to over $80! That was in early 1995, and the report is still here in the files.

What did you learn from that?

I learned that you shouldn't worry about $2. If you really know what the stock price *trend* is going to be, that's more important. You can't always pick everything off at the exact bottom. You are going to have to be willing to run with something and sometimes come into a stock mid-stream.

So instinct and courage are very important?

They are. And I think that it is something that you've got to go through once or twice before you understand that it's okay not to pick it off at the exact bottom. Investors deal with this all the time. It's hard to build the full position at the bottom. When you're talking about something going from $12 to $80, missing a dollar or two doesn't matter. Trying to be too perfect in this business is impossible. You can't be perfect. It's a percentage game — that's a weakness that I have to fight.

But it's a path that all analysts and fund managers tread, inasmuch as timing calls is the hardest part of the job and we tend to sell too early or buy too late.

I always sell too early, too. Almost always [*laughs*]!

Do you use charts? Would they help in timing calls?

I don't really use charts in any meaningful way. I remember one time I recommended Schlumberger[9] when the psychology was very negative on the group. A senior analyst at CSFB made a copy of my report, stapled SLB's chart to it, and wrote a note that stated, "The chart looks horrible. The market knows something you are missing." With that call I picked off the exact bottom on SLB for a multi-year period. If I had let the chart control me, I would have missed it. I kept that note for years to remind myself not to be one-dimensional. I look at charts more now than I used to, but only because I just know so many people are looking at them.

Another piece of data.

Yes. In fact, in my industry, charting as I have tracked it and listened to the chart calls over the years, have been about as contrarian an indicator as you could have ever hoped for.

Contrarian?

Yes. About as wrong as you could possibly get. Creating the extremes in the tops and the bottoms. The inflection points seem to be the real weakness of that approach. Given the lack of liquidity in the oil service sector, you have to "fight" the charts to put a meaningful amount of money to work. Now, notwithstanding that, I do like to look at relative strength sometimes, just to get a sense of the broader trend. I also look at cross-over points and moving averages in order to understand where people expect major inflection points. But overall, charts are way down the list for me as an investment argument or case. And when people call me all excited and breathlessly say, "Have you seen the chart? I think it looks great," one of my favorite responses is to say, "Yes, I was looking at it, but whoops, I had it upside down!" [*laughs*]. But everyone looks at them because everyone looks at them, which is a bizarre concept. For the buy-side, it probably makes more sense than it does for the sell-side. I'm not the guy making the investment. I'm the guy coming up with information and ideas that an investor can fit into his framework. And most investors can read a chart better than I can, so if I'm making my calls off a chart I'm not adding any value.

And where does a sell-side analyst add the most value?

The buy-side are by and large better investors than the sell-side; otherwise the roles would be reversed. There are lots of very bright investors that know how to make investments and time the market. They all have very different perspectives, very different objectives, and portfolios with a range of different industries in them. Consequently, they can examine other opportunities and can weigh what I propose as an opportunity against other alternatives. As an industry specialist I'm missing the macro view, and if I try to understand all of it, I won't be an industry specialist anymore. The most value that I can add is the information that I can provide for them, and perhaps even challenging their thinking. I get a lot of people who call me and say, "What's wrong with this?" or "Why don't I do this?" And they generally want me to say, "Here's what could be wrong with what you're saying." Even if I agree with them, they will still want to hear what might be a problem with their logic. They also want to have somebody to simply go back and forth on an issue with. I find very few clients are going to say "What do you like in the sector?" and then just buy those names. There is a lot more due diligence that goes on than that, at least most of the time.

What's the hardest part of the job?

The maintenance part is tough. The routine is a real grind at times. In energy, we work very closely as a group and try to be creative in regard to maintenance. When we find something that has really become painful to all of us, we try to find some way to alter it. For example, with quarterly earnings announcements the whole team (Jim Clark, Phil Pace, Ken Sill, and I) believed that the entire process had become mundane and low value-added. There was a time in the past before conference calls became pervasive when we were some of the only people getting an analysis of the numbers out quickly. We were writing them up, and faxing or emailing the analysis out. No-one else was doing it in any big way. Others *might* comment on the numbers the next day, or mail out a review of the numbers. But now there is a whole army of people getting the quarterly earnings out, writing them up and faxing them out in a timely fashion. We have thirty companies in my area under coverage, so it's a lot of paper to generate and, what's more, the press releases have become more comprehensive, the conference calls have become more comprehensive, and so there is less value that you can add to the process.

It's dull?

Exactly. It becomes very dull and boring, particularly when things are as expected.

And one quarter isn't a trend.

Right, and we used to talk to the companies individually rather than on a conference call. We still talk to them individually, but most of it is covered publicly on a conference call. We therefore determined that we needed an analytical tool that is incremental and fast. So we created a system — in fact, Jim Clark thought of this: 'Measurement While Reporting.' It's a play on a term within the oil service industry called "Measurement While Drilling". We get the incremental data, we have the database, we drop the new data in, and it produces comparative trends for this company versus all the other companies in the industry. It's automated to a large extent. Then we focus briefly on the key incremental data that came out of the quarter, write four bullet points that cover those items, and it's done. The clients get it quickly and it has everything that is needed, as well as comparative data. Through this approach, we created a way to make a required maintenance item a little more interesting for both us and our clients.

Are there any other parts of the business that are tough?

Yes, misinformation and off-base rumors. I find these the most frustrating thing to deal with. Even somewhat outlandish stuff has to be chased down to some extent. You have got to deal with stocks dropping 10%, and you know from the second that you hear it, you think, "That's garbage." Sometimes investors have exactly the opposite view from us. They think, "Awesome opportunity" — a chance to buy this stock 10% lower than I have to pay otherwise." The press creates some rumor out there, often due to an utter lack of knowledge and ability to filter noise. But, what is most frustrating is when industry analysts create the off-base stuff because they lack anything better to talk about, or because they don't want to do the work of chasing the information down before they go out with it.

What advice would you give anyone coming into this business?

Don't get too aggressive in your recommendations or style too early, and don't go out there and be a gun-slinger, flash-in-the-pan type. Be rigorous, figure out what it is that drives the stocks, and develop a framework that is value-added. Don't copy what others are doing and saying. In fact, I would suggest not even looking at what the competition is doing, to avoid being biased by it. The clients benefit from unique perspectives, not just another individual reiterating the current groupthink.

What do you think can be taught in this business and what can't?

That is a tough and interesting question. I believe that first-hand experience is valuable. Maybe I'm just thick-skulled, but some things are hard to really grasp until you've been through it at least once. For example, in a volatile cyclical like the oil service sector, when times are good it's hard to imagine how quickly the cycle can fall apart or how much business can deteriorate when the cycle turns. But then it happens again. Even when things start changing, the pressure is always there to ignore the turn. The system always wants to draw you into reiterating your position quickly. And even if you say, "Wait a minute, this thing could go down another forty, fifty percent," the companies, the salesforce, the product manager, and investors are calling and pushing for you to recommend the stocks again. In that environment it's critical to have the strength of your convictions and the confidence of your firm. Otherwise, you get dragged around by market psychology. I don't believe that the ability to have strength in your convictions can be taught, it has to be developed through experience. The confidence of the salesforce and management is also not likely to be granted immediately.

So, it's basically an issue about knowing how to manage the white noise and knowing how to change your calls in a smart way.

Correct. That's very difficult for someone that is new at the job. Mistakes are unavoidable in this business. Often the nature of the pressure from the system only serves to compound errors. The tough part is that people are most vulnerable to mistakes early in their career, and they are most vulnerable to losing their job early on as well. People get fired in this business. You either make it or you don't. I think back to my starting class — there are maybe three of nine that are still in the business, and what's more, half of the starting class were gone within two years. If you're not careful, the sales desk will write you off in your first year and then you are dead forever. You have to be savvy, humble, and a nice person, but also firm in your convictions. If you can endure or manage the stress, it's a healthy environment and it keeps you humble. This is a very humbling business. If you aren't humble, it will eventually make you humble.

What are the common mistakes that you think the average investor makes when it comes to the stock market?

We have been in a multi-year bull market, so being long has worked. Buying stocks has worked, and the average investor right now is only thinking about buying. Possibly more risk is being taken than is realized. Most people don't measure the risks and don't balance long positions with short postions. Some people are making investments on incremental information with very little understand-ing of what is discounted or already priced into the stocks. In a bull market, investors are often right for the wrong reasons. If we ever have something other than a bull market, it's going to be a bit painful. The other odd phenomenon is that people always seem to want to buy something after a big upward move. I guess it works as long as there is significant underlying growth. It hasn't been a particularly successful approach in the energy sector.

What was your best call and what did you learn from that?

I'm such a skeptic that a good call for me occurs when you can actually make money on anything in my sector! But one does come to mind that stands out, and that was Cooper Cameron.[10] This company came public through an exchange offer. Cooper Cameron's financial performance had been a disaster for several years. It was a mess, horrible numbers, and thus very difficult to value. I enjoyed the challenge. An exchange offer is very much like an IPO; investors had to want to own Cooper Cameron and to trade shares in something else to get shares in Cooper Cameron. So, investors must be convinced that the price you set is attractive. CSFB was retained to do the exchange offer, so I had the challenge of setting a value on the company. What was most fun about the deal was that two of my top competitors were aggressive in issuing reports that said we had significantly overvalued Cooper Cameron shares in the exchange ratio. They were convinced that the company was going to continue to generate horrible returns. What they didn't assess properly were the changes that were coming, both internally and externally, and the underlying value of the assets. The company actually had everything going for it: the emerging cycle; strong assets, attractively valued; and, most importantly, a new management team that was very strong. I was convinced that you had to look at this stock on asset value, return *potential,* and earnings *potential*, rather than on its track record and a multiple of current results. It was going to be a very different company. Nonetheless, it was controversial. I loved the investment opportunity and was vocal about it; my competition didn't like the stock and they were vocal about it. It came out at US$9 on a pre-split basis in the summer of 1995.

So you went out on a limb based on your view of management and the potential they could unlock in the business?

Yes. I was out on a limb all by myself, with my top competitors at that time telling the market we were wrong big time.

And what happened?

By the end of that year the stock was over US$17, while the peer group was fairly flat. At one point in 1997 the stock was over US$80. From 1995 to the present, Cooper Cameron has been the best performer in the sector, significantly outperforming other large service companies.

Did that call put you on the map, or was it just the icing on the cake?

A single call never does it. Clients need to see consistent, high-quality work. I was just squeaking by with the number one ranking already in 1995. But it was a close race between myself and Jim Carroll. Jim was the dominant analyst in the oil service sector for years — very tough competition, a great analyst. He is now on the buy-side and he is an enjoyable client to interact with. And I'm so glad he's on the buy-side.

And what does it take to get to number one?

The first thing for me was a lot of prayer and then some good

fortune, if you call it that. Second, you have to be pretty disciplined
— in fact, very disciplined. You need to be differentiated in terms of
product and approach, particularly if the competition is tough in
your sector. You also have to properly assess your own strengths and
weaknesses, to know how you can best succeed. You have to have a
realistic perspective on yourself within your environment. For
example, all my competitors were doing a lot of marketing when I
started covering the group; they were always flying everywhere and
visiting investors, seemingly trying to one-up each other on travel. So
I figured that the frenzied marketing approach was pretty well
covered and that my competitors were probably better at it than I
would be. So I focused on having a better product and doing in-
depth research.

Do you phone clients much?

No, not really. I'm just not the "smile and dial" type. I wish it was the
way it used to be in the old days, as I understand it. You did your
work, and investors would call you when they wanted to know
something. I'm not good at creating something to say every day. I
only know what to say when I really have something to say, and then
you can't physically call all the clients that you should in a reasonable
timeframe. Technology is however helping to solve this
communication problem.

Do you get pressured, though, to make junk phone calls?

Not now. I felt some pressure in my early years on the job. I did force
myself early on to make calls. You just had to. But you have to play to
your strengths, and in my case it's my industry knowledge and
technology, as well as the fact that I have a disciplined industry
framework. I learned a lot about frameworks and marketing from my
partners, Jim Clark and Phil Pace. Clark is a Williams undergrad and a
Harvard Graduate School guy, so he's a lot more balanced and
articulate than myself, and Phil Pace is blessed with the most pleasant
of personalities.

And when you market, is it telemarketing or face-to-face?

I travel with Jim Clark or Phil Pace. We market together in teams.

Better value for the client, better for you.

Yes. Better for the client, better for you. There was a lot of resistance to it at first. We had salespeople who refused to let us come to their region in pairs. But it does a couple of things — it forces you to get on the same page as somebody else. That requires a level of discipline, and often you have to put your pride aside because you have to come to a conclusion that you can all accept. It's not all that hard when you have a lot of respect for the people you work with. And that's been really good for me career-wise, to be sharpened by somebody else. The other critical factor is integrity. Being honest makes such a big difference — people say, "What about this?", and I say, "You know, I don't know. Let me see if I can find out and get back to you." Mentioning a competitor by name, a client once said to me, "You know, that guy always knows the answers. He never says, 'I don't know,' but I'm glad *you* do from time to time." This issue of integrity and trust is the key for analysts today, especially given the level of corporate finance work that is required these days.

You are working for both the buyers and the sellers of equity.

Correct. You have to work for both. You have to, but you can do it with integrity. The balancing act is the toughest part of the job. It's challenging, but it can be done. If you have the right perspective and you have the right priorities, then it can be done.

How do you judge success?

Typically, success is viewed as being based on the performance of your calls, your institutional rankings, or whether you won the big deal. I remember days when I was very affected when a stock didn't go my way. If you made the right call you felt good, and if you made the wrong call you felt bad. It's important to care about your calls, but you have to have perspective. You have to have a way of dealing with the stress. I judge success by whether or not I'm meeting my priorities in life and not whether I'm the highest-paid guy or the top-ranked guy. I never expected to be the top-ranked guy in my sector. Being number one is a gift, a blessing, it's gratifying, I enjoy it, and it's fun, but it's just not the most important thing to me. The most important things to me are my faith in Jesus Christ and my family. Work is third, if that. It has always been down on the list, never higher than third, and it's never going to be higher than third.

Is it harder to stay number one than to get to number one?

I was so surprised that I got to number one when I did. In fact, I'm still shocked, because I think about how incapable I was when I got to number one! It truly depends on your competition in each area. The competition in the oil service sector was much stronger when I achieved the top ranking than it is now. And if analysts like Jim Carroll or Ken Miller came back, it would be a lot tougher again. The level of competition can change quickly. Even if you have a big lead, you can't get complacent. I have seen how fast a lead can evaporate.

And what was the major reason you think you got to number one?

A lot of prayer and then some good fortune, if you call it that. The consistency and integrity of the product was more important than the stock calls or the marketing. It doesn't come overnight. I believe that my understanding of the sector and my ability to run my business have improved every year. I want to learn something new every year. I believe that you can always create new ways of looking at things and improve your product. Sometimes I'm amazed that I used to say X without knowing Y. I'm stunned I didn't see it before. It's astounding how you keep learning in this business; that's what keeps it fresh.

Another issue is the oversupply of research and the torrent of data that fund managers are hit with. How do you allow or accommodate for that?

I've always put a lot less emphasis on the written material delivered by the postman. Looking back, I can remember the heat that I used to get in the early 1990s when I wouldn't write up quarterly results, publish them, and mail them out. I believed that if a company has just reported something, an immediate breaking piece of information, it's of little value to publish it in a written report and *mail* it to somebody. I was a big believer in faxes earlier on, before it became popular. Analyze breaking information, write a quick note, and fax it out — to me, that made a lot more sense than the mail. Big studies with shelf life, those I publish and mail out. But I have never done the time-sensitive stuff that way. Today this is fairly standard, given how swamped the clients are with research and given the improvements in communications technology. Now everybody is faxing and emailing and voice-mailing.

So, how do you get through to the clients?

I think that one of the big benefits for somebody that has been in the business for a while is that the clients tend to call you. That is the beauty of it. I would hate to start over again. It's tougher now, even with a differentiated product, to be heard over the din. What you find is that a lot of people don't come with anything new to put in front of people. New analysts start out looking at what the leading analysts are doing and they do the same thing. Their salespeople often market them by saying he's just like so-and-so. The clients don't need somebody new to do the same thing that somebody else is doing. So you have to bring something new to the market. Be creative. I believe that a good sell-side analyst ought to be able to list the new products that they have developed and the new ways of examining things. After someone has been in the business for a while, they ought to be able to look over the last five or ten years and say that there have been five to ten things that they did that were new and creative and different from what anybody else did. And if you're not starting that process, which most new analysts aren't, you're not going to have a major impact.

And what was it when you were starting out that helped you to get noticed?

When I first came into the business, there were several things that were fortunate for me. One was a new trend that turned out to be pretty massive, which was extended-reach and horizontal drilling. Since I was an engineer I was really digging for new technologies being applied in the business, so I was kind of fortunate to happen across extended-reach drilling which was a fairly minor business until 1990. But it was something I was intrigued by in 1989 and wrote about in a big way and made a big push on in 1989, and then it happened. It helped establish me as someone who understood industry trends. The irony is that, as I look back on it, I'm not sure there was really any way for an investor to make a significant profit from it.

But it got you noticed?

Yes. It helped identify me as somebody who had something different to say very early on in my career, and I got noticed right out of the box because it came to fruition. I saw other guys try to imitate that, even the leading analysts at that time, either directly or through spin-off concepts. One of the guys picked this other thing called coiled tubing and tried to make this into a big trend as well. And it was interesting, but it wasn't a paradigm shift, and it wasn't going to be the kind of thing that would get him where he wanted to be. But still, he was trying to head down a direction that helped me a lot, which is differentiating yourself through demonstrating an understanding of the business. That was a break.

Was there anything else that helped?

Another item that helped me was that while everyone focused on the rig count as an indicator of industry activity, we identified certain shortcomings in that data. We developed a massive model called QualRig, which computed the monthly drilling and completion expenditures real time. It tracked more closely with the revenues of oil service companies than the rig count did, and identified the impact of shifts in regional activity that take place on a regular basis. Mix-shifts are very important, because a rig drilling in Kansas generates about one-tenth the service revenues of a rig drilling in the North Sea. Analysts were looking at rig counts, but they were missing these big trends in spending patterns. The industry noticed that this new model was worthwhile as well. The chairman of Baker Hughes Jim Woods gave me a lot of credit, saying publicly, "We have been counting rigs for more than forty years and here comes this young buck who changes the whole system."

How important is the firm you work for in getting a rating?

I believe that the firm is very important. If you are at a firm that has broad distribution and a strong salesforce, you do a lot better. So, it's critical. Even more important than that is being at a firm that fits you.

Culturally?

Yes. I made a mistake in overlooking the importance of cultural fit once. Very briefly. I spent twenty-four hours at another firm, a good firm, but it wasn't right for me. I reversed that decision and came back to CSFB. It was, perhaps, the most embarrassing thing that I have ever done. I came back without a package, which appeared to be the most naive thing I've ever done.

What are some of the common mistakes you see from junior analysts?

Credit Suisse First Boston has built an outstanding position as the leaders in returns-based analysis of stocks. With that focus I have seen some analysts build too narrow a framework, relying almost exclusively on EVA. I listened to one junior analyst covering a company where his only questions for management boiled down to "What are your returns going to be next year?" You might as well just cut to the chase and ask them what their earnings are going to be. Moreover, to believe that just because you are studying returns and modeling in an EVA framework that you are adding value from an investment standpoint and are covering all the important bases is kidding yourself. I haven't seen any big EVA advocates on the sell-side put up the numbers on stock performance. I want to look at all the *inputs* that drive the returns, but more importantly the inputs that drive the *stocks*. A common mistake from young analysts is that they find some sort of model or framework like EVA that sounds appealing and they believe it's the solution for everything. They ignore its flaws and use it exclusively as their framework. A good framework should be theoretically sound and multi-faceted. If you want to use the EVA model, you still have to begin with the inputs and figure out how you get the returns, because *you* have got to decide whether the returns are going up and whether the rising returns as measured by that model will drive stocks or not. You can't rely on management's opinion on the direction of returns. *You* have got to figure that out.

But you went to business school and were trained that way too, weren't you?

Well, yes. I loved business school. I enjoyed finance theory. Fortunately, at Gordon College and MIT they taught us to think critically and to understand the flaws in the methods. This kind of training helped me to grasp pretty quickly what you could apply and what you couldn't apply to the investment process. Even still, I was a bit idealistic coming out of business school. With an engineering background and good business school training, I initially thought I'd model the sector on a computer in no time and I would be on the beach, making calls. I learned pretty quickly how complicated the system dynamics are in the investment world. And what's more, some of the theories have significant flaws. For example, in the capital asset pricing model, the whole volatility and risk area is very problematic. I'm convinced that stock *volatility* is the wrong proxy for measurement of business risk. And some of what is pushed as new techniques is just DCF[11] or ROI[12] repackaged in cute new terms. I don't have any patience for re-branding of old techniques that still have the same inherent flaws. For example, EVA is often used as a management accounting tool for internal investment decisions — does the proposed investment at the end of the day exceed your hurdle rate or cost of capital? Nothing terribly new about that question. You want to brand *new* things and ideas — not old things. Re-branding something that already exists adds no value. ROI has been around a long time and it has some distinct weaknesses, but EVA has exactly the same weaknesses. It's useful only if you understand its flaws and know how to use it in the investment process. But it had better be only one element of a multi-faceted framework.

So, find out what works for you and for your industry and stick with it.

Yes, start with determining what drives the stocks and what skills you have to add value in the process. Furthermore, you cannot let other people make your stock call. That is a critical factor . You can't let your salesforce, product manager, or the company executive make your stock call. You've got to make your own call, and you have to live with it or die with it. Don't get me wrong: I highly value the viewpoint of certain salespeople, company executives, and our product manager, Terry Cuskley, who is terrific. Some of these inputs are invaluable in building perspective; there is a lot that you can learn from them. But at times, you have to fight the tape and go with what your framework concludes. You need to be able to tell people that "This is what it tells me, and I'm going to go with that for these reasons." There are times that you are going to be wrong (at least 30% of the time), so I would also recommend being polite and measured in the process. If you are haughty, then you will get the backlash at some stage. Deservedly.

How important is consistency?

Huge. The product has to be consistent. But there is another element to consistency that is important as well. And I learned the hard way that there is a lot more to loyalty than people ascribe to it. Loyalty to your clients and loyalty to your employer. Loyalty is an unusual trait on Wall Street. You get into a pattern, a groove that works, you have associations with lots of people in the firm, whether they be salespeople, bankers, or traders, and you can benefit enormously from understanding how each other works. And it's easy to say you had a bad call and it's nice to move to another firm and get more money at the same time. Even if going the distance with the same firm costs you a little bit of money, I believe that there is some real value in sticking with the same group of people you are with. Not just the firm, but the people that you work with at the firm. I have derived an enormous amount of benefit from being at one firm for thirteen years (apart from one day). Yes, I made that mistake for one day, leaving the firm, but coming right back was the best thing that I ever did. Strangely, I knew it was the wrong decision before I went, but we all make those mistakes.

❋ ❋ ❋

For Gordon Hall, understanding stock-market and economic cycles is the number one key to success. Moreover, Hall's experience and views demonstrate that it is possible to make money in sectors or stocks that suffer from low growth rates and declining pricing power. However, it is important to understand the leads and lags between stock-market expectations, and where industry fundamentals are or are likely to be over your investment horizon. The key features of Gordon Hall's approach are:

- Understand where a stock or a group of stocks are within the fundamental/economic cycle. That way, you will be able to more clearly understand what the market is pricing or discounting relative to the stock's or the sector's current fundamentals and prospects. To put that in its proper perspective, you will also need to understand where the stock or sector is trading *relative* to its historical trading ranges.
- When investing in cyclical stocks, timing is very important. Don't be afraid to buy when pessimism is at its worst or to sell when optimism is at its highest.
- Net earnings are a relatively bad indicator of economic reality; cash flow, rather than earnings-based multiples, is a more useful investment yardstick.
- EVA is not a panacea, and cost of capital issues (due to technical/ statistical issues concerning the beta of a stock) can distort the picture. However, while the *absolute* level of returns can be subject to interpretation and debate, it is the *direction* and future trends of returns that are more important and will most likely dictate the future direction of the trend in the stock's price.
- Don't get distracted or obsessed by quantitative methods. As an engineer with an undergraduate degree in mathematics and a Masters of Science in Finance and Operations, Hall quickly learned the limitations of computer modeling and quantitative methods, and that successful investing is as much about soft issues and psychology as it is about math. Moreover, making informed judgments about qualitative issues such as management, and geopolitical events or risks, are also important factors in stock price performance.

- Don't think that you can always buy at the exact bottom and sell at the all-time high. Hall's experience with Smith International, where he delayed the release of a report because the stock price was beginning to run and he preferred to wait for a pull-back (which didn't occur for years), demonstrated to him that it is better to participate in a positive trend in a stock price rather than try to finesse your entry point to the extreme. In other words, it is impossible to be perfect and the stock-market is a percentage game.
- While rumors are grist for the stock-market mill, negative rumors are often a great chance to buy stocks at a discount to their usual price. The cliche "buy on the rumor and sell on the fact" can, on many occasions, work in your favor, but you are likely to be better off as an investor when you treat rumors as an opportunity to add to your long-term positions rather than as short-term trading opportunities.
- While economic fundamentals within a sector can be difficult, prices can nevertheless move due to the fact that most sectors will trade relative to the broader market which is being driven in many cases by growth stocks. In those situations, the gap between price and value can be stretched for an extended period of time. For sell-side analysts, develop strategies to know how to deal with that paradox, and for investors, these situations present great money-making opportunities.
- Management is a key investment parameter, so try to gauge whether there is potential value that may lie within a company that management, or another catalyst, can unlock. Hall's against-the-market call on Cooper Cameron, which subsequently went from US$9 to US$80, was largely based on his perception of management and the *potential* returns and earnings for business.
- Understand your strengths and play to them. Moreover, you need to develop a framework for analysis that works for you, as there is no single key to success.
- As you are likely to be wrong 30–40% of the time, humility is an

important quality. Moreover, as a sell-side analyst, integrity and loyalty are qualities that are often overlooked but have nevertheless also played a significant role in Hall's success.

---

1   Raytheon Company provides products and services for defense and commercial electronics, engineering and construction, and business and special mission aircraft. At the time of writing, the company had a stock-market capitalization of US$10 billion.

2   Hewlett-Packard Company designs, manufactures, and services products and systems for computation and communications. Products include computers, calculators, workstations, printers, disc and tape drives, and medical diagnostic and monitoring devices. At the time of writing, the company had a stock-market capitalization of US$101.6 billion.

3   Now trading as PE Corp-PE Biosystems. The group manufactures and distributes instrumentation, reagents, and software for the pharmaceutical, biotechnology, environmental testing, food, agriculture, and chemical manufacturing industries. At the time of writing the company had a stock-market capitalization of US$8.8 billion.

4   Millipore Corporation develops, manufactures, and sells products that are used primarily for the analysis, identification, monitoring, and purification of liquids and gases. Millipore operates around the world. At the time of writing, the company had a stock-market capitalization of US$1.4 billion.

5   Teradyne Inc. manufactures automatic test systems and related software for the electronics and communications industries. At the time of writing, the company had a stock-market capitalization of US$8.4 billion.

6   Economic value added, or EVA as it is often referred to, differs from most other measures of corporate performance by charging profit for the cost of all the capital a company employs, debt as well as equity. Capital is also adjusted to reflect economic reality by taking into account off balance sheet debt and adding back unwarranted write-offs against equity. The result is better information and insight about a company for its managers, which enables them to make better decisions. EVA is not particularly new as the concept, a registered trademark of Stern Stewart & Co., was first written about by Alfred Marshall, the English economist, in 1890.

7   The beta of a stock is a measure of its relative risk. It is the co-variance of a stock's price with the market index, and is standardized by dividing by the market variance. A stock with a beta of 1.0 would be expected to move in line with the market, whereas a stock with a beta higher than 1.0 would be expected to rise or fall at a greater rate than the market.

8   Smith International, Inc. supplies products and services to the oil and gas exploration and production industry. Products and services include drilling and completion fluid systems, solids control equipment, waste management services,

drilling tools, sidetracking systems, and liner hangers. At the time of writing, the company had a stock-market capitalization of US$2.2 billion.

9   Schlumberger Limited provides resource management services and technology products, services, and systems for the oil industry. The company offers seismic data acquisition, well construction, and productivity services, wireline logging, and other oil field services. It also provides services to utilities, energy service providers, and other industries. At the time of writing, the company had a stock-market capitalization of US$43.9 billion.

10   Cooper Cameron Corporation manufactures oil and gas pressure control equipment for oil and gas drilling, production, and transmission for onshore, offshore, and subsea applications. Products include valves, wellheads, chokes, blowout preventers, and assembled systems. The company also manufactures gas turbines, centrifugal gas and air compressors, and other products. At the time of writing, the company had a stock-market capitalization of US$2.4 billion.

11   Discounted cash flow, which is the net present value of the future cash flows discounted at an appropriate hurdle rate.

12   Return on investment.

12

William Low and Alistair Veitch: The Weighting Game

"If you get it right 51% of the time you'll be better than the market, but the real measure of your success or performance will be down to the issue of how you weighted that portfolio."

Based in Edinburgh, Scotland, William Low and Alistair Veitch are a director and vice president, respectively, of BlackRock International Ltd., a leading provider of global investment management and risk management products. As of December 31, 1999, BlackRock had global assets under management of US$165 billion. Low and Veitch are both members of a Pacific Basin team that has managed mandates in this region for over ten years. Low has over twelve years' experience in investing in the Asia-Pacific markets; Veitch also has extensive experience in Asia since beginning his career as an equity analyst in the early 1990s.

A key feature of BlackRock's approach to investment is their emphasis on risk management and portfolio diversification, as well as a strong fundamental investment approach to company analysis which is also augmented by proprietary risk management systems. Low and Veitch could be described as "active" managers who combine fundamental analysis with a disciplined quantitative framework. Their investment process first involves stock selection based on proprietary screening systems. Companies that rank highly in the screening process are then subject to extensive fundamental analysis. Factors such as strength of management, cash flow, product and customer diversity, balance sheet strength, and company and industry life cycle position are all reviewed to confirm the results of the initial screening process. The final stage of their investment process involves risk analysis which is assessed at both the stock and portfolio level. Particular emphasis is given to sector, industry, and, where appropriate, geographical diversification. The overriding goal of this investment style is to minimize risk while maximizing returns relative to a particular benchmark. The optimum weighting of portfolios and attention to risk management are important ingredients for success, because, as Low attests, overweighting a bad stock call can be far more detrimental to performance than underweighting a good stock call.

How did you get started in this business?

WL: I started in investment management in 1987. I had done a degree in geology, but back then there were no jobs as the oil price was around US$10 a barrel. Therefore I had to look at something else. Fortunately, friends in my course were applying for jobs in investment management and stockbroking and I thought it looked like an interesting career. I ended up being a trainee at Dunedin Fund Managers. I had no previous conception that this was a field I wanted to work in. I just fell into it.

AV: I'm a bit different from Will insofar as it was always my goal to work in the stock market because my father works in the industry, so I was weaned on the equity markets from a very early age. Consequently, the markets have always fascinated me, and it was always something that I intended to do.

Have you both always been on the buy-side?

WL: Yes, we have.

What was your first big stock call?

WL: That's an interesting question, because in the very early days as a trainee, and specifically in the first two or three years of my career, I didn't have much direct input into buying stocks. But some of the better stock calls we made weren't about individual companies; they were more about picking the right large stocks at the right time. An example of that would be HSBC[1] in the early 1990s, when the stock was friendless and unloved and most people hated it and everyone was buying Hang Seng Bank[2] instead. So, we started buying HSBC right at the bottom when everyone was selling it. Hutchison Whampoa[3] was another example; we were buying it when everyone was selling it because they didn't like the launch of Rabbit[4] and subsequently the formation of Orange,[5] as most people thought that management was eroding significant amounts of the shareholder value. That pessimism was more than fully discounted for in the share price, and so we took advantage of that. They were two rewarding stock calls for us. And it's making calls like that that have been the real drivers of our performance, rather than making calls on small stocks.

AV: From my perspective, it's very hard to find standout winners in Asia, because unfortunately, there are few companies that are consistently going to add value. It's very difficult to find an example — the exception, of course, being HSBC, where we found a company that was an acorn that later grew into a large tree. With HSBC, it was a case of a change in the way management ran the company, combined with a change in the dynamics of the banking industry. However, following the Asian crisis, I think now is a more interesting time trying to pick big winners, because when I started out in this business it was the beginning of the Asian bull run and everything was performing, including the rubbish. So, success was more about the risk that you were prepared to take and managing that, rather than about finding great companies. We were positioning ourselves more for the bull run in *the markets,* as opposed to focusing on individual stocks.

So, you tend to focus more on the large, liquid stocks?

WL: Yes. We avoid getting caught up in small, trendy stocks. Unfortunately, it's a sad indictment on Asia that there hasn't been an Asian equivalent of Microsoft,[6] or Dell,[7] or another great global franchise that was built up over the years. If you can think of one, please tell me!

Have you always covered emerging markets, or have you also covered developed markets?

WL: Developed and emerging markets.

What are the key differences in investing between the two?

WL: The main variables behind share price movements don't differ between developed and emerging markets. It's just the emphasis of how these key valuation variables operate that can be significantly different. In emerging markets the main drivers of share prices are liquidity and the influence of the macroeconomic cycle. In developed markets, although the macro cycle and liquidity are important, their *relative* importance is diluted by more company-specific issues.

AV: That's right. In emerging markets the underlying criterion tends to be growth, and the *perceptions* of that growth are much more sensitive to changes in the discount rate. The growth in capital and the incremental return on capital that the new investment will generate are both important, but ultimately they are not as important as the disount rate to which it is related. When times are good, the return on capital is high and the discount rate that you use for the long term is low. But when it flips over and goes in the other direction and the discount rate is high and the returns are low, the growth rate expectations are also lower. Consequently, you get much more volatility in terms of the main criterion you're using when you do a valuation based on a DCF,[8] EVA,[9] or whatever cash flow-based method you use. By comparison, in the developed markets, those factors are a lot more stable, and *management* can add a lot more incremental value by focusing on the way the company is being managed.

WL: Another thing is that it's not really always about stock picking. Emerging markets can have their own unique cycles which are unlike other markets' cycles, especially when they've just been discovered. In Asia, you have many examples of this. When Indonesia opened up for the first time in the late 1980s, there were only a handful of listed companies — ten or twenty — so stock picking based on the fundamentals of the company didn't matter then, as stock prices would go up several-fold when investors were allowed to go into the market for the first time.

Liquidity flows were the major drivers of stock prices back then?

WL: Yes, for certain markets. You had exactly the same phenomenon in China, and later in Russia as well.

AV: The interesting thing is the dynamic created by the foreign cash flows. The dynamic of monetizing healthy current account surpluses and the subsequent balance of payments impact on what are, generally speaking, quite small economies in relation to the foreign capital that can flood in, can be very powerful. It tends to create a self-fulfilling prophecy: the discount rate keeps falling as a result of these liquidity flows, which in turn keeps justifying the valuations, which consequently keeps fueling the future growth potential, which in turn gets monetized, which then creates demand for future investment. And, of course, the stock market keeps going up. So, it becomes a gigantic snowball.

How do you find the point where this phenomenon or psychosis starts to reverse — the inflection point?

WL: The initial decision is deciding that there *is* going to be an inflection point. That's the, relatively speaking, easy part. The hardest part is picking when it's coming to fruition. For example, let's take the China phenomenon in the early 1990s, especially 1993, when all sorts of stocks were going through the roof. Stocks like Cafe de Corale[10] went up several-fold on the argument that it was going to be the McDonald's[11] of China. We thought this was overly optimistic. We had invested in the company as fundamental investors previously, but we felt that it had become overvalued. There was, of course, the risk that the stock could go up another 20–30% beyond what we thought was peak value, but ultimately the stock price collapsed.[12] So, timing is always the most difficult thing to gauge. To pick a potential inflection point, you have to have a very strong sense of what's overvaluation. Another example would be Malaysia — the stock-market cycle in that country is a classic monetary phenomenon. For example, we could turn bearish on the market from a macro standpoint based on the fundamentals of the economy and think that the market will refect this, and yet the liquidity cycle and equity markets ran a lot further than anyone expected. So, timing and picking the inflection points can be *very* difficult.

AV: From my perspective, I bear in mind what I perceive to be my required long-term rate from the investment, what I perceive the long-term achievable growth rate in capital and return on capital will be of the business, and with these inputs I calculate my long-term value on the company. I then adjust my decision according to what is going on in the shorter term. And if the short-term share price moves further away from my long-term fair value, I get increasingly more concerned. At some point the share price is likely to be making key assumptions that we feel are just unachievable, and it's at this point that I begin to feel that the inflection point is near. The share price is like an elastic band and at some point it will spring back. This methodology won't give us the exact timing of the inflection point, but it will give us some idea of how risky the trend is becoming.

What sort of benchmark returns do you look for?

AV: A lot of it is instinctive. A lot of these markets don't have any long-dated bond markets, so you have to make some assumptions about what the underlying structural long-term nominal growth rate is going to be.

So, there is no magic pudding — you must set your own standards or criteria and stick by them?

AV: Yes, you have to have an independent mind but also keep a close eye on what the market is telling you.

How do you deal with the conundrum of setting your own standards but also being judged by a benchmark index and quarterly performance?

WL: Our clients do measure our performance against a benchmark, and therefore we do use technology to measure the level of risk that we are taking for the client.

Could you elaborate on that?

WL: Technology is used to help us measure and understand the risks we are taking and not necessarily to limit it or to tell us what to do. Instead, the systems we employ enable us to measure how much of our weighting decisions versus the benchmark are due to country/ currency bets, sector bets, and individual company bets. The benchmark isn't adjusted on a timely basis and can be a flawed representation, particularly in the era of the New Economy.

Is risk measured in the traditional way in terms of the standard deviation of returns?

AV: Basically, yes, though the systems we use provide information on many aspects of risk, including tracking error. This enables us to seek greater alpha[13] while controlling the level of risk.

What was the worst stock call you ever made, and what did you learn from it?

WL: I think a good example of that is a stock that we used to own several years ago in Hong Kong which owned the global Singer franchise and which had a lot of potential selling electronic products under the Singer brand name in the emerging markets. It looked great in theory and on paper, but it never delivered anything to the bottom line.

What did you learn from that?

WL: I think that the lesson with all bad stock calls is that you realize you have to be very careful in assessing management, because they can fool you or mislead you.

How so in this case?

The company had a strong habit of raising money from shareholders very regularly, but there were never any incremental returns on that capital. So, not surprisingly, management was never going to deliver what we expected. The stock was an underperformer and we ended up selling out of it.

What happened to the company subsequently?

WL: It filed for bankruptcy in September 1998.

Do you learn more from those situations than you do from your successes?

WL: Very much so.

AV: From my perspective, the most recent bad call that I've made is disbelieving the potential of the Indian software companies. I saw it as something that had only short-term potential. Much against my expectations, the share prices have continued to rise. So, from the perspective of getting it wrong, it's a clear and annoying case of a lost opportunity, rather than something that's cost us cold, hard cash.

On reflection, what was the message for you in that?

AV: Stock selection is all about looking at what companies are returning at the moment, and then asking how that dynamic will change. In some cases we have overestimated the ability of certain companies to keep reinventing themselves and moving up the technology curve into more value-added businesses. When that catches you by surprise, you have a losing investment.

WL: I think another aspect of that argument is that, if you look at Asia over the last twelve years, what you find is that companies haven't really delivered what they should have over that period. So, against that perspective, it has been very easy to be quite skeptical about Indian software companies, for example, and in many cases that has been a very healthy attitude to have. If you had been an out-and-out bull in Asia over the past seven years and not had a degree of skepticism, you would have suffered or at least have struggled. So, that's something you have to be very careful about. On the other hand, you can be too skeptical and miss all sorts of opportunities, and maybe the Indian software sector is an example of that. But there are plenty of examples where having a healthy degree of skepticism has helped us to avoid incurring losses.

For example?

WL: The Red Chip[14] bubble back in 1997 was a complete nonsense. It was amazing the number of regional rated analysts who helped to create and support that bubble.

How do you avoid those types of situations?

WL: Our style of investing is neither purely top-down nor purely bottom-up. It's very much a mixture of both. The risk that we take in terms of asset allocation or sector selection can be driven by either a top-down or bottom-up view. We do have top-down views on the markets and will take positions on the future prospects for individual countries. This has been more noticeable in recent times in Asia due to the volatility in interest rates and economic prospects associated with the Asian crisis. Going forward, we expect that these macro factors will become less important and the majority of our decisions will be based on a bottom-up criterion.

Once you've made the top-down country decision, do you drill down by sector or just go straight for companies based solely on value? For example, property companies might look very cheap, but they can also be very risky.

WL: Our primary focus is to buy companies that we like and to know why we are investing in them. We don't buy bad companies just because they are perceived as "value." Investment styles come in and go out of fashion. We concentrate on knowing our companies and understanding why we are investing in them. If a property company is growing, generating cash, has strong accountable management, and offers value, we will own it. If it is just cheap on historical valuation criteria, we won't own it. The sector decision is generally derived from where we find the attractive companies.

AV: If you look at the fraças that occurred with the recent downturn in the Asian markets, the basic value criteria collapsed because of the underlying volatility in analysts' assumptions, and just the way companies were operating, was starting to fall apart. So, what we've been developing over the last two to three years is more of a "looking through the cycle" valuation methodology.

Could you elaborate on what that means?

AV: We have systems that allow us up-to-date information on all the traditional valuation and momentum measures, but we look to see whether stocks are attractive using more rigorous, longer-duration valuation models. This added value, particularly during the depths of the Asian crisis. Now, the way that works is that we don't directly say "This company is worth $X," but rather, what we do is look at it from a *relative* viewpoint, because a lot of the companies within industries across markets and within markets will have the same underlying dynamics and the same underlying return profiles. And in view of that, we can put subjective elements on top of that, like how are management going to improve or destroy the fundamental demand for their products, for example.

Is that a uniquely BlackRock Edinburgh approach, or is it adopted across the group globally?

WL: It's something that we actively utilized here in Edinburgh across all international markets.

Do you believe that stock markets are efficient?

AV: No, not at all.

WL: Absolutely not.

But aren't you implying that your model *is*? What has vindicated your belief that your model or approach is valid? You could be right for the wrong reasons.

AV: True, but it has been a combination of our *processes*, experience,
and the specific valuation models that has enabled us to fairly
accurately call the recent low of the Hong Kong market, and it's also
worked well for us in other markets too. Models are useful tools, but
since markets aren't efficient throughout their cycles, the timing of
decisions becomes key.

WL: That's right. If you start from the top down, my view is that the
most important thing is picking the inflection points in markets, or
sectors within markets, because they can be a major driver of your
investment performance. Recognizing that an inflection point is
about to occur and adjusting your portfolio accordingly is key,
because if you realize that an inflection point has occurred and
adjust for the new dynamic, that can really help your performance. I
think one of our successes is that we have been good at identifying
these critical points. As Alistair mentioned, the process has worked
well for us in Hong Kong, but take Thailand as an example as well. We
were very bearish on Thailand and had nothing in Thailand at all
going into the Asian crisis. We believed it was a bubble economy
where the market was living on borrowed time and that it would
catch up with them. And that's exactly what happened. When we
started reinvesting in Thailand in September 1998, we bought in at
twenty points from the bottom of the market.

AV: The interesting thing about Thailand is that we weren't buying
the safe, steady stocks. We were going into the aggressive, even
"bankrupt" stocks. We were putting a base under the underlying
market and saying that the fundamental problem was the yield curve
or the discount rate, but, despite that, the risk of bankruptcy was
beginning to diminish. When we combined that with the
improvement in debt restructuring, we could perceive future returns
that were compelling.

Did the banks figure at all in that analysis?

WL: They did. But what really drove our thinking was trying to pick companies that had franchises, because there was a lot of paranoia back then that a lot of these companies were going bankrupt. There is no doubt that that was a realistic proposition; in fact, many companies have gone bankrupt since. But what we decided, based on the franchises of these companies was that if there was ever going to be a future for Thailand, if there was going to be an upturn in the cycle, then something like Bangkok Bank,[15] which was probably the strongest banking franchise in the country, would be a survivor. Another example was Total Access Communications,[16] which is one of Thailand's key cellular telephone franchises.

So, you focused on buying businesses and not stocks?

AV: That's right. But what was interesting is that we didn't go in with a very finite, short-term approach. We didn't sit down and pick our companies based on "That's a winner, that's a winner, that's a loser." We adopted a basket approach where we were basically looking and saying, "Given our estimate of what the prospective returns of all banks look like, the underlying value of the country's banking franchise is $X."

How did you determine $X?

AV: The theory was very straightforward, but like all these things it required a lot of subjective inputs, primarily: what we thought the prospective long-term sustainable return on assets would be, what our long-term return on equity was, and what would be the deposit and lending growth rate. The underlying valuation for the banking system then was below what we considered to be the franchise value.[17] We didn't necessarily know how the banking system was going to adopt or farm that franchise — that is, *who* was going to survive or *who* would be around after the dust settled — but we did know that the system would be around and it was more likely that the bigger banks would be the ones to survive. The main risk, however, was how much of that franchise would be taken by the foreign banks. Perhaps the market was pricing that risk correctly, because the market was implying that the country's banking franchise was going to be owned by the foreign banks. But the moment we saw foreign banks buying into the listed local banks and not looking to set up their own franchises — just buying into the listed equity — we realized that the underlying franchise value was going to remain in the stock market and not in the hands of the foreign banks.

So, sometimes the signal to buy can be quite subtle and go unnoticed?

WL: Yes. It's sometimes the simple things that flag to you that it's time to reappraise the market. Indonesia is a case in point. If you had asked equity strategists or economists at the end of 1998 what they thought of Indonesia, invariably they would have said, "It's a write-off. Hyperinflation and all that." If you had then asked, "What do your other clients think about it?" they would likely have said, "Oh, most of them don't even want to discuss it." People had mentally written it off as a country. They thought it was going to have the sorts of problems that Latin America had with hyperinflation and so, for that reason and political reasons, it wasn't even worth looking at. To us that was a little red flag, because when almost unanimous negative sentiment begins to grow in a market, invariably that's the time to go looking. We did almost exactly the same thing in Thailand.

AV: And what was interesting was that because of our experience in Thailand, we knew that it was a model that was working. We had seen what was happening in South Korea and Thailand, and the macro environment was being set up in exactly the same way by the IMF. So, we were very confident that our approach and the positions that we took would work. We didn't necessarily know about the timing, but we were confident that it would work as long as we bought companies that had fundamentally decent franchises.

But Indonesian banks couldn't have figured in that portfolio, could they?

WL: That's right; they couldn't, because of the problems in the industry and the fact that it was very hard to pick whether the franchises were going to survive. Moreover, there was so much recapitalization required that, at that stage, it was very difficult to predict which bank one should buy. But one thing that we were very sure of was that the cost of capital would come down significantly, so our portfolio was biased toward companies that would benefit from a huge fall in interest rates and who also had strong franchises.

AV: And benefit from a strengthening of the rupiah as well. Companies like Astra International,[18] for example, were perceived by the market at that time to be in significant financial difficulty, and investors were backing away from the stock. That's what interested us.

Why?

AV: Astra had a severe U.S. dollar debt problem. Furthermore, it had something like 120 banks to deal with in restructuring its debt. Motor vehicle sales were down 98% and the market was pricing in from an enterprise value[19] perspective, a high rupiah discount rate, a high value of the U.S. dollar debt versus the rupiah revenues, and no restructuring or debt haircuts for the banks. In fact, the market was pricing the stock as if the banks were going to end up owning all of the company's assets and motor vehicle sales were going to stay where they were. But the underlying dynamic was that the company had significant operational leverage and it was very likely that, in the next five or even ten years, motor vehicle sales would be back up to their previous levels. So, when a share price is factoring in excess capacity that is unlikely to be utilized, you must look at those situations, but you also have to have the courage of your convictions that the company won't go bust.

WL: I think there was another overriding belief that we had at the time. Because of the uniqueness of Asia and the poor structure and process of the bankruptcy laws, we believed that, in reality, trying to make a company bankrupt was *very* difficult. The bottom line was that the company wasn't going to go under. At the same time, Alan Greenspan was bailing out the world and, in doing so, he was bailing out Asia. As I mentioned before, we knew that the chance of these companies going under was pretty low, because it was a completely different legal system to what we had in the West. As the companies were unlikely to go to the wall, we were attracted to buying core business franchises, especially those that were priced at deep discounts.

AV: For some of the valuations at that point, we actually *removed* the equity risk premium, because we perceived that the risk to the debt holder was the same as the risk to the equity holder. Everyone was factoring in an *enormous* risk-free rate and then adding an *enormous* equity risk premium to get to their underlying valuations. Consequently, there were some crazy valuations out there.

For example?

Indonesian cigarette companies were trading at very low multiples. If you looked at the franchise value of those companies who sold their product in a country of just under 200 million people, Philip Morris could buy that *entire market* for just under five hours worth of revenue! So even on a relatively simplistic argument, that was a franchise that was worth substantially more than the market was valuing it at.

What sorts of returns, therefore, are you seeking to generate?

AV: We continuously seek to provide our clients with out-performance versus a benchmark index. Our track record shows that we are a top-quartile performer over a five- and seven-year period.

What do fund managers want from the sell-side?

AV: I'd like to see a stronger fundamental understanding of how a business operates and how a company operates within its industry. At the moment, there is far too much maintenance research from the sell-side which focuses on trying to second-guess what the company accounts will look like one or two years down the track. When you think about it, the underlying valuation one or two years out based on the cash flow is such a small amount that it's almost inconsequential, especially in Asia. But what's happening is that the sell-side is getting distracted and focusing on the fact that they may be 5% or 10% out in their earnings per share forecasts which, in the broad scheme of things, is nothing, because the forecast number that they are 5% or 10% out on means little. So as Asia develops, and more companies try to consistently add value for their shareholders, management input is going to become a more critical investment issue. Furthermore, as we will be seeing more and more industry consolidations, where there will be a few winners and a lot of losers, we're far more interested in understanding the changes in the underlying industries themselves and how the managements of companies are adjusting to those changes. But, unfortunately, there is very little research from the sell-side focusing on those issues.

WL: I would agree with that. Strategic thinking is very important to us. The sell-side is very good at telling you about how things are today, or indeed, how they were yesterday. In fact, they are *very good* at telling you what the companies' managements think of their businesses. They should focus more on highlighting what the financial result is and what are the important or significant *messages* contained within the result.

So, you are more interested in identifying turning points in industries or companies and structural shifts in company results?

AV: Yes. Furthermore, it's not just forecasting the bottom line that's important; it's the *structure* and *drivers* behind that result that are important. The tendency on the sell-side is just to focus on the bottom line and if it's in line with their expectations, then that's considered a good result. Another thing that is important for us is to be able to identify structural shifts in economic policy.

Such as?

AV: It's no longer sufficient to argue that, because the risk-free rate looks like it's falling, you should buy the market. For example, as Asia changes the way it does business, interest rates won't be as important a driver of valuation as has been the case in the past. And as central banks begin to move away from currency pegs and, hopefully, adopt a more appropriate monetary policy in light of their underlying economic environment, you won't get the same booms and busts. If you're operating under a more inflation-targeted interest rate policy where you try to create a more stable economic environment in which the corporates will be operating, how company managements operate in and respond to that environment will become the critical investment issue. This is opposed to the old way of thinking, which was: "Interest rates are coming down, so buy the market."

WL: That's right. Companies have to manage for long-term growth rather than just the business cycle. Most managers in Asia have managed to date only for the latter.

And the relatively high level of extraordinary income and asset disposals contained in the net earnings of Asian banks, combined with excess capital, isn't creating much in the way of shareholder value either, is it?

AV: That's correct. And it's not just in the banking system, it's right across the board. This type of thinking means that the focus will start to move away from just earnings per share growth and more toward the quality and durability of cash flow and more efficient use of capital.

WL: Another aspect of the liquidity and business cycles that has generally underscored strong Asian stock markets is that minority shareholder rights have never really been an issue, because people traditionally made plenty of money by playing those cycles. But now as investors start to hunt for consistent and durable long-term returns, it will be the companies that look after minority shareholders and are more efficient users of capital that will be rewarded by the share market.

What role does the sell-side have in all of this?

AV: Making these markets and companies more efficient requires effort on the part of four parties. The central banks can adjust their monetary policies and help make these economies and their exchange rates more "efficient," but it's probably up to both the buy and the sell-side to take responsibility, together with the managements of these companies. In the past we could wash our hands of that, because the attitude was one of, "Well, there are no minority shareholder rights, so why should we bother?" But post the recent crisis in Asia, capital is going to be more rationed, and so in order to make sure that there is no next bubble, it's up to the buy- and sell-side to make sure that capital is allocated more efficiently and that the companies generate better-quality and more sustainable returns. In other words, companies need to manage shareholders' capital in a way that creates value and not just rely on the liquidity and business cycle.

WL: That's right. One of the big lessons from the Asian crisis has been that we are starting to see better disclosure, greater transparency, etc., but it still has a long way to go. Fortunately, there are some companies that have realized that if they start to respect minority shareholders' rights, there are benefits to that. They are beginning to understand the implications of that for their own cost of capital and their stock-market rating.

AV: But the important point is that if, over the next year or two, the various central banks don't adopt the correct macro policies, the foreign banks don't improve in the local allocation of debt, and the portfolio- or index-based investors buy indiscriminately, then the whole corporate governance issue will probably diminish in importance. The attitude is likely to be one of, "Well, we went through the bad times but the good times are back, so nothing really needs to change."

Is it easier to be popular or contrarian?

WL: It's easier to fall into extremes of either style. Some people love to be contrarian all the time, but that won't always be a fruitful or profitable investment strategy.

AV: It also depends on where you are in the cycle. For example, if you are doing the popular thing at the inflection point in a cycle, you could end up being the greater fool. However, if you are on the uptick of a cycle, then by definition, you will want to do the popular thing and your stance will change as you move through the cycle. Subsequently, at the inflection point, you'll want to take more of a contrarian viewpoint. So there isn't necessarily one investment philosophy that you can adopt. You have to remain flexible in your thinking.

WL: Whichever cycle you pick around the investment globe, whether it's a long-run one in the United States or what has been a short-term one in Asia, they all tend to last several years. So, looking for inflection points every day is a dangerous pastime. Consequently, understanding the formation of cycles and where you are in that cycle is where you should put in most of your effort and hard work.

What's the ratio between talent and sheer hard work?

WL: At BlackRock we believe that there are four main drivers to obtain consistent outperformance for our clients: people, process, technology, and research. The people provide the talent, the process and technology help with the implementation, which leaves the vast majority of our time to be spent on the key fundamental research decisions. A change in our strong views or picking important inflection points doesn't occur every day. Notwithstanding that, picking those turning points and key stocks, and getting them right, is very important, because it sets the tone for your longer-term performance.

AV: That's right. It's crucial to find the right stocks to invest in, and also to time the inflection points, but there is a talent in terms of how you implement it.

In what sense?

AV: The important part is in going out and meeting the companies, meeting brokers, doing the financial analysis and valuation work. But a lot of talent is required to gauge how you should weight a particular stock or theme in your portfolio in terms of the associated risks.

WL: The hard work aspect of the job also extends to the fact that, in reality, creating longer-term performance isn't about making a lot of winning stock calls; it's about, *on average,* making more winning stock calls than bad ones. Every successful fund manager will take some torpedoes at some time. There's no question about that. But you've also got to have as many winners as is consistently possible.

Do you believe in dollar cost averaging?

WL: Yes, but as long as you are buying good stocks, because cheap stocks can get cheaper. Thailand at the beginning of 1998 was a good example of that.

AV: I'd also agree with that and add that as long as it's in companies that are generating a return that is above their cost of capital, because they'll be the companies that will continue to see their share prices trend up.

At what point are your assumptions about creating shareholder value recognized by the market and reflected in the company's stock price?

AV: There are a range of investors, including ourselves, who have a process or framework that is value-driven. It's a bit like an elastic band, insofar as you can say that a stock is cheap from a value perspective, but it doesn't necessarily mean that, versus growth stocks, that valuation discrepancy isn't going to continue or be quite stretched for a long time. So, there is always an assumption that if you use a particular process it will always work and that a stock is cheap. But unfortunately, you'll never know at *precisely* what point in time that valuation discrepancy will be recognized by the market, because there are a lot of other cross-currents out there affecting investors' perceptions of absolute or relative value.

WL: It can quite often be off-the-wall things that make you or the broader market decide whether your perspective is right or wrong. Take the Australian stock market, for example. While it has changed in some ways, it's still a relatively small, insular, inward-looking market that is dominated by a handful of large local institutional investors who love to hate certain stocks or sectors. There are times when you can virtually predict whether they are going to fall in love with one particular company or sector or valuation methodology, and we've been able to improve our portfolio performance by picking those inflection points.

For example?

WL: When there is sector rotation, such as switching between banks and industrials, or away from resources into banks. As a broad rule, if every broker is saying that a company or sector is a buy, then chances are it's a sell!

Notwithstanding that, how difficult is it not to have too rigid a view of a stock or sector?

WL: That's a dilemma for both the buy- and the sell-side. There are examples over the last few months where our rigidity or strong opinions on companies or sectors has meant that we've missed opportunities, but by the same token, there are cases where our prejudices have worked very well for us, as was the case in Thailand. But there are other things that we missed that we kick ourselves about, and the reality of the job is that you'll miss some things, but you aim to get more things right than wrong.

AV: It's important to realize that sometimes you have to have a very strong view, but if you're wrong, then move on. The last thing you want is to have to keep revisiting an issue month after month after month. It's better to take it on the chin and focus on the things that are going right, and not on what you've got wrong. Otherwise, you risk being caught in the headlights of an oncoming car.

Do you look at charts?

WL: We do, but we're not driven by them. This business isn't a science, and so there isn't one unique method or system that's always going to work. I think that, in general, you are wasting your time looking at charts, because there's a lot of noise in them. But notwithstanding that, occasionally they do tell you something.

For example?

WL: When a price or chart is breaking down and you get no feedback from your analyst or the market as to why, then it can be really telling you something.

AV: If a price is making a new high and has a lot of momentum, then you know that there is a psychological game going on. As Will mentioned, it can work the other way too, when a price is on a downward spiral; in that case, the charts can have an impact on the general psychology of the market as well. Now, it doesn't mean that you throw fundamental analysis out of the window, because you must still ask yourself whether the price behavior is justified. But you need to treat charts as one of the *psychological* variables that has an effect on share prices.

WL: In other words, charts can be a red flag to make you reappraise what your view of a stock is. If a stock's chart is breaking down and you have a positive stance on the stock but it's becoming increasingly apparent that no-one else likes it, then you must ask yourself the question, "Am I missing something here?" There could be very good reasons as to why other people don't like the stock and you haven't picked up on them yet. On the other hand, when your stocks are having a good run and the chart also looks good, you know you have a winner.

Is the thrill of a good stock call as intense as the pain of a bad one?

AV: Yes. They are equal but polarized emotions. You love it when you get it right, it's equally as painful when you get it wrong. I suppose it's a bit like having your head in the oven and your feet in the icebox, but on average, the temperature's fine!

WL: I think it also depends on the nature of the underlying call. For example, if you make a contrarian, against-the-market call that is ahead of the market and you get it right, that's a far more satisfying call than buying a stock that doubles and slightly outperforms the broader market. The really annoying bad calls are when you think to yourself after the event, "That was stupid. I did something really silly there and should have done something about it." For example, when you buy a stock and it falls 50% and the market rose 40%. That's *really* galling. Fortunately for us, that doesn't happen too often.

Does that tend to happen when you lose your independence of thought and just follow the crowd?

WL: It varies, really. Everyone makes mistakes in this business, so it's very important to make sure that you learn from them and don't make the same mistake next time around.

AV: You have to remember that it's not just an issue of whether you get the stock call right or wrong. It's as much about the *weighting* that you put on that stock within the portfolio, because if you get it right 51% of the time you'll be better than the market, but the real measure of your success or performance will be down to the issue of how you weighted that portfolio. It comes back to what we talked about earlier about the ratio between the grind and talent — the grind part is getting the binary stock calls right at least 50% of the time. However, talent is about knowing how much money to put into those calls on a risk-adjusted basis. The worst thing about being wrong isn't the fact that you feel stupid or angry about it, it's about what was the *cost* of being wrong. And when you compound your error by overweighting a bad call, that's when you really get mad with yourself.

That can work in the other direction too, can't it?

WL: Absolutely. It's almost as equally maddening when you buy something where you have a lot of conviction and it turns out to be a market darling, but your weighting is too small. So getting the binary call right is only half the challenge; weighting it correctly is just as hard.

Do markets change, but people don't?

AV: "Climbing the wall of worry" is a phrase commonly used in stock markets. When things change, more often than not, people at first deny the change. And when markets reach inflection points, the usual response is one of denial. But when it keeps going and becomes the trend, that's when the panic sets in. And that's why the phrase "climbing the wall of worry" is so apt for stock markets, because you can sit there with a stale position and hang on believing that you are right and the market is wrong.

If markets priced in change instantaneously, then that would be it. But markets don't work that way; there is always a *drift* from one position to another at inflection points, and so there is always this "wall of worry."

If you're on the wrong side of that inflection point, what do you do if a stock call is going badly for you?

WL: The first thing is that you keep reappraising why you made the stock call in the first place. You need to find out why the stock call isn't working and, if need be, get out, because cheap stocks can get cheaper and cheaper. Also, you need to figure out if you've missed out on a longer-term negative secular trend that is developing and whether you are just at the early stage of it, because you don't want to get sucked into dollar cost averaging a potentially bad situation. If, on the other hand, it's just negative sentiment that will dissipate, then you should look to add to your position, as it's potentially a great buying opportunity.

AV: That's right. You don't necessarily sell out. You need to reassess *how much* you should have of that stock in your portfolio. This gets back to the earlier issue we were talking about in terms of the importance of weighting your portfolio correctly and limiting the cost of your bad calls.

WL: The worst thing you can do is lock in underperformance and sell out when pessimism is at its worst — which is what the sell-side plays to — and invariably, it is momentum investors who fall into that trap more than most. I can think back over the last ten years and recall sticking with stocks that looked bad and which all the brokers hated. But we stuck with them and, at times, bought even more.

Could you give an example?

Memtec[20] was a case in point. It was an Australian technology company which we got into too early, and then the stock fell a long way. Most sell-side analysts in Australia became disillusioned with the stock. The attitude was, "It's disappointed, don't trust them, it's going nowhere." But we bought more and, though it took a while, the stock eventually went up 400%.

So, is successful investing about temperament — about not compounding your mistakes?

WL: Absolutely.

How do you judge success?

AV: Inevitably, it's against your peer group and against your own personal and professional standards. A fundamental part of that is finding stocks that add value to your portfolio.

WL: For me, it's also about getting the results for our clients and about getting professional respect from the people we deal with for doing a good job. This is because there are a lot of people in this industry who get very well rewarded for doing a very mediocre job.

How important is having a long-term perspective in achieving success?

WL: It's very important for the buy- and sell-side alike. For example, one of the dilemmas we have with the sell-side is its short-termism. This is caused by the structure of that industry. That makes it very difficult for fund managers, as there is a lack of consistency and track record in a lot of the sell-side houses.

That raises the issue of whether there is a fundamental conflict between the buy-side and the sell-side?

AV: There are four parts to this: the buy-side, the sell-side, the corporate financiers, and the companies themselves. Sometimes the buy-side and the companies have different priorities. The result being that the advice that those two parties are getting is different, and perhaps not what direct consultation between the companies and the *owners* of the companies should be, and which, to be honest, is likely to be far more objective and more in both parties' interest.

WL: It also gets back to the issue of what does the sell-side fundamentally do to help the buy-side make their decisions? They can probably split their clients into two camps. First, there are those that just want to be told what to do and they do it. Second, there are those that want to hear about the thought processes and the ideas about how you look at and think about stocks and companies. Whether you recommend it as a buy or a sell is fundamentally far less important. For example, we want to hear the logic of how you construe your view of a company, because the vast majority of the decisions to be made are *our* decisions and more often than not, it's based on different data collated from different brokers. But we do remember brokers who stand out from the crowd and who really help us to understand the logic behind what might be driving markets or a company's share price.

AV: A broker's recommendation is only a barometer, inasmuch as you can tally up all the buy and sell recommendations and it gives you a sense of the underlying *sentiment* toward and confidence in a particular company. What's more, if every broker has a buy recommendation on a stock, it's likely to be a sell, because it's a barometer that the stock is likely to hit an inflection point sometime soon as the market is becoming too optimistic.

How important is patience for the average investor?

WL: Very important. It gets back to what we were talking about earlier, about how easy it is to lock in underperformance. You can lose patience and get bored with a stock or a company and flick it out at a loss. And then sometime later the stock moves, and all you've achieved is that you've generated commissions for brokers and potentially locked in underperformance.

AV: I think that while patience is important, it's still not as important as having the courage of your convictions. These issues are all related, but I think that courage and conviction are more important, because it's what you *do* with the stock. Do you add to or subtract from your position? If a stock is underperforming and you still have the courage of your convictions, then patience isn't a matter of sitting on a stale position; it's a matter of *adding* to that position, because when it does turn and you are proven to be right, you make more money off the back of the courage of your convictions. In other words, it's about knowing and feeling that you are right and acting on that.

What other qualities do you need to succeed in this business?

WL: A large dose of common sense. For example, I came from a non-financial background and my undergraduate degree was in geology, but that hasn't prevented me from doing a good job. While I had to undertake some financial training early on in my career, I'm still strongly of the belief that a lot of this job is common sense.

AV: You also need to understand your weaknesses and be able to understand, to a certain level, how companies and industries work. But you also have to be able to admit to yourself that you'll never understand the business in fine detail — in terms of that final bit of cost or a certain level of revenue — but you can have a commonsense level of input, inasmuch as you should ask yourself, "Would this business provide something that I would be interested in?" This is similar to what Warren Buffett[21] says: he never invests in companies that he doesn't fundamentally understand or whose products he can't relate to.

How do you define common sense in an investment context?

WL: A good example of common sense in investing is if you take the Red Chip phenomenon in Hong Kong, a market where, traditionally, making returns for the benefit of minority shareholders was never easy. These businesses were created from paper virtually overnight. Supposedly, they were going to add gigantic value to shareholders, as assets from China were going to be injected into them. The stocks went up two, three, fourfold in a very short space of time. Now, common sense suggested that if making money was that easy, then that model could be repeated in every other part of the world. But it's never that easy. When you looked closely at the dynamics of what was supposedly going to drive this phenomenal increase in shareholder value, it was a nonsense.

AV: The crux of it was that the Chinese were selling these assets into these vehicles, but the marketplace, because of the hype, was putting a different valuation on the *same* assets. This is where common sense comes into it, because the market believed it was smarter than these astute mainland Chinese businessmen who were selling these assets at a discount to the market. Call me old-fashioned, but I have yet to meet a Chinese businessman or trader who would sell me a dollar for eighty cents!

In view of that, how do you view the Internet stock phenomenon?

AV: There is no doubt that the Internet will change how companies and consumers will interact, and that this will provide significant opportunities for those involved in this new era. However, there are many business models being developed, not all of which will be successful. We are endeavoring to ensure that the better ones are core holdings in our portfolios.

What, then, is the best way to play that market?

AV: First of all, it boils down to how much you have in that sector — the portfolio management aspect — because at the end of the day, there are a range of returns and valuations for what you think this sector is capable of providing. You have to try and work that out, but no-one seems to have done that yet. So, investing in the sector means you'll have to have the courage of your convictions as well as a lot of patience to allow your theories and views to work. However, the big risk in Internet stocks is that they may just be overvalued. Moreover, the volatility in the sector is high, and the higher the stock prices go, the higher the risk. Therefore, you can't run a portfolio of Internet stocks in a static manner. To manage that type of portfolio, which is characterized by extreme and demanding valuations, high volatility, and high forecasting risk, takes a huge amount of skill to manage.

In a more general sense, what skills in this business can be taught and what can't be taught?

WL: Common sense is something that can't be taught — either you've got it, or you haven't. This business is as much an art as it is a science. There are no exact answers. Experience also counts for a lot, because the longer you look at these markets, the more you see the same errors and mistakes being made, and patterns or cycles reappearing, especially in emerging markets. So, experience and a track record are very important when it comes to investing.

Is the average investor better off just following the gurus, rather than trying to do it for themselves?

WL: No, I don't think so. I think that a guru only states *publicly* what he thinks when it suits his own position. There are no holy grails or oracles out there to guide us. It's a very tough business to consistently make above-average returns, and you have to keep working very hard at it.

What is the toughest part of the job?

AV: Timing is always the toughest part. Implementing a decision at the right time, whether it's a buy or a sell, can be very difficult, because you have a view, and it is generally speaking a strong one, and you may believe that a stock is worth $X, but you don't know by when. For example, you might believe that an Internet stock could be worth 50% of its current value, but it may not necessarily be tomorrow that the market is going to acknowledge that. And that gets back to the "climbing the wall of worry" issue that we spoke about earlier, where you might think the market's wrong, but how do you adjust to or cope with that?

WL: Another issue that makes the job very difficult at times is the deluge of data and research. The growth in technology over the last decade has meant that the amount of information at our disposal compared to ten years ago is unbelievable. Consequently, time management and information management is something that is becoming difficult for all fund managers to deal with. It's very easy to fall into the trap of thinking, "If I read everything, I'll know more," when in fact you don't. You just drown in data and, at times, irrelevant information. You end up getting lost and losing your focus about what you should really be thinking about.

AV: Another issue that follows on from that is trying to understand the full impact that technology is having on companies and industries, in terms of the ways they operate or do business. That's a major challenge for all investors.

Is technology also having an effect on the volatility of share markets?

WL: To an extent. For example, in terms of increased media coverage and the availability and speed of transmission of data, yes, there has been an impact on volatility. But I think that's as much a symptom of the increased participation in share markets. There are a lot more brokers, individuals, and fund managers involved now than, say, ten years ago, and that's had a clear impact on volatility. When you overlay that on top of the fundamental volatility of the economies or business cycles that drive these markets, then yes, it has had an impact.

AV: I think what has also contributed to the recent increase in volatility of markets is the greater divergence in opinion as a result of the greater supply of information.

To what extent has technology had an impact on the craft of stock picking and stock selection?

AV: I think that the impact of spreadsheets has been tremendous, because it quantifies the objectivity and allows for a greater emphasis on the subjectivity of the inputs. Because valuation models and the profit and loss and balance sheet models are now a lot more commoditized, as fund managers, we have moved on from the stage of rewarding sell-side analysts just because they had a model. We now rely more on analysts for their inputs and ideas, for the subjective part of the modeling process. In other words, the mundane part of the business, "the model," used to be regarded as an art form, and that's no longer the case. Furthermore, we have far more standardization, so comparative analysis is easier. Consequently, I think stock picking or stock selection processes have significantly improved as a result of technology.

WL: I'd agree with that, but there is also a risk of an overreliance on spreadsheets. It gets back to what we were talking about earlier, which is that some people want to believe this is a scientific process. Consequently, it's easy to get sucked into believing that if you build a huge spreadsheet model it's going to give you "The Answer." But it's not. One of the worst things you can do is simply extrapolate existing trends and, unfortunately, spreadsheets lend themselves to that sort of error. You have to be *very careful*. As Alistair was saying, you have to spend more time thinking about the subjective inputs and be conscious of not engaging in linear thinking or extrapolating existing trends.

In view of that, what advice would you give someone considering entering the buy- or sell-side?

AV: Go and work in the industry that you plan to cover, because a fundamental understanding of the industry is far more important than number crunching skills, which can be learned or even delegated.

WL: I would agree with that, or at least, go and work in an environment that allows you to study the industry that you want to cover.

What advice would you give them about the way they should think about valuation?

AV: Share prices don't really move off the back of a change in two-year assumptions because, when you think about it, the next two years account for perhaps less than 5% of the value of the company. And that's the root of another problem: the bulk of your valuation is beyond two years, which by definition has a higher forecasting risk, and not many brokers' forecasts go beyond two or three years. So, you should think about taking a longer-term perspective on valuation and not get too obsessed about the next one or two years.

Would it be better to have a range of valuation scenarios?

AV: Absolutely. The best you can do is to have a range, because there is a range of prices that you can justify for a stock based on the subjective assumptions that you are making. But notwithstanding that, it's very important that the nearer you get to your *base* valuation, the less risk there is and the more compelling the investment case becomes for you. By contrast, the market is likely to price a stock at the top of its valuation range when the company is nearing the end of its business cycle.

WL: Another aspect of valuation that is important is relative valuation arguments — that is, across markets or across regions. I would advise anyone entering the sell-side to start thinking more about cross-market comparisons and not become too focused on one market or company. That may require becoming part of a regional or global team, but I think that's where you are likely to become more *strategic* in your thinking about valuation and be able to add a lot more value to the buy-side.

Can too much success be a risk in this business?

WL: Yes, it can, because you risk not becoming a good listener and spending most of your time telling people what you've done, rather than listening out for what you should do next. Moreover in this business, the moment you start to relax or rest on your laurels, you can be guaranteed that something will come out of left field and knock you over.

Are there any years that stand out for you as particularly good or bad?

AV: The recent decline in the Asian markets stands out, because it brought home many issues pertaining to valuation and risk, as well as the problems with Asian companies' balance sheets and the way they did business. The weaknesses in those business models were clearly highlighted and it has served as a wake-up call for a lot of people. Fortunately, we were on the right side of the Asian crisis and it brought home to me the fact that when you get it right, bear markets are more satisfying than bull markets.

WL: The recent crisis has vindicated for us the validity of the thought processes behind how we approach investing and how we look at markets. But notwithstanding that, one of the most difficult years for me was 1993, not 1997. In 1993, the markets had shot up across the board in Asia. You had places like Malaysia that had just ballooned and were considered one of the best foreign markets in the region. But what was driving that market were speculative stocks and asset injection stories, and consequently we were underweight. So, it was quite depressing to watch all that happening and to personally underperform that year. But ironically, we were also quite happy to sit back and watch some of our competitors trading aggressively and punting on all these speculative stocks, because we *just knew* that there would be a reckoning and that we would be vindicated at some stage. And so, while we significantly underperformed in Malaysia in 1993, we more than outperformed in 1994, because we had only invested in companies that had decent franchises and were delivering growth.

So, the greater fool theory still has a place in the stock market?

AV: Absolutely, and especially in Asia. You can play the greater fool theory and do quite well, especially as the retail investor is such a dominant force in the various markets. But if you are fundamentally driven, at times you're going to be frustrated, look stupid, and underperform. However, there are also times, such as the last two years, where you will significantly outperform. But it's not an enjoyable environment in which to make money, because it's so volatile, and liquidity and the retail investor are such powerful forces.

WL: That's right. In fact, one of the trickier aspects of our jobs is understanding that, in Asia, the retail investor can dominate at certain points in the cycle in certain markets.

Isn't that generally true for most markets when they are getting to the top of their cycles or peaks?

WL: Yes, it is. History has shown that most major equity cycles have had a dominance of retail money when they are at the top end of it — historically, the U.S. stock market has been a good example of that. But in Asia it's even more ubiquitous, so consequently, you will have periods of underperformance, and they can be tough to go through. However, you can take some comfort from the fact that your risk-adjusted returns are probably better than the overall market's.

Does being physically removed from the markets you invest in help your objectivity, or is it a handicap?

AV: We believe it's an advantage, but we have to combine it with regular trips to the markets that we cover. We can't sit in an ivory tower here in Edinburgh and pretend that we know everything that's going on. The good thing however is that when we begin our day, the Asian markets are closed, and so we can ignore the brokers' "story of the day" or the morning news flash. When we start our day, a particular stock may already be up 20% or 30%, but we can spend the day reflecting on or thinking about whether that stock price movement was justified.

WL: Another aspect is that, by being on the other side of the world, the "noise factor" is significantly reduced for us. Furthermore, because our style is to invest for the medium to longer term, being on the other side of the world is a help to us. If our clients wanted us to manage short-term funds and be involved in every hot stock or story going on, then we may benefit by being physically located in the markets, but that's neither our style nor our mandate.

❋ ❋ ❋

For William Low and Alistair Veitch, there are three key elements to successful investing:

- You must have the courage of your convictions and be prepared to buy when other people are selling (and vice versa);
- you must get at least 51% of your stock calls right and weight them correctly. This also includes making sure that the cost of making a bad stock call isn't too high; and
- you need to understand when a market or a stock is approaching or has reached an inflection point.

Their investment philosophy and style is also underscored by a number of other important principles:

- Understanding the formation of investment cycles is crucial. Therefore, most of your efforts should be applied to understanding where you are in any given investment cycle. While inflection points don't occur every day, identifying those points and getting them right will set the tone for your longer-term investment performance.
- To help identify inflection points, you must have a base case valuation for stocks and markets. Moreover, due to the impact of liquidity, occasionally you will need to be prepared to see markets or stocks overshoot by 20% or 30%.
- When markets or stocks reach turning points, more often than not, people deny the change. Therefore, don't hang on to a stale position in the belief that you are right and the market is wrong, otherwise you could be "climbing the wall of worry" for quite some time.
- If a stock call isn't working out, be objective and reappraise it and, if need be, get out, as cheap stocks can get cheaper. However, don't lock in underperformance by selling out of a position when

pessimism is at its worst. Furthermore, when a stock price is moving against you, try to understand whether (a) you have missed a long-term negative secular trend that is developing, or (b) the price weakness is due mainly to short-term negative sentiment which you can take advantage of.

- Buy businesses or franchises, and not stocks. Management quality is a key investment issue. Try to understand what is the value added by management to company performance, as opposed to the underlying economic and business cycle.

- Successful investing isn't about making a lot of winning stock calls; it's about, *on average*, making more good calls than bad ones. If you get 51% of the binary calls right, your ultimate performance will still, however, be determined by how you weighted those calls. Two of the worst things that can happen to any investor is overweighting a bad position and underweighting stocks that substantially outperform.

- As any period of valuation discrepancy and the timing of price discovery can be difficult to predict, patience and a long-term perspective are required in order to narrow the gap between price and value. Furthermore, when the sentiment toward a stock or a market is universally negative, that is often the time to go looking for businesses or franchises that are selling at deep discounts.

- Successful investing is as much an art as it is a science, and there is rarely an exact answer. Therefore, respect the fact that while computer models, spreadsheets, and quantitative methods can bring discipline and objectivity to the investment process, don't become overreliant on them and believe that they contain "The Answer." They are only one aspect of a multifaceted decision-making process and, in many instances, strategic analysis and qualitative issues will be of greater importance in picking winners.

¹ HSBC Holdings plc is the holding company for the HSBC Group, one of the largest financial services and banking groups in the world. At the time of writing, the company had a stock-market capitalization of US$99.7 billion.

² Hang Seng Bank is a subsidary of HSBC Holdings plc and provides commercial banking and related financial services. The company has 146 branches in Hong Kong and China, and at the time of writing had a stock-market capitalization of US$19.1 billion.

³ Hutchison Whampoa is a Hong Kong-based investment holding company whose operations include real estate, ports and related services, retail and manufacturing, telecommunications, media, energy, infrastructure, and finance. At the time of writing, the company had a stock-market capitalization of US$52.8 billion.

⁴ In 1992, Hutchison Whampoa Limited invested in a mobile telephone operator, Rabbit, which lost US$183 million over the next twelve months. The investment nevertheless allowed Hutchison to gain a toe hold in the UK mobile telephone market via the launch of Orange, which was later sold to Mannesmann AG in 1999 for US$14.6 billion.

⁵ Orange plc operates the Orange digital PCN telecommunications network in the United Kingdom and sells related telecommunication services. The company provides a broad range of mobile voice and data communication services. At the time of writing, the company had a stock-market capitalization of £27.6 billion.

⁶ Microsoft Corporation develops, manufactures, licenses, sells, and supports software products. The company offers operating system software, server application software, business and consumer applications software, software development tools, and Internet and Intranet software. Microsoft also develops the MSN network of Internet products and services. At the time of writing, the company's stock-market capitalization was US$473 billion.

⁷ Dell Computer Corporation designs, develops, manufactures, and directly sells standard and custom-specified computer systems that include desktop computer systems, notebook computers, workstations, and network server and storage products. At the time of writing, the company had a stock-market capitalization of US$105.5 billion.

⁸ Discounted cash flow.

⁹ Economic value added, or EVA as it is often referred to, differs from most other measures of corporate performance by charging profit for the cost of all the capital a company employs, debt as well as equity. Capital is also adjusted to reflect economic reality by taking into account off balance sheet debt and adding back unwarranted write-offs against equity. The result is better information and insight about a company for its managers, which enables them to make better decisions. EVA is not particularly new, as the concept, a registered trademark of Stern Stewart & Co., was first written about by Alfred Marshall, the English economist, in 1890.

¹⁰ Cafe De Coral Holdings Limited is an investment holding company whose principal activities are fast food, institutional and hospital catering, specialty restaurant operations, and food manufacturing. At the time of writing, the company had a stock-market capitalization of US$211 million.

[11] McDonald's Corporation develops, operates, franchises, and services a worldwide network of fast-food restaurants. The company's stock-market capitalization at the time of writing was US$57.6 billion.

[12] From HK$5.65 on November 30, 1993, to HK$1.46 on November 28, 1997.

[13] Alpha is usually defined as the excess returns required above a benchmark. For example, a hedge fund's benchmark may be the yield on ten-year U.S. government bonds, whereas an index-based fund's benchmark would be a particular stock-market index.

[14] Offerings in "H" shares, which were Hong Kong listing vehicles that allowed large companies from mainland China — or "Red Chips" — to tap international capital.

[15] Bangkok Bank Public Company Limited is Thailand's largest bank. At the time of writing, the company had a stock-market capitalization of US$3 billion.

[16] Total Access Communication Public Company Limited provides cellular mobile telephone throughout Thailand. The company also sells cellular handsets and other telecommunications. At the time of writing, the company had a stock-market capitalization of US$1.5 billion.

[17] While there is no exact way to determine the franchise value of a bank, statistics such as goodwill to deposits (i.e., market capitalization minus shareholders' funds, divided by retail deposits) and similar ratios are used as proxies as a measure of relative franchise value.

[18] PT Astra International Tbk's principal activities include the distribution of automobiles, motorcycles, and related spare parts. The company is also involved in financial services, wood-based operations, heavy equipment, agribusiness, infrastructure, electronics, information technology, and consumer goods industries. At the time of writing, the company had a stock-market capitalization of US$1.1 billion.

[19] Enterprise value is defined as a company's stock-market capitalization plus the market value of its debt less cash plus long-term liabilities plus deferred tax plus minority interests.

[20] Memtec Limited researches, develops, and produces membrane and other filtration and separation products. The company was acquired by US Filter Corporation in September 1997.

[21] Warren Buffett is chairman and CEO of Berkshire Hathaway and is widely regarded as one of the globe's most astute investors. He is the third-wealthiest person in the United States, with an estimated net worth of US$31 billion.